THE CHINESE EARTH

THE CHINESE EARTH

STORIES
BY
SHEN TS'UNG-WEN

TRANSLATED BY
CHING TI
AND
ROBERT PAYNE

COLUMBIA UNIVERSITY PRESS
NEW YORK

First published in 1947
All rights reserved. Reprinted by arrangement with George Allen & Unwin, Ltd.

Preface to the Morningside Edition and "About the Author" copyright © 1982 by Columbia University Press

Library of Congress Cataloging in Publication Data

Shen Ts'ung-wen, 1902–
    The Chinese earth.
    Reprint. Originally published: London : G. Allen & Unwin, 1947.
    1. Shen, Ts'ung-wen, 1902–   —Translations, English.   I. Title.
PL2801.N18A27 1982   895.1'35   81-18150
ISBN 0-231-05484-X   AACR2
ISBN 0-231-05485-8 (pbk.)

Clothbound editions of Columbia University Press books are Smyth-sewn and printed on permanent and durable acid-free paper.

Columbia University Press Morningside Edition, 1982
Columbia University Press
New York

Printed in U.S.A.

For
JACQUELINE BAUDET

CONTENTS

Preface to the Morningside Edition	3
Introduction	7
Pai Tzu	15
The Lamp	22
The Husband	41
The Yellow Chickens	61
San-San	70
Under Moonlight	88
The White Kid	103
Three Men and a Girl	114
Lung Chu	137
The Lovers	152
The Fourteenth Moon	160
Ta Wang	167
The Rainbow	177
The Frontier City	190
About the Author	290

PREFACE TO THE MORNINGSIDE EDITION

THE *Chinese Earth* was put together in 1946 through the efforts of the well-known British author Robert Payne. It was based on *Selected Works of Shen Congwen* (Shanghai: Liang You, 1936), with additional stories from some of my other books. All these stories were written between the mid-1920s and the mid-30s. The translator was Mr. Jin Di (Ching Ti), now an Associate Professor of English at the Tianjin Foreign Languages Institute. He was then teaching English in the Department of Western Languages and Literatures of National Peking University. Since he was a close friend and neighbor of mine, it was easy for him to consult with me frequently, while working on the translation, to clear up problems connected with the people and places mentioned in the stories. Mr. Payne did much to improve the style and diction of the translation, and after it was finished, he arranged to have it published by Allen and Unwin in London in 1947.

I was born and brought up in a small mountain town in western Hunan Province. I was a wild boy, hard to manage and unwilling to subject myself to the discipline of old-fashioned private tutors. I preferred to make contemporary society my textbook, and studied all kinds of people and human affairs. A sore disappointment to my family, as soon as I graduated from elementary school I was sent away from home to live on my own. I became a First Sergeant in the local army and did clerical work. For five years I traveled with the army, leading an unsteady and difficult life. But I had the opportunity to read many old Chinese books. Later I felt the last ripples of the Literary Revolution, growing out of the Movement of May 4, 1919. I was convinced that Vernacular Literature was becoming the mainstream of a new epoch of Chinese literature. Hoping to find more knowledge, a brighter future, a freer life, and an independent livelihood, I left my home region in West Hunan in the summer of 1922 and went to Peking, at the age of twenty. I was fortunate to carry with me in my mind strong and vivid impressions of what I had seen: the large-scale slaughter of Miao people in my native region before and after the Revolution of 1911, which overthrew the Qing dynasty; the even more widespread fighting, killing, robbing, and burning under warlords large and small after the Revolution; and life in the towns and villages on the Yuan River and its five tributaries, where I had traveled for five years, and where the ancient poet Qu Yuan had also traveled. I had become familiar with the people of this area, with their customs, beliefs, and feelings, and with their distrust and dislike of the authorities. Holding lowly positions and always on the move, I had associated with peasants, craftsmen, and boatmen. I understood them and sympathized with them, and found most of them to be basically good. Their joys and sorrows blended with the beautiful mountains and rivers into a panorama that became a permanent part of my life. Thus I managed to survive in Peking for six years—the first three years were indescribably hard—making a living with my pen. By 1935 I had published more than thirty separate volumes of fiction and essays.

All my life I have liked and admired the work of artisans and craftsmen. In Peking I saw the finest products of Chinese handicrafts, from prehistoric pottery to eighteenth-century porcelain and other objets d'art; I fell in love with Chinese arts and crafts. In 1950, when I began to work in the Museum of History in Peking, I found that the objects available in every branch of Chinese material culture were incredibly rich and numerous, and highly important for the historical study of Chinese civilization. The work I did in the Museum and (since 1978) in the Institute of History of the Chinese Academy of Social Sciences in Peking, brought out many fresh subjects and problems for study.

In October 1980 I came to the United States—my first trip

outside China—at the invitation of Yale and other American universities, to lecture on my contacts with the Chinese literary world in the 1920s and 30s, and on my work since 1950 in the history of material culture. I enjoy meeting old and new friends in America, seeing Chinese collections in American museums and libraries, and discussing problems of mutual interest. I have great hopes for expanded Sino-American cultural co-operation. Those who have come to my lectures and spoken with me know how happy I am in my present work.

When I gave a lecture at Columbia University, I met two gentlemen from Columbia University Press who, at the suggestion of Professor C. T. Hsia, came to ask me whether I would let the Press reprint *The Chinese Earth*, long out of print. I agreed. It pleases me that readers in the English-speaking world are interested in the stories I wrote many years ago. If the book appeals to them, credit should be given to Jin Di and Robert Payne, who put the stories into English. I want to thank them and those who are preparing the republication. I am grateful to Hans Frankel of Yale University for translating this preface into English.

North Haven, Connecticut
January 1981

SHEN TS'UNG-WEN

INTRODUCTION

THE mantle of Lu Hsun has fallen on the shoulders of his friend Shen Ts'ung-wen, who is prolific, where Lu Hsun wrote only with the greatest difficulty and whose attitude to life, for good or ill, has nothing in common with the mordant humours and self-criticism of the elder writer. When Lu Hsun's coffin was being drawn through the streets of Shanghai, surrounded by the peasants and students who loved him, it was noticed that someone had inscribed on the pall the words: "The soul of China," in gold letters. But Lu Hsun had spent his life castigating all that was decadent, bad, morose, stupid and foul in the Chinese soul as it existed in the time of the civil wars, and it was left to Shen Ts'ung-wen to celebrate the abiding virtues of the people who alone among the nations of the world have made goodness a philosophical principle of government. That they have often failed in this, as they failed in other things, can be seen in the later writings of Lu Hsun; but of the natural goodness of the character of the people there is almost no trace in the bitter satires which succeeded "Ah Q." Lu Hsun wrote of the towns; Shen Ts'ung-wen writes of the country. Lu Hsun saw the impact of western commercialism on the unprepared minds of his countrymen. Shen Ts'ung-wen, with perhaps more reason, regards the invasion of the west as something so unimportant in the long history of the Chinese race that it hardly ever enters his stories. Lu Hsun chiselled every sentence he wrote from his own breast-bone; Shen Ts'ung-wen writes with difficulty, but he has trained himself to write under all circumstances, with the result that he has produced probably more books than any other living author. He writes boldly and delicately, with a cunning understanding of the great depths of life and its delicate details. Though he regards Lu Hsun with the reverence which he accords to all great writers, he belongs to the traditional scene of

Chinese culture, with its vigour, its entranced love of colour and shadow, its remorseless and interminable pursuit of the nature of love. Lu Hsun is dead, and his shadow looms large over all the writers of the present time: but Shen Ts'ung-wen is still living, and through him there speaks the soul of another China, more vigorous and more closely related to the historical impulses of the race.

"I desire nothing except the pursuit of beauty," he once wrote. He has found beauty everywhere, but more particularly in his native province of Hunan, with its waterways and great lakes, its red hills, bleak winters and handsome youths. Where other writers continued along the paths of social criticism, he determined to put down on paper the lives of the peasants and soldiers whom he had known. He had no other aim. In the preface to one of his books of short stories he wrote: "The critics who ask me that I should concern myself with the social system, or with some political beliefs, do not disturb me, for I know that what they demand of me is impossible. On such subjects I have nothing to say. When you read my books I beg you to forget the preachers, and I only ask of you that you should try to understand the momentary sorrows and joys of the people, a glimpse, nothing more . . ." And yet by the sheer breadth of his understanding of the common people Shen Ts'ung-wen has in fact provided the basis for the only possible social criticism. In *The Chinese Earth* you will find the people of China as they really are. He has hidden nothing, revealed everything; and what is strange is not that the world he has created is beautiful, but that it is so complete. We see the golden rivers and the lakes, the lamps in the streets of the prostitutes, the lovers singing in the chrysanthemum-covered hills, the sailors walking through the mud and dirt of the streets or climbing the ratlines of the high-prowed junks which sail down to Changsha like Spanish galleons; and somehow everything is as we expected it to be. A small girl is beating a drum, a funeral procession, with all the mourners clothed in white, winds mysteriously through the dusk, a young soldier disinters the body of a beautiful girl, the lovers kill themselves in the blue cave and the pagodas shine like candles on the night of the murder, and we are not surprised, for surely—we say to ourselves—China is a large country where anything may happen, and what is strange is only that his stories should be so credible and that we should believe so implicitly in the China he describes. We know Pai Tzu and Lung Chu as we know our brothers. The sufferings and joys of Green Jade are made real to us by the perfect art and unfailing vision of the author. For the first time a Chinese writer has given us the tastes and smells of his country. He has written of China as she was in the past, is now and forever shall be, unchanging in spite of change, cruel, vindictive, beautiful, calm, merciful and good in the pure honesty of her unchanging youth; for this is one of the dicta that you will find on every page of these stories—that China is young.

In his autobiography he has described his life up to the age of twenty. He was born in the village of Feng Huang Ting (Phoenix Hall), on the borders of Kweichow, Szechuan and Hunan. At the age of six he was sent to a local primary school. He was always playing truant. "All day long I wandered along the mountains and the orange orchards, watching, listening, smelling—the odour of dead snakes, decayed straw, the skin of the butchers which always retained the scent of blood, and then the smell rising from the kilns after rain, where the porcelain was being burnt—listening to the sound of a bat, the sigh of a cow when it is being felled, the rattle of the great yellow-throated snakes and the faint sound of fish jumping in the water." He would gaze for hours at the doorways of shops, and he was continually asking himself questions. Why were the donkeys blindfolded when they stood at the mill? Why were iron bars harder for being immersed in water? How could a sculptor convert a piece of wood into the living image of a buddha, and why was the gold foil on the statues so thin? He asked himself thousands of questions about *things*, and later he began to ask himself interminable questions about people. There were no answers to these questions at school; so he continued to play truant, even when his father threatened to cut off one of his fingers unless he desisted. He spent very few days in school. Most of the time he wandered along the shores of the river. "The influence of the rivers in my life has been tremendous; and perhaps this is why my emotions are fluid, and not set hard. My schooling took place along the river banks; the most happy time of my life was spent there; and I believe that it was from the river that I learnt to recognise beauty and use my mind."

His grandfather had been Governor of Kweichow, but his father and uncles were all officers in the army. At the age of twelve he was sent to a military training school. Two years later he followed the regiment to Huai-hua. "I stayed there for about sixteen months and saw seven hundred executions by decapitation. I learned how torture was employed, how men behave before execution; and I saw so much stupidity that even now I have no idea how these things can be related." To this period of his life belong the stories "Ta Wang" and "Three Men and a Girl." He made friends with the secretary of a commanding officer who lent him an encyclopaedia which he proceeded to learn off by heart. He has related in "Ta Wang" his admiration for the great masters of calligraphy, and now he began to train himself in this most difficult and accomplished art. He is still a good calligraphist; his calligraphy is rigorous and free, and according to Chinese scholars resembles the stem and blossoms of a plum-tree. He began to read omnivorously. Among the books he read were those extraordinary adaptations of Dickens rendered in the Purist Chinese classical style which began to appear at the turn of the century.

"Of Dickens I can speak only in reverence," he says in his autobiography. "He tells me everything I want to know—he makes no attempt to explain—he only records. I am a man who watches events as they pass, and I refuse to measure the significance of things by their social values. I am interested only in the quality of the delight which things exert on my senses. I am never weary of 'watching' things, but I have no understanding of 'ethical beauty.' " And though he insists too much and too often in his autobiography on his completely amoral attitude to life, it is significant that he places beauty higher than truth, and believes that the artist must be the bond-slave of beauty before he can be an artist at all.

When he was young he was supported by his uncle, but when his uncle died hd joined one of the revenue offices in Hunan which were under the charge of the army. He fell in love and wrote poetry in praise of a "tall, white-faced girl," whose brother later stole a thousand dollars from his cashbox, forcing him to flee for his life. For a while he lived in a miserable tumble-down inn in Chang Teh until his savings were exhausted. He decided to sail to Chenshow. On the boat he made the acquaintance of a ruffian who boasted of having seduced forty virgins, but what Shen Ts'ung-wen admired more than anything else was the quality of the man's imagination. "Every woman he spoke about seemed to have a particular individuality of her own, yet he could describe them all with a few careful strokes of the brush. It was due to him that I learnt to be able to draw the portraits of young women, especially those young women whom others refuse to consider in their works, and it was from him that I learnt to depict them with art and grace. . . ." He was still unemployed when he reached Chenshow. Six months later he returned to the army, and once again he began to read the ancient Chinese classics. He began to study the ancient bronzes. He began to read newspapers avidly, and when the army set up a printing press he worked with the compositors. About this time he suffered from fever, and during the delirium of convalescence he reviewed his past life. He told himself that he had done nothing except wander about China. He looked like a beggar-boy. There was nothing to show for his life except the continual nightmares of the executions. He had seen life in the raw, but he was still callow, he knew hardly anything about Chinese literature and he suddenly determined to go to school. As soon as he had recovered from the fever he left for Peking. At the little inn where he stayed on his first night at the capital, he wrote in the hotel-keeper's book a brief summary of his life up to that time: "Shen Ts'ung-wen, student, aged twenty, born in Feng Huang Ting, Hunan."

As usual he was desperately poor. He was determined to make his living by writing, but Peking was a hard school in the early 'twenties, and it was not until two years later that he began to receive attention. In 1924, at the age of 22, he became one of the editors of *Modern Critic* and fell for a while under the influence of Yu Ta-fu. Meanwhile Hsu Tse-mo, the most famous and the most beloved poet of his generation, accepted one of his stories for the *Peking Morning News*. He studied for a while in Peking University, wrote voluminously, and taught in Tsingtao University. His life was still hard. He learned to write by an act of will, fighting against time, delving forcibly into the sources of his inspiration. A weaker man might have succumbed to the necessity of producing copy under pressure, but what distinguished him from others was his extraordinary talent for producing work of high quality under the worst imaginable circumstances. It was hack work, but many of his best stories were produced at that time. In the eight years from 1924 to 1932 he produced forty books.

As his fortunes increased he left Peking and settled in Shanghai. The change was inevitable, for the centre of the literary renaissance was now in the south. With Ting Ling and Hu Yeh-ping he founded a publishing house and edited a magazine called *Red and Black*. Both projects went bankrupt, and he was compelled to return to a ceaseless output of stories. The stories, however, were improving. He began to pay more attention to style; he read the ancient T'ang and Yuan Dynasty novels, and he realised that he was still at the stage when he was learning his trade.

To the majority of Chinese readers Shen Ts'ung-wen is distinguished in at least three separate fields. He was the first to discover the Miao tribesmen for literature, he was the first to write simply and accurately about the Chinese soldier and peasant, and he is the greatest stylist of his time. He prefers the short story because it offers him a certain definite compass; he complains against the *longueurs* and artificialities of the novel. In the preface to his *Selected Works* he has described his aims: "All I attempt to do is to understand my momentary sensations and images. I believe that a writer should isolate himself almost completely from the outside world, for all writing must be individual, impregnated with the personality and the sentiments of the author. To achieve this we need to assert ourselves thoroughly. . . . There are people who attempt to build towers or palaces on sand and water, but I only wish to build a small Greek temple among the hills—a temple of stone. I would like my temple to be solid, harmonious, tiny, not rococo. In this temple I shall enshrine 'human nature.' I am a countryman, and I say this without pride or modesty. A countryman, with his deep-seated stubborn ways, with his own loves and his own hates, is entirely different to the man of the city. A countryman is conservative; he is obstinate; he loves the earth; he does not lack wit but he is devoid of cunning. He is serious about everything, perhaps too serious, so that sometimes he even appears to be foolish. As a child, I wandered along the shores of rivers and lakes, always suffering hunger and cold. Under-nourishment retarded the growth of my body but gave wings to my imagination. . . . I would like you to cross the gulf which separates the man of the earth from the man of the city; I would like you to see in the countryman his burning passion and eternal devotion, his health-giving worship of wisdom and the beauty of humanity, his hatred and disgust over selfishness and stupidity." When he came to speak of *The Frontier City*, which is perhaps the greatest of his works, he said: "This is the design of a small cottage, contrived in a little space and with comparatively little material. Though the materials making up the building have been economically used, I have flooded the whole landscape in air and sunlight. I have tried to describe a certain mode of being which is natural, vigorous and not contrary to mankind. . . . The whole story is a commentary on the word 'love.' If I have described this well, then even if the whole world perishes, love will remain in my story."

The selection of the stories in this book has been made by Shen Ts'ung-wen. We have to thank Yuan Chia-hua for permission to include his translation of the story called "The Lamp," and Wang Tseng-tsien for much helpful criticism and advice.

CHING TI
ROBERT PAYNE

Pai   Tzu

THE junk was anchored beside the quay at Chengchow. The passengers went ashore down a gangway whose two ends rested on the stone steps of the quay and the gunwale. And those who went ashore balanced themselves carefully on the long plank.

There were many junks anchored along the shore, so many that their innumerable masts were thrust up into the sky at random, and the ropes hung in a tangled confusion. On every junk blue-clad sailors stood about, holding their long pipes in their mouths. Their hands and feet were exposed to the wind—hairy like those of the elves out of a monster's cave in a child's imagination. They were like those heroes who are called "Flying Hairy Feet," and they had many oportunities of showing their prowess, especially when they shot up the tall masts to disentangle the ropes round the pulleys. Then their feet and hands seemed to be equipped not only with hair but with something like hooks, for they scaled the slippery masts as fast as though they were flying. And to show that this was no serious hardship, they would sing carelessly in the shrouds as their hands worked among the ropes. And if there were men on the masts of neighbouring junks, the singing would be joined to and fro between them.

The other sailors looked on from below. They did not dare to climb the masts, and they seemed to resent the old helmsman's order to remain on deck. They would swear wistfully, and all the while the acrobats on the masts were making the women laugh.

"Oh, fall down, my son, and crush yourself to death!"

"Ah, grandson, let's hear you sing when you have fallen down dead!"

Hearing these taunts, the acrobats would sing all the more

happily, and they would change their tune from "A Song of a Flower" to a "Song for my Children," while the "children" looked up gaily at the singers high above them.

Meanwhile, too, innumerable dark-skinned men were using their hairy hands to roll large iron casks from the deck on to the beach. There had been all kinds of things stored on the deck during the last twelve or twenty days, and now they were carried ashore and from there hauled up to the warehouses by women labourers. But still there were people with time on their hands, and they would hear above all the other sounds of the place the singing of the sailors in the topmasts. Their hearts beat rapidly, for no sooner had a red lantern taken the place of the singing than the singer came to the listener's side. It was night now. Lamps hung on the masts. There was something mysterious in the swift-flowing river at night.

On rainy and windy nights the junks would be canopied over with oil-cloths, under which the sailors huddled, listening to the wind and the rain. The waves would roar like mad people, and the junks would pitch and roll in spite of being roped together. But the sailors were perfectly detached, they neither liked nor disliked these things, for their life on board ship raised them above likes and dislikes. Nothing troubled them—neither the moon nor the setting sun nor the morning dew. What did arouse their interest was whether they were fed beef or sour cabbage for dinner, and whether the anchor was dropped in midstream or at a port. They preferred beef to sour cabbage, and they were more cheerful when they settled down by the quay.

Men were going down the gang-planks in the rain, and walking over the muddy beach towards the town. There was one of them, Pai Tzu, who was never tired of climbing the masts and singing all day, and he was not in the least fatigued in the evening. Like many other sailors that night, he walked carefully down the gang-plank, his belt filled with coins. He stepped on the beach, and there was neither moon nor starlight, and a fine rain was falling in his face. His feet stirred slowly in the mud—it was impossible to hurry, for his feet were wreathed in the mud, and he journeyed towards a red lamp burning in a house up the street, seeking to find something which would cause his heart to break into flower.

From the beach you can see innumerable lamps like these. Under each little lamp there would be one or a group of sailors. The lamplight would not be strong enough to fill the entire room, but gaiety would fill their breasts and their eyes would be half-closed. The lamplight, their rough voices, their songs and their laughter would flow out towards those who stayed behind for lack of money, and just as it is everywhere else in the world, they would curse the happiness of others. And the hearts of those who could not afford to go ashore flew to these familiar houses, and at the same time their minds would be flooded by their past experiences, and for them perhaps it was still better, for they did not have to risk slipping and falling into the mud.

The wine, the smoke and the women—all these things were dear to them, and they let themselves sink into the atmosphere, completely oblivious to the world or their own past and future. And each woman was the centre of their real and daring dreams, and they were prepared to pour on her person all the money and all the energy they had stored up in a month. They did not demand sympathy and they did not think of pitying themselves.

Pai Tzu, one of those who were looking for happiness, reached the door of a house, knocked, after the manner of sailors everywhere, and whistled loudly. The door opened, and his body was tightly girdled by two arms, although only one of his muddy legs had been thrust through the door and the other was still outside the threshold. And now another face was laid against his newly-shaved rough face, which had been burnt by the sun and washed clean by the rain. Although he could not have said so, her perfume and her way of embracing were perfectly familiar to him. Her face was so soft and so scented . . . He moved his face and met her wet tongue.

"You wretch!" she exclaimed, as he bit it, and at the same time she tried to release herself from his grasp. "I thought you were floating on the Tung-t'ing lake by the water made by those Changteh prostitutes!"

"Your father wants to bite off your tongue!"

"I'll bite off your——"

He went into the room and stood under a red lamp. The woman stood by his side, simpering. He was a head taller than she was. He crouched down and took her by the waist, as though he was pulling on the oars, making her head bend forward.

"Your father is tired of pulling on the oars. He wants to push a wheelbarrow!"

"Push your mother!" said the woman, as she began to search his pockets. Each time she pulled something out and threw it on the bed she shouted its name.

"A bottle of snow-cream . . . some paper . . . a handkerchief . . . a tin . . . What's in it.

"Guess!"

"Guess your mother! So you have forgotten to bring me the powder?"

"Look at the brand, open the tin and see for yourself."

Being illiterate, she saw only a picture of two girls on the wrapper. She moved closer to the lantern, opened the tin and sniffed—and suddenly sneezed. For some reason this made Pai Tzu extraordinarily happy, and he snatched the tin away from her, placed it on the unpainted table, seized her in his arms and lifted her to the bed. Then the bright lantern illuminated the muddy foot-prints on the yellow floor.

Outside, the rain fell unceasingly. They could still hear laughing and singing. The rooms were partitioned with thin unpainted boards, so that sounds even lower than those which accompany smoking opium could be heard from the next room. But Pai Tzu and his woman were too preoccupied to listen to anything that happened outside.

His footprints dried up and were more sharply etched on the floor than before. The light shone on their two bodies lying on the bed.

"Oh, you're strong, Pai Tzu—strong as an ox!"

"If I wasn't, you wouldn't believe that I had behaved properly down the river."

"Well, tell me—dare you swear you are clean enough to enter the Temple of the Heavenly King?"

"Um... Perhaps your mother would believe in oaths. I don't have any faith in such things!"

And she knew that he could only behave as roughly as a young ox. At last he gasped, relaxed and lay quite still in the bed like a bundle of wet hemp. Then his hands groped over her ripe breasts and he began biting them with his mouth, and afterwards he bit her underlip, her arms, her thighs... It was still the same Pai Tzu who climbed the masts and sang songs in the sun.

The woman, lying on her back, laughed at the tricks he was playing.

After a while they made a Great Wall with an opium tray which lay between them, and they lay on either side. And while she twirled the little greasy ball of opium, which he would smoke later, she sang songs for him. Pai Tzu smoked quietly, and sometimes he sipped tea. He felt like an emperor.

"Now listen to me, woman, those females down the river—really they are quite charming."

"Then why didn't you join your soul with them?"

"Perhaps they wouldn't have taken it!"

"You're only giving me what they don't want."

"Ah!... How long did I have to wait my turn? How many others have come here before me?"

She made a wry face, allowed the little glistening bulb of opium to fall into the pipe and handed it to him, hoping that he would keep his mouth shut and talk no more nonsense.

Pai Tzu smoked, but he persisted in speaking.

"Tell me—anybody here yesterday?"

"Mother's! I've been waiting a long time for you. I counted the days, I knew that corpse of yours would be coming..."

"H'm... You'd be quite happy if I were drowned in Blue Wave Rapids..."

"Yes, yes, of course I would be happy," she answered, slightly offended.

Pai Tzu enjoyed making her angry. Seeing her long face, he removed the tray to the end of the bed. Now that the Great Wall was down, the situation changed abruptly. Something new was taking place. By the bedside hung his muddy legs, and round the upper part of his legs there was wrapped a tiny pair of feet bound in red silk.

Pai Tzu plodded slowly under the heavy rain towards the muddy beach. In his hands he held a piece of lighted hemp, which illuminated the ground for a space of three feet around him. The lighted hemp shone on the innumerable reflected rays of falling rain, and Pai Tzu walked through them unprotected, his feet stirring the muddy water. Having accomplished his business, he was now going back to the junk.

Although the rain was heavy, he did not hurry. He was afraid of slipping and falling down, and there was something sheltering him from the rain, or rather making him forget about the rain altogether. He was thinking of the woman. Everything else was irrelevant. He did not think whether the woman had fallen asleep or was embracing another man. He remembered her body perfectly: there were curves and quiet pastures, there were hills and caves. It seemed to him that he could still caress it, still describe those curves even though he was a thousand miles away from her. Her movements and her laughter were like a leech in his heart. What she had given him compensated for a month's toil, compensated him for all his sufferings on the junk, the sun, the winds, the rains, his losses in gambling, everything. He enjoyed his happiness in advance. In another month he would return. And now he would work more cheerfully, eat more cheerfully, sleep more cheerfully, for he had fulfilled all his desires.

His money was gone, but it was well-spent. But not all of it was spent—there was still a little for gambling at cards. Yes, it had been worth doing. Singing in a low voice, he climbed up the gangway and suddenly he decided not to sing the song of "Eighteen Caresses," for the old woman of the junk was feeding her child at the breast, and he heard her voice as she coaxed the child and the sound of sipping milk.

The Lamp

Two years ago, when I was teaching at college, I took my present lodgings, where I use the front room as my study, and the inner room as my bedroom. It was May. Curiously enough, the electric light was always going out. Towards evening, while my rice-bowl and chopsticks were set ready on the table, I would glance contentedly at those dishes which were always tasteful to me, though simple in appearance, and I would think of paying a sincere tribute to my cook. Then the lights would go out, and I would have to postpone my supper indefinitely. Sometimes after supper, when I was comfortably seated and reading some book or other, or a visitor had called to consult me on various matters, then again the light would go out. More than once a friend of mine and I would be deciphering an unannotated piece of ancient Chinese calligraphy in cursive script, or pondering the genuineness of some antiquated seals, when an unexpected darkness compelled us to stop our work, sighing. My friend, himself a painter and calligraphist, usually the gentlest of men, could not suppress his anger, and he would curse the electric light company for their irresponsibility.

These mishaps did not improve for about a fortnight. Enquiries and complaints were sent in from various quarters, but the electric light company merely published an apology in the newspapers, saying that the defect was due entirely to a change of weather. Meanwhile the price of candles went up by five dollars a packet, as I learnt from my cook, who never forgot to remind me of the nuisance, placing a candle beside my plate when he brought in my supper.

My cook was an extraordinary man—honest and perfectly trustworthy. When quite young, he had been among my father's retinue travelling in the north-west and north-east, penetrating as far as Mongolia and Szechuan. Once he went in my native town, watching dutifully over my grandfather's tomb. Last year he served in the southern revolutionary expedition in their advance towards Shangtung. He was chief cook under the company commander of the 71st Regiment. In Tsinanfu he witnessed the most shocking atrocities committed by the hostile armies upon the civilians; and one night, amidst the spluttering of machine-guns, he left his regiment, losing all his personal possessions. Soon he found his way back to Nanking. Perhaps it was from an acquaintance that he learnt my address, for he immediately wrote to me. He would be pleased, he wrote, if I would allow him to superintend my household. In reply I told him that it might be a good idea for him to have a holiday in Shanghai, but to undertake my housework seemed out of question as I live a very simple life. Besides, I would try to entertain him and help him out of his financial and other difficulties until the time came when he would return. At last he arrived. He wore a grey uniform which looked so worn and so tight that I imagined that it had been tailored in Hunan three years ago when the National Revolutionary Army marched through the province. His stout, bulky figure was framed in an army uniform entirely unsuited to him. He brought with him a small bag, a hot-water bottle, a toothbrush and a pair of maple chopsticks. The hot-water bottle hung at his waist, the toothbrush stuck out of his left upper pocket and the chopsticks were fastened across the bag according to the custom in the army. The ideal servant, for whom I had been searching day and night, stood before me. Fastidious as I was, I could find nothing disagreeable in him. Without the exchange of a single word between us, I was conscious of the simplicity and nobility of his heart.

We found a great number of things to talk about. Our topics ranged from my grandfather to the mysterious grandson, whom my father would delight in imagining, but whose existence was still problematical. This servant of mine poured out an uninterrupted flow of conversation. He was never weary of discussing my family affairs, nor were his own personal experiences ever exhausted. Imagine him—a man of about fifty, who had travelled nearly always on foot over the greater part of China; had witnessed the turmoil following the Boxer Rebellion and the overthrow of the Ch'ing Dynasty; had fought many battles in the civil wars; had tasted a great variety of foods and had entrusted himself to many strange beds; had climbed over mountains and swam torrential rivers. He was a classic, a masterpiece which one could never finish reading. And as I listened to him, my profound interest and keen curiosity was intensified. Whenever I had a moment to spare I would ask him about whatever was uppermost in my mind, and I was never disappointed.

My landlady's maid would charge me sixteen dollars a month for my board, two meals a day. She was a shrewd woman from a village north of the Yangtse river. I enjoyed whatever she could spare of broad beans and cuttlefish served alternately, and there was scarcely anything else. Occasionally she would give me some pork a little sweetened, or fish, not fried, but steamed in the rice kettle and seasoned with soya-bean sauce. As a guest the newcomer remained silent as he regarded my meals for two days. On the third day, however, he was out of patience, and asked for money. I gave him ten dollars, without in the least knowing what he was going to do with it. But that afternoon he returned secretly with the cooking utensils, and it was not till suppertime that he appeared, wearing his old soldier's uniform, bringing in the rice-bowls, and smiling as he explained that the meals were prepared with his own hands, adding that they would probably improve if he was allowed to carry on. The simplicity of his carriage and the appetising flavour of the dishes filled me with reminiscences of army life, and throughout the meal we talked of nothing except the rank and file. After supper he cleared the table and went to the kitchen. Left alone, I sat at my desk, reading in candlelight the exercises sent in by my students. Suddenly the door opened and in the old soldier slipped. I suspect that in the faintly-lit room I may have possessed some of the dignity of a company commander. The retired sergeant-major announced himself and hung at the door. "What is it?" I said. He came towards me, bearing in his hand a piece of paper on which he had written an account of the day's expenditure. I realised that he had come to settle the account. I felt embarrassed and a little annoyed. The serious expression on his face did, however, suggest that he was performing the duty of a cook, and I was soon reconciled to a smile. "Why do you bother?"

"I think it is better to make things clear. If we cook by ourselves, you know, we'll save a great deal of money—sixteen dollars a month would be more than enough for both of us. For cuttlefish and stale rice every day, you have to pay sixteen dollars!"

"Isn't it too much work for you?"

"Too much work! Why, cooking rice and vegetables is nothing compared to moving boulders out of the river-bed. You—you're a gentleman of leisure!"

Another glance at his scrupulously honest face, and I could no longer raise any objections. And so I agreed to let him undertake the cooking of my meals.

The old soldier acclimatised himself readily to the new circumstances in Shanghai, but his old uniform still looked a little out of place. I suggested that I should find a tailor for him, and asked him for his preferences in style and colour. He nodded, but made no answer. Shortly afterwards, learning that I had received an unexpected sum of money, he asked if I could spare him ten dollars, and that evening with the ten dollars in his pocket he went out and bought two suits of cotton flannel tailored after the manner of a Sun Yat-sen uniform, and a pair of second-hand shoes set with spurs. He showed me these things with an air of pride and contentment.

"Well," I said, "what makes you so fond of that uniform? You are no longer in the army. Why don't you wear a long gown like me."

"I am always a soldier, sir," he replied. And so he is known among my friends as the "army officer cook."

At first the trouble with the electric light was not serious. Occasionally it would go out for a short while. Later on, however, the matter became worse, and we never had supper without a candle. Then one day the soldier found an old lamp, trimmed the wick to the shape of a triangle, cleaned and polished it, and set it on my table. Such an old-fashioned lamp might well be considered a curio in Shanghai, but I said nothing, knowing his obstinacy. Besides, it was useful. And in case the electric light should go out, I placed the lamp on my desk when I began to work after supper. Facing the transparent crystal lampshade and the faint yellowish glimmer which issued through it, often I would be immediately translated in company of the soldier into the dream-laden, fantastic atmosphere of a dilapidated temple of a small village inn—an inn situated in the neighbourhood of a whole battalion of soldiers and horses. I had loved these things, but they were now remote and out of my reach in Shanghai. At that time I was no longer able to suppress my scepticism and weariness over the details of my work. What was I doing? Every day I entered the lecture-hall, and there I stood by a small square table in front of an audience, looking serious and dignified, and at the same time I felt hypocritical and conscience-stricken. I talked rubbish, but this rubbish was nevertheless supported by quotations from different and sometimes contradictory authorities. I would be hypnotised by my own arguments, and then suddenly the bell would ring and I would notice a student who had fallen asleep with his head in his arms. A crowd of students would gather round me, plying me with incessant, irrelevant questions, till at last I escaped to my own rooms, hoping to find peace there. But when I returned home, I found books, papers and manuscripts lying all over the place. I had to push them aside before I could find enough space on the desk to deposit the students' exercise books. Then I would heave a sigh of relief and quietly read through their exercises. Oh, I was tired of it all. I yearned to escape altogether from the world. I would rather take up the post of clerk in a meat-tax office and listen to the frogs croaking in the little pools in the courtyard after heavy rain and set myself to imitating the style of our ancient authors.

But there in front of me lay the old-fashioned lamp under whose flickering glimmer I caught a glimpse of the old soldier looking the acme of contentment. It was this soldier who could make me forget for a moment the day's toil and the troubled evening air. He instantly transformed himself into an object of devotion.

"Do you know any soldiers' songs?" I asked him.

"Of course," he replied. "How can a soldier not know those songs? Only the songs of foreigners are strange to me."

"And the folk-songs?" I continued.

"What kind of folk-songs?"

"Are there different kinds of folk-songs. 'Cloud over cloud is climbing in the sky.' 'The sky is flooded by the billowing clouds.' Don't you know them. They are all beautiful, and I did not understand them in my childhood. Then I joined a guerilla detachment and we were so wild that we considered dog's meat the rarest delicacy, and these songs were never far from our lips. Not even the gods could have been happier than we were in those days."

"They're prohibited among the regular troops now," he answered. "You are punished if you even whistle them."

"Then you must think me an outlaw? The songs were like charms to me in my youth. I often wonder if they can still be heard among the young who 'live in the mountains under a blue sky.'"

"I am afraid the world has changed since those days," he

said musingly. "All good virtues and refined customs have been swept away by a mysterious whirlwind. Just look at this queer lamp. Last year when I was living with your father in the country, all the lamps I came upon were like this."

It was clear that he shared the preference of the country gentry for seed-oil lamps rather than gasoline.

We indulged in day-dreaming; we were both intoxicated. But unfortunately the landlady's clock in the corridor struck nine, and the old soldier immediately stood up and bade me good-night. I entreated and even threatened him to resume the conversation, but he did not hear me, went into my bedroom to have a last look round and returned to salute me awkwardly and at the same time charmingly, as though we were still with soldiers in the camp. Then he hurried down to his own small bedroom.

Why should he be in such a great hurry? I asked myself. Perhaps he was afraid to interfere with my work, or perhaps again he feared to intrude on my proper bed-time. A moment before he had looked so eager, so brimful of stories he wanted to relate, and suddenly he had stopped, postponing till to-morrow the continuation of his stories. Nine o'clock was the curfew hour in his unspoken military testament. Left alone, I felt a profound loneliness creeping over the corners of my heart. Concentration was impossible, and every effort to resume my work proved to be futile.

I was bewildered before his inexhaustible resourcefulness. I thought of writing about him, but how could I transform his beautiful, pure soul into sedentary prose? Both his complexion and his voice had led me to see life under a different aspect, and I had to own that what I knew and wrote about was altogether too shallow and prosaic. A pair of sunken eyes, faintly melancholy, yet not entirely lacking hope in the future, bare of eyelashes, peeping out at you from under brownish eyelids. You read the ever-present eloquence in his eyes, but you failed to transpose these things into words.

Sometimes I would gaze at him without uttering a word. Sometimes, when we were talking about the wars, he would pause abruptly and assume a pensive expression at the mention of the houses of the peasants burnt to the ground and their cattle seized and led away in triumph. He seemed to be groping in the dark corners of his brain for words which possessed meaning, but all words seemed powerless now. He stared in silence. There was an understanding between us. Long afterwards a gentle and perfectly charming smile crept over his face, and with a nod of the head our painful thoughts were turned into another direction altogether as he sang a short song. He never dreamed of the wavering of my heart in those moments. There were times when his most casual gestures filled me with horror at the thought of my Chinese friends, who were so stupid and so righteous. There were times indeed when it seemed that the peaceful soul of this most ancient and oriental people was being driven by the tides of the present into an incongruous world of struggle and turmoil. With melancholy and restraint they lived out their lives of compromise in a new world, while their dreams were still centred upon a world of light. Listening to him, I would suppress my tears with the greatest difficulty.

Sometimes, secretly agitated, I would grow irritable, and then I would ask him to entertain himself instead of waiting idly in my room. At such moments he would glance at me speechless and walk quietly away. Immediately afterwards I would call him back. "Would you like to go to the theatre?" I would ask apologetically, giving him a few dollars and adding that he might do as he pleased with them. He would stare at me with a forced smile, politely take the money and then turn to walk downstairs. As usual I worked till midnight before going to bed. I heard the old soldier softly opening the door before disappearing; at ten o'clock a faint squeak at the door announced his return. I hoped he had been enjoying himself at the play, or drinking wine, or gambling, and thinking that the money had been enough. I did not bother him with questions. At lunch the next day I was surprised to find a well-cooked chicken on the table, but I refrained from enquiring how it had come there. We smiled, and I could read in his brown eyes the vague and tender words he had left unspoken. "Let us drink," I said. "You used to drink a great deal, didn't you?"

He hesitated, and answered with a delightful smile: "Oh, I have some good news for you. Nearly all the wine-sellers here only sell alcohol. I tried many shops before I came to one belonging to a countryman of mine, who offered me some really delicious rice-wine."

He hurried downstairs and returned with a small bottle of white wine. He poured half a cup for me. "Just drink this—not too much!"

Though almost a teetotaller, I could only do my best to comply with his wishes. Then he filled the cup again, and emptied it in one throw. He relished its sweet and sour fragrance. Smiling and saying nothing, he took the bottle downstairs. Next day we had another chicken. In Shanghai in those days a chicken cost only a dollar.

The old soldier never showed much enthusiasm in the college where I was working. Once he enquired about the future of the students after graduation, and seemed to feel that they were all becoming magistrates. He wanted to know, too, the amount of my salary, and if it fluctuated as it did in the army during the civil wars. All he wanted to know was the potential number of magistrates and whether my monthly salary was sufficient for my living expenditure. His interest was centred on me alone. Out of pure kindness he became increasingly inquisitive about my personal affairs. At first he would agree with me about everything. Later on, he would find excuses to intrude upon my time, and he no longer paid any attention to my reluctance, and seemed to be imposing upon himself all kinds of duties and obligations for my sake. I could not reproach him in a harsh voice or drive him away by kicking him downstairs. He said very little, though sometimes he would complain against invisible and imaginary enemies, the suspected causes of the present unfair treatment of myself. His sense of justice could never be reconciled to the fact that a man of my age remained unmarried. Nevertheless, as time went on, I became more and more embarrassed by his endless talkativeness. Once I told him rather bluntly that being neither rich and respectable as a gentleman nor young and promising as a student, I was helpless about the matter and had decided to give up any further attempts. I thought he would give up criticising my negligence, but on the contrary everything became worse. He began to keep an eye on all my fair visitors. Whenever a lady friend or a girl student called, he would go out and buy fruit and bring them in on a neat tray. Then he would back out and stand silent on the landing, or sit on the stairs playing the vigilant eavesdropper. And when I was seeing my visitor off, he was always there, pretending to be looking for something. He would cast a casual glance at her, and there would follow fitful enquiries about the visitor and the impression I had formed of her, and he would even comment on her manners, her way of smiling and speaking. More irrelevant was his queer application of the Chinese laws of physiognomy. By observation of the voice, features, figure and gait, he could tell whether the woman in question was to be fruitful or virtuous, to enjoy blessedness or a long old age. At first I paid little attention to the things simmering in his mind, but after a while I began to notice the extraordinary behaviour he evinced in the presence of myself and my fair visitors. It was curious. In his innocence and simplicity, he seemed to think he was dutifully fulfilling a solemn rôle when he attempted to induce me to marry a woman; and perhaps he was looking forward to the great moment when, wearing a smart uniform newly purchased from the market, he would stand gracefully at the entrance of the East Asia Hotel and receive the guests who had come to celebrate my wedding. And perhaps in exactly the same uniform, he would one day accompany my young son, dressed like the son of a general, to play and frolic in the park. He may have indulged in still more fantastic dreams. Some day perhaps I would return in honour and accompanied by my family to my native city, and he would come before me, riding a magnificent horse, the first to enter the city gates, returning the greetings of the relatives and friends who had come out to welcome me. Then he would spur the horse to a gallop, while the whole town rejoiced . . . Ten years before, he had cherished similar hopes for my father, and again later for my elder brother, but they were all frustrated. He seized upon me as a drowning man seizes upon a straw. In the old days my family was flourishing and renowned in the neighbourhood. When it began to decline, I cannot exactly tell. According to the old soldier, my father, his master, returned home in despair after a series of adventures in Mongolia and the north-west. He had fought the mounted bandits and been injured, and there resulted the constant ache along his spine and sides, a disease which never left him, and reduced him to a premature old age. He retained the rank of colonel, and even offered his services to the medical corps of my province. My elder brother followed in his footsteps. Eventually, as a result of his haphazard wandering, he acquired the rough manners and courage characteristic of the north-eastern provinces, and the noisiness and extravagance of the Shanghai tradespeople. He, too, returned home and practised as a professional artist. With my younger brother, a man whom the old soldier regretted that he had never met, things took a different turn, and a revolutionary age began. He entered Whampoa military academy in Canton. There was icy vigour and boiling-hot blood in this younger brother of mine. As a platoon commander he led a few dozen soldiers and gallantly fought out some battles in Hupeh and Kiangsi, but as soon as the revolution of 1927 was over, he mysteriously left the army and returned to civilian life, bitterly lamenting the bloodshed and corruption and all the inconceivable stupidities of humanity. Now he idled away his days as an honorary staff-officer of the lowest rank, with pay but without any known duties. I did not follow in the path of my father or my brothers, and it was this, perhaps, that gave the old soldier grounds for his selfless dreams of my future.

Before the old soldier I was continually oppressed with melancholy and shame. And yet I dared not question his dreams. Once I told him quite frankly that I enjoyed being a teacher and writer, and wanted nothing more, but he could see only the surface of my life and suspected great unplumbed depths.

At that time there was a young girl, a revolutionist, who would occasionally call on me and stay for a long while. Usually she brought along her own writings, and whatever the season she would wear a blue gown. She had perfect confidence in me, and confided in me completely. For a while the old soldier's entire interest was centred upon her. He behaved like a mother, and nothing—however trivial—escaped his attention. When my lady friend came, he would always find some excuse to linger for a few minutes in my room with the clear desire of being introduced to her. I had no desire to hurt him. I even told my young friend about him, his rugged past, his honesty, his sincerity. And gradually she grew friendly with him. The weather-beaten old soldier, whose heart had been hardened by slaughter and famine, began to melt like wax, and by some mysterious process he came to the conclusion that I would be committing a terrible crime if I failed to be united with her in matrimony. And in a serious and rather reproachful manner he would sometimes discuss the matter with me when we were alone.

At first he was shy when she spoke to him, but later when she began to ask him about his own past, he opened out, smiling an unnatural smile and answering politely and yet with some lingering embarrassment. Before long, familiarity brought courage, and he would try to turn the main topic of discussion to my daily affairs. He implored her to advise me on my way of living, as for example—I should work less, pay more attention to my food, dress like a gentleman. These conversations, of course, were conducted in my presence. He dwelt on the gentle and noble manners of my father, the great esteem of my countrymen for my brothers, the grace and sweetness of my mother. And all the time he was trying to explain in the most awkward manner imaginable, how a young woman should behave to her husband and her father-in-law. On points bordering on exaggeration and while speaking in a subdued voice, he would smile upon me indulgently, lest I should be annoyed and make unnecessary corrections. As soon as he saw that the young lady was moved to sympathy, he imagined his solemn duty fulfilled, and casting a contented glance at me, he would ask permission to go downstairs to prepare tea and refreshments. His quick steps on the stairs spoke of a light heart.

One day he saw me at my desk addressing a letter to my mother. His curiosity was intensely stimulated, and he asked if I had mentioned the young lady. "The extraordinary lady," he said, and I knew that he meant extraordinarily charming or extraordinarily suitable. I did not reply. I knit my brows. "Hm, hm . . ." he backed away, grumbling. His eyes seemed to be saying: "Well—only a joke—out of pure goodwill, I assure you! Please don't mind!" He went towards the furthest corner of the room, as though dreading that I might throw the inkstone at his head.

One day the lady in the blue gown called while I was away. The old soldier received her and for a while acted as her only interlocutor. (Afterwards I realised from his gestures that he had treated her in a very polite and yet intimate manner as befits a servant before the mistress of a household.) At last, not knowing when I would return, she went away. As soon as I arrived, I had to listen to his report on her, and his interminable irrelevant digressions. And then suddenly she reappeared. It was nearly supper time. Guessing that I was about to invite her to supper, he immediately showed his excitement and hurried downstairs. Half an hour later he brought in several surprisingly sumptuous dishes. I do not know where he learned his new style of cooking. Instead of seasoning everything with pepper, he made everything sweet to suit her taste—even the roast fish was seasoned with sugar and sour sauce.

When the table was cleared he brought in the dessert—apples and a pot of boiling-hot tea. Though nothing more was wanted, he hovered around for a few minutes before going downstairs. And now, overwhelmed with excitement, he began to drink, and to his intoxicated eyes there was displayed a picture of his master and mistress, and in the depths of the cup he may even have seen the young boy, who was also his master, a boy dressed in a splendid army uniform exactly like the foreign children he would meet in the streets. And this visionary young master, with two small white legs in a brand-new pair of leather shoes, walked perfectly steadily, and behind him there followed the faithful servant —himself! He had given way to the wildest dreams on learning that I was supping together with the young lady. But nothing could be more pathetic. My young lady friend had come to tell me that she and her sweetheart were leaving for Peking next month, and they would be married there. The word "marriage" mysteriously reached the ears of the old soldier, ears as wonderfully keen as those of a battle-horse, and without knowing anything else, he confidently interpreted the word as the culmination of all his long-deferred hopes. After she had gone, I sat down at my desk, rejoicing over the happy news, and yet unconsciously I must have been a little depressed. Suddenly a reddish face protruded from under my nose, and I saw that he had been drinking.

"Well, you've had a drop too much, haven't you? How on earth did you manage to provide so many beautiful dishes? My guest appreciated your cooking tremendously."

He had been smiling all the time, and now he was as frisky as a kitten. "I feel very happy to-day," he said.

"You ought to be happy."

He was in an unusual mood and inclined to argue with me. "What do you mean—I ought to. I can't see why. I've never been so happy. I emptied half a bottle of white wine."

"Well, buy some more to-morrow," I said. "Try always to have a bottle handy. Whatever happens, you should have enough to drink in spite of the shortage of everything here."

"I've never drunk so much in my life," he replied. "I ought to be happy. Do I always look unhappy? When I think of your father and his bad luck, really I can't feel happy at all. And when I think of your elder brother and his delicate health . . . I've never seen your younger brother . . . He's a leopard, a golden-striped leopard, hot-tempered but very agreeable. Once I thought I would follow him through the enemy's lines, with a gun in my hand, climbing barbed wire and things, challenging those rough northerners and sticking a bayonet in their chests . . . learning from him how to throw one of those hand-grenades which describe a parabola in seven seconds . . . But you know, I heard that all the fourth class of the officers at Whampoa were killed in the battle of Lungt'an. Two months ago someone came and told me you could still smell the bodies. Oh, there must have been a friendly star hanging over the head of third master. He would go out hunting the wild-boar on horseback. A hero, isn't he? And I am unhappy because he was never promoted to divisional commander. You can't make me happy. You are not at all healthy. Why the hell don't you . . . "

"Go to bed earlier? I have so much work to do."

"Yes, you don't trust me—that's it. You think I'm just a stranger. I've got the ears of an old horse. Nothing escapes me. I know everything. I'll soon be drinking in honour of the happy marriage. You are keeping the secret from me. All right, I'll pack right now, and leave to-morrow."

"Now tell me what you have heard. Have I ever kept anything secret from you?"

"I know, I know . . . Oh, I beg you . . . You really can't imagine how I feel in the depth of my heart!"

Suddenly he burst into tears. A middle-aged man, a sturdy and stubborn soldier, now began to weep like a little child. I realised that his tears were tears of relief and delight. Evidently he believed that I was soon going to be married to the young lady who had just called.

I decided that it was impossible to keep him any longer in the dark. He was quite certain that his assistance would always be needed, and now it seemed that he would be in charge of everything. At last he had found his ideal mistress, and while his old dreams displayed themselves in more tangible forms, he could no longer hold back his tears. I understood his feelings. Suddenly, wiping away the tears with his hairy, massive hands, he asked me if I had fixed the date, and suggested that I should consult the blind fortune-teller who was usually employed in such delicate situations.

I was embarrassed. I did not know whether to laugh or to cry. I dared not rebuke him. Besides, he was not really drunk. It was only that he was firmly convinced that I had no right to keep it secret from him. He suggested that I should immediately write a telegram to inform my people seven thousand *li* away. He pronounced a sincere eulogy of the lady, and I gathered that from the conversation he had had with her earlier, he was convinced that she would make an ideal daughter-in-law in my mother's eyes.

I tried to calm him. I explained in detail exactly what had happened. With his mouth slightly open, he stared at me and listened intently. At first he was puzzled, then aghast. He believed every word I said, and his immense dejection weighed heavily on my heart. In the end I decided upon a white lie, and told him that I was in love with another lady who resembled in every detail the girl in the blue gown. But apparently he was still dubious. From his small brown eyes two streams of tears flowed down, and he seemed to be paralysed.

The clock downstairs struck ten.

"It is bed-time now. Let us postpone the talk until to-morrow."

And suddenly struck by my unexpected entreaty, he awakened to his mistake. With a forced smile he apologised for drinking too much and for behaving like a lunatic, and he swore that he would never drink again, and then asked if I would like some carp for dinner to-morrow. I said nothing. Seeing the peeled apple-skins on the gilt tray, he picked them up slowly before bidding me good-night. As quietly as a fish he slipped away and gently closed the door behind him. I heard his slow heavy steps plodding down the stairway.

The clock struck twelve . . I was still sitting up and groping among the intricate labyrinths of human affairs. My mind was no longer quiet. I was aroused from my dreams by a noise, at first barely audible, which sounded on the stairway, gradually approaching my door. It must be the old soldier, I thought, coming to remind me of bed-time. Hastily I turned down the wick of the lamp. I heard a gentle sigh in the darkness outside. "Well," I said, breaking the dark silence, "I've just finished and I'm just going to bed." There was no reply. After a while I went to the door, but he had already gone downstairs.

After this comedy, he gave up drinking and changed considerably. If I asked him about wine, he would say no genuine wine was sold in the shops—only alcohol. He no longer talked about women; he paid no attention to my fair friends, but he was still interested in my work and he no longer urged me to save money for my future home, and he no longer criticised my shabby and unclean clothes. His disillusionment was so complete, and there was no longer any possibility of patching together his shattered dreams; and he was even more wretchedly buried in loneliness than I was.

Once more the lady came to bid me good-bye before leaving for Peking. Once more she came to dinner. This time, however, besides the ordinary dishes, only one vegetable dish was added. The old soldier seemed rather sullen as he carried them in—I was secretly amused, for he was so touchingly serious with things bearing on his own joys and sorrows. Henceforward the lady in the blue gown made appearances in my study. Not long afterwards I heard that she had been arrested with her husband in Tientsin. I did not tell the old soldier.

Some time ago I promised him that as soon as the summer vacation opened, we would go down together to my native town in the south. For seven years I had not seen its familiar blue sky nor stepped on its familiar soil. It was six years since he had been there, and now it was early June and there were only eighteen more days before the vacation. Then suddenly the civil war broke out, and one day he asked me for some money to travel to Nanking. He said he was going to have a holiday there. And now, as he grew more reticent and reserved, I found it increasingly difficult to please him. Day after day he did the cooking and all the trivial affairs of the house, and sometimes he would quarrel with the landlord's maid for borrowing things without telling him. I began to think a holiday in Nanking was just what was wanted. And then he left—and never returned. I do not think he joined the civil war. He did not die. I like to think of him still serving as cook in the army, and sometimes when he is stationed in a ruined monastery, he will get up early in the morning and, accompanied by his mate, he will go to the market in search of provisions. He will take a rest in the rice shops, chat with his friends and stand on the river bank watching the sails float by. In the evening he will sit on a bullet-case made of wicker-work, and there, under the reddish glare of a lamp, settle his accounts with the corporal; and as he tots up the lists of vegetables, writing in his cramped handwriting on a scrap of waste paper, he will curse under his breath. At night he will lie down on a wooden bed, covered with a patched cotton quilt. So I imagine him living for ever, or at least for another twenty years. He has never written to me; and yet I am certain that he is still living in the world.

That was how the lamp found its way to my desk. Occasionally I still use it. Sometimes, when I am writing about those things which are familiar to me, when I am plunged in meditation, I will switch off the electric light and burn this oil lamp instead. In such moments I see the old soldier as in a vision, his red face, crumpled army uniform, this steward of an ancient household. And the soundless tears torrentially flowing from his small brown eyes.

The Husband

THE spring rain has been falling for seven days. The river is swollen; and since the river is swollen the opium-boats and the flower-boats anchored near the beach are now very close to the bank, and are moored to the posts of "the houses with hanging feet."

Any idle man, taking his tea in the tea-room called the "Four Seas Spring," and leaning against the window commanding a view of the river, can see the tower, the smoking rain and the red peaches on the further bank, and he can see the boat-women serving their guests with opium-pipes. It is only a short distance from the boats, and there are often voices calling from above or below. And when he calls and a woman answers him, they talk together with wild, rough words; and then the man in the tea-room pays his money and walks down the wet and ill-smelling lane until at last he reaches the waiting boat.

Once in the boat, and for a payment of from half a dollar to five dollars he can smoke and sleep as he pleases, and enjoy himself with the woman, a woman with large hips and a plump fat body who lives in the boat, and who will serve him throughout the night.

The woman in the boat calls this "business," and to speak truthfully their merchandise neither conflicts with morality nor spoils their health. They come from the country, from the families of farmers who spend their lives tending fields and reaping the rice; they leave their villages, the mill-stones, the calves, the arms of their young and strong husbands, and following some chance-met acquaintance they come to do business on the boats. Soon they lose their rural appearance and become urbanised; they develop vices which are useful only in cities, and soon they are ruined, but their ruin comes so slowly that it is hardly noticed. Yet there are some women who retain all the characteristics of the daughters of farmers, and this is why there are always so many young women available for the flower-boats on the small river of the city.

It is all very simple. A girl who is not anxious to bear children can go to the city, and every month she will send what she earns in two nights to her honest and hard-working husband, who lives on the farm in the country, leading a perfectly satisfactory life, retaining the title-deeds of the farm and all the profits from the rice. So it happens that many young husbands, after marrying a wife, send her into the city, while he lives quietly on his farm.

And whenever the young husband thinks of his young wife on the flower-boat, or when New Year comes round, it behoves him to meet his wife, and so he dresses in a suit of starched, clean clothes, hangs on his girdle his pipe and his tobacco pouch—the pipe which he held in his mouth all the time he was working—and carrying a full basket or hamper of potatoes or dumplings, he makes his way to the town and enquires from all the boats on the quay, in the manner of a man searching for a remote relative, until at last he finds the boat where his woman lives. Then, having made sure of her whereabouts, he goes on board, lays his pair of cloth shoes very carefully outside the cabin, hands what he has brought to the woman, and at the same time he examines her up and down with amazed eyes. For the woman has, of course, entirely changed in the eyes of her husband.

Her great pile of gleaming hair, her fine eyebrows artificially plucked with a pair of small forceps, the white powder and scarlet paint on her face, her city manners and city dress—all these things confuse the husband who comes from the country. It is easy for the woman to notice his stupidity. And she begins to speak at great length, saying: "Did you get that five dollars?" or "Have the pigs produced piglings?" The tone in which she speaks has naturally changed, and he cannot recognise her in the free and gentle-mannered woman who has nothing in common with his country wife.

But the man who is her husband, when he hears his woman enquiring about money and the pigs breeding at home, realises that his position as master has not been entirely lost sight of on the ship, and that the lady has not forgotten the things of the country; and so he grows bolder, and slowly takes out his pipe and a flint. He is then surprised a second time when the pipe is suddenly snatched from his hands by the woman, and a cheap cigarette is thrust into his rough palms. But it is only a momentary surprise, and the husband smokes the cigarette and begins to talk . . .

In the evening, when supper is finished, he is still smoking the cigarette, which appears new and interesting to him; and a guest arrives. A boat-owner or a merchant, wearing a pair of cow-hide boots with a large silver chain shining from his many-pocketed girdle, a man full of strong wine, staggering on board the boat and shouting for kisses and sleep. The loud, rough voice, and the pomp of his progress, remind the husband of the great men of the village—the village headmen and the country gentry. Seeing this man, and needing no instruction, he crawls timidly into the after-hold, and hides there panting; and then, looking out aimlessly on the dusk of the river, he picks the cigarette from his lips. Night has changed the river. Lamps shine along the banks. The husband thinks of his fowls and the little pigs back home, because these little things are his friends and he is far away from home and near to his wife. A faint feeling of solitude creeps over him, and he wants nothing more than to go home.

But does he go home? No. His home is ten miles away, and there are jackals, wild cats, soldiers wandering in the night or on guard. They are all such troublesome things, and though he would dearly like to return, he has no means to accomplish his desire. The old woman in charge of the boat will entertain him at the theatre called the "Palace of the three Gods," and he will enjoy tea with her at the "Four Seas Spring." Furthermore, since he has come a long way to the city, he must look at the lamps of the city and the people of the streets. So he stays there, sitting in the after-hold, enjoying the view over the river, waiting till the old boat-woman can come to him. At last, when it is time to go ashore, he sidles along the gunwale towards the bow. And having gone ashore, he will return in exactly the same way, careful to make no noise lest the man smoking opium in bed should get angry.

When it is time to go to bed, he listens for a while to the sound of the drum on the watch-tower, and looking through a crack in the wall he notices that the guest is still there. He says nothing, but lies down on a new quilt. At midnight, when he has fallen asleep, or still in a half-dream, his wife finds a free moment and creeps into the after-hold to ask him whether he would like some sugar-candy. Being his wife, she cannot possibly forget his fondness for having a piece of sugar-candy in his mouth, and though he says he has fallen asleep and has already tasted some sugar-candy, she pops some in his mouth. Then she leaves him, curiously ashamed of herself. Meanwhile the husband, still sipping the sugar-candy, goes peacefully to sleep, having wholly forgiven his wife and allowing her to entertain the guest in her cabin.

There are many such husbands in the villages. These villages produce strong women and honest, faithful husbands. The women come to sell flesh, and the men all know the benefits that can be derived from such merchandise. They are wise. The women still belong to them; children, should they be born, will belong to them; and part of the money earned will belong to them.

The boats lay along the bank of the river, so many that a stranger could never count them. The only man who knows how many they are, and who can recognise every boat and every woman on them, is the old water sheriff.

He is a man with only one eye. They say that he once killed a man in his youth, and during the fighting lost one of his eyes. But his single eye has seen what two eyes have never seen. The whole river looks to him. His power over the small boats is more complete than the power of the Chinese Emperor over China.

When the river is swollen, the sheriff is busier than ever. He has to look everywhere; he must know where the boat lies in which a baby is crying for milk, because the parents have gone ashore; he must recognise at once the boat in which people are quarrelling; and he must see whether there are any boats in danger of floating away, because there is no one to guard them. To-day, however, something on shore had affected the life of the river. Three small robberies had taken place, and according to the police, they had searched everywhere, even to the little clefts in the earth, and they could find no trace of the stolen property. It was all very wonderful, but it meant hard work on the part of the water sheriff. He had received his instructions: the police who always lie had ordered him to accompany the armed water police and search the boats at midnight.

He received the information in the morning, and there was plenty for him to do during the day. Above all, he was determined to do his duty to the people who had so often treated him to "fine wine and good meat entertainments." So he wandered among the boats, chatting with the people there, enquiring whether anyone knew of a stranger of unknown origin.

Now the men who are selected as water sheriffs are generally rulers of the water, and they know everything concerning the water. Originally he lived on the water, and it is just those people who are to be found on the side removed from law and government whom the officials make use of in order to dispose of the affairs of the river. When he grows old and rich in the vicissitudes of the world which is every day changing, having brought up a family and drunk much wine, having attained a life of comfort and ease, he at last achieves the dignity of an honourable and peaceful man of the world. He assists the government, and at the same time he maintains close and friendly relations with the people on the boats. Thus he establishes a moral code. He is respected equally with the officials, and he is the adopted father of many of the prostitutes.

At this very moment he was jumping along a plank which led to the newly-painted bow of a boat. The boat was moored under a "house with hanging feet," the house of a store where they sold lotos seed. Everything was quiet. He knew whose boat it was, and as soon as he dropped on board he called out: "Maid the Seventh!"

There was no answer. Neither the young woman nor the old pander appeared. The old man was very knowing, and he thought perhaps there was some young fellow playing about on board, and he stood there looking round the bows, waiting for a while.

Then he called again. He called for the aunt and for Wu Tu, the little sharp-voiced, sharp-faced maid of the boat, who remained on board whenever the others had gone ashore to buy rice. She would boil the rice on their return; she was often beaten, and she was apt to weep. But no sound came from Wu Tu. He thought he heard something in the cabin, a sound like a human breath; and it seemed to him that the people on board had not gone ashore, and they were not sleeping. So he bent down and looked in through the opening of the cabin, and shouted into the darkness, "Who's there?" but there was still no answer from within.

He grew angry, and shouted in a loud voice, "Who's there?"

"It's me!" a man's voice could be heard from within, a voice which was unfamiliar to him, and timid and fearful. And this voice continued to say, "They have all gone ashore."

"All gone ashore, eh?"

"Yes, they . . . "

As though he feared that simply by answering like this he would offend the newcomer, and that there was some duty to be performed, the man crawled out of the darkness, steadied himself by holding the sail-yard and looked up at the newcomer in utter confusion. He was shy and afraid, and he did not know what to do.

He saw first of all a pair of high and tall pigskin boots, seemingly oiled with persimmon oil. Above these he saw a brown, many-pocketed girdle of soft deerskin and two crossed arms with hairy hands, and on one of the fingers there was an incomparably large gold ring. Above this he noticed a square face which seemed to be made of innumerable pieces of orange peel. Imagining the man to be a customer, he began to speak in a tone of excessive politeness mingled with flattery, and attempting to imitate the city people, he said. "Master, pray take a seat inside. They'll soon be back."

From the way in which he spoke, and from the way he wore his new starched clothes, the sheriff knew at once that he was a farmer newly arrived from the country. He had intended to leave as soon as he discovered that the women were not on the boat, but now the young man aroused his interest and he stayed.

"Where do you come?" he asked, gazing at the man with fatherly kindness, lest he be uneasy. "I don't know you."

The husband thought for a while, and it occurred to him that he had never seen the visitor before. "I came here yesterday," he said.

"Is the wheat out yet?"

"Oh, wheat—our wheat in front of the mill—ha, ha—and there's that little pig of ours, eh? . . . "

And now the husband, as though suddenly aware that his replies were not what were demanded, and remembering that he was talking to a townsman of some position and that he should not say "eh," should not say "little pig" and "mill," knew that he had said the wrong thing, and could not go on.

Because words failed him, he gazed at the sheriff timidly and simpered. He wanted to be understood and to be forgiven.

The sheriff understood all this perfectly, and knew from his conversation that the man was some relation to the boat-woman. "Where has Maid the Seventh gone?" he asked. "Will she come back soon?"

This time the husband replied still more carefully. He said: "Came here yesterday," and a little while later he added: "Came here last night," and it was not till then that he announced that Maid the Seventh, the old boat-woman and Wu Tu had gone ashore to worship at a temple, after having asked him to guard the boat. And in a further effort to explain why he was keeping guard over the boat, he explained to the sheriff that he was Maid the Seventh's "man."

Now Maid the Seventh usually called the sheriff "papa," and since this was the first time that the sheriff had made the acquaintance of his son-in-law, he needed no prompting to enter the cabin.

In the cabin there was a small bed, with quilts of flowered silk and red chintz neatly folded together. Guests could sit on the side of the bed. And though the room looked dark from outside, enough light came through the opening to make it look bright inside.

The young husband, looking for cigarettes and matches for his guest, made such clumsy movements that he accidentally overturned a small vessel containing chestnuts. Round chestnuts shining like black gold began to roll about the dim floor of the cabin. The young husband tried to pick them up and put them back in the small container; he had no ideas of how to entertain the guest with them. And his guest made himself perfectly at home, picking up nuts from the floor and cracking them with his teeth, and saying that this season's nuts were really delicious.

"They are delicious—yet you don't like them," the sheriff said, noticing that his host was not eating them.

"I like them. They grow on the tree behind my house. There were so many of them, and they burst out so splendidly from their green, thorny covers," he smiled, and he was as happy as though he had been speaking of his own son.

"You know, chestnuts as large as these are rare," the sheriff went on.

"I selected them."

"You selected them?"

"Yes, I was keeping them for Maid the Seventh—she likes them."

"Are there monkey-nuts at your place, too?"

"What are monkey-nuts?"

The sheriff began to explain. "There are monkeys who live on a high mountain, and when men come and insult them they throw down heaps of chestnuts each one as large as your fist. And because people desire these chestnuts, they deliberately use foul words, and come and take the monkey-nuts away."

Through the chestnuts the young husband found someone who could sympathise with him. He told the sheriff all he knew about chestnuts, and what happened in the chestnut groves, and went on to talk of a place called Chestnut Cave. He then went on to talk of the extraordinary solidity of ploughs made of chestnut wood. He was in desperate need of someone to talk to. All through the previous night there had been drinking and opium-smoking in the cabin, and he remained in the small after-hold. When he tried to talk with Wu Tu, he found her as drowsy with sleep as a pig. There should have been an opportunity for him to talk with his wife about country affairs in the morning; but the woman had said that she wanted to go ashore and worship at the temple at Seven Mile Bridge, and she had told him to guard the boat. He had been sitting there waiting for a long time. Nobody came back. After a while he began to look at the strange scenery of the river, where everything was new to him. The river tormented him. He lay in the cabin thinking of the flooded river and of the innumerable carp which would fall into the bamboo fishing nets if he was back in the country. Afterwards he would string them through the gills with willow twigs and set them in the sun. He was counting them, but he had failed to complete his calculations when the stranger appeared on board. At that moment it seemed to him that all the carp' had jumped back into the water.

The guest came, and the young husband decided that he was a man who was eminently satisfied with conversation. So he decided, too, to take the opportunity of saying all the things he had intended to say to his wife.

He spoke for a long while about country affairs. He spoke of the mischievous temper of a small pig, about the millstone cut recently by a stone-cutter, and finally he told the story of an extraordinarily small sickle.

"Isn't it strange?" he said. "I swear I searched for it everywhere—under the bed, in the doorway, in the barn. I searched everywhere. It was hidden away. I scolded Maid the Seventh because of this. She wept. But we didn't find it. 'There is a ghost throwing stones. There is a spirit making walls around you.' It was in the rice-basket after all —it had been lying in the rice-basket for half a year. All covered with rust like scab. Do you understand? How could it come to be in the rice-basket for half a year? Oh, I remember it all now—I used it to sharpen a bamboo stick. I cut my hand. It was bleeding, and I was so angry that I threw it away. . . . I ground it near the river for half a day, and it was quite good again after that. It could still eat your flesh, and you would be wounded unless you were careful. I haven't yet told Maid the Seventh about it. She can't have forgotten how she cried. And do you know, I've found it again, ha, ha, I've found it!"

"A very good thing, too."

"Yes, I'm glad I found it. I used to suspect that Maid the Seventh had dropped it into a stream, but I didn't have the heart to ask her. Now it's all right. I wronged her. I said: 'You can't find it? Very well, I'm going to beat you.' I didn't touch her, though. All the same she was really frightened when I got angry. She wept half the night."

"I suppose a sickle can be very useful for cutting grass."

"Oh, useful, eh? It's useful in many ways. Such a pretty sickle, such a delicate sickle. What do you mean—cutting grass? With a sickle like that you can do anything—peel potatoes, carve a flute, anything! And its so small, and worth three hundred coppers—excellent steel. Everyone ought to have a sickle like that, don't you understand?"

"Yes, yes, I understand. Everyone ought to have a sickle like that. I follow your meaning," the sheriff said.

He imagined the sheriff understood everything. He opened out his heart to the sheriff, and he even said that he hoped she would provide him with a baby in the coming year, words which he should only have spoken to his own wife on the same pillow. He went on for a long time, saying many wild things and many silly things; and it was only when the stranger stood up and was about to leave that he remembered he had not asked his name.

"Your honour, please tell me your honourable name. Leave a card here, will you, so that I can tell them who came."

"Tell her a tall man came, and that he wore the boots that I am wearing, and tell her not to receive guests to-night. And tell her I am coming."

"You mean—tell her not to receive guests. You're coming?"

"That's right. I'm coming. And I'm going to invite you to have a drink, because we are friends."

"Yes, we are friends."

The sheriff patted the young husband on the shoulder with his big fleshy hands, and then, jumping ashore at the bow, he went on to another boat.

When the sheriff had gone, the young husband began to wonder who he was. It was the first time he had ever talked with such a noble person. He would never forget the excellent impression the man had made on him. Not only had they talked together, but the man had called him friend and promised him a drink. He imagined he was one of Maid the Seventh's constant visitors, and suddenly he was overwhelmed with happiness and burst out singing in a low voice an old folk-song from his native village:

"The river is rising,
The carp come and lose themselves in our nets,
The large ones are as large as large sandals,
The small ones are as small as small sandals.

At noon, when everywhere people were cooking rice in their boats, he watched the smoke like a piece of thin silk spread evenly over the water. Smoke penetrated everywhere, entering their nostrils and making them sneeze. But the wet firewood on Maid the Seventh's boat could not be kindled, and he was still at a loss to know what to do. He heard the cook in the restaurant near the river beating the rim of a cauldron with a ladle, he heard cabbages being poured in the cooking-vessels of a neighbouring boat, but still Maid the Seventh did not return. He could not kindle the wet firewood, and so the small iron furnace remained cold. He tried for a long while, but in the end he gave up.

There was nothing to eat. He felt hungry and sat down on a bench, drumming with his feet on the boards. He began to think of the tall man who had come on the boat, a tall man with a face like pieces of orange peel, a face which resembled the mixture of red lees and red blood, and he remembered the man's commanding presence and his foul-mouthed order to the husband: "Don't let her have any guests to-night—I'm coming." Why did he say that? What right had he to say that?

He could not sing any longer. His throat was parched with jealousy, there was no more happiness in him, and when he tried to kindle the firewood again he lost his temper and threw it all in the river.

"God damn you, firewood—go and drown yourself in the ocean!" he exclaimed.

The firewood, however, was picked up by people living in

another boat only a short distance away. He saw them pick up the firewood, and it seemed that immediately afterwards they were lighting a fire with it; and soon the fire was well kindled, and there were sounds of loud crackling. He was so ashamed that he decided to return home.

But he had hardly walked down the street when he met Maid the Seventh, and there was Wu Tu walking hand in hand with his wife, and in Wu Tu's hand there was a perfectly new two-stringed violin. He had never dreamed of such splendour.

"Where are you going?" his wife asked.

"I'm on my way home."

"I told you to look after the boat, do you hear. What are you doing? Has anyone done anything to you?"

"I'm on my way home. Let me go home."

"Go back to the boat."

He gazed at his wife, noticing the determined expression on her face. Yes, he had seen the violin. He knew it had been bought for him. "All right, all right," he murmured vaguely, and his forehead was damp on his fingers. He came back to the boat.

Shortly afterwards the old pander-woman returned, carrying in her hands some pig lights. She walked quickly, as though they were stolen by her, and she was afraid of being arrested by the police. Her cheeks were crimson; she was gasping for air. As soon as she reached the boat, the young wife cried out from the cabin:

"Do you know what my husband is up to? He was going to leave the boat."

"You mean—he was going to leave without seeing the show?"

"We met him at the end of the street. He was angry because we did not come back soon enough."

"That's my fault—Buddha's fault—the butcher's fault. I shouldn't have quarrelled with him for half a day over a penny, and he shouldn't have filled the lungs with water."

"No, it's my fault," answered the young wife, who was sitting in the cabin with her husband. Suddenly she began to change her clothes, and intentionally exposed her fascinating red silk corset.

The husband's eyes were rivetted on the corset. He was speechless. Something unspeakable was rushing and burning in his blood.

Outside the old woman and Wu Tu were discussing the firewood.

"Who washed the rice? Who stole the firewood?"

"Maybe he couldn't kindle the fire . . . Maybe that country brother of hers only knows how to kindle pinewood."

"Didn't we get a bundle of firewood yesterday?"

"Well, it's all gone now."

"Then go along to the bows and get another bundle, eh?"

Meanwhile the young husband said nothing, and his eyes were fixed on the two-stringed violin. But later, when the cabin was filled with smoke, his young wife told him to bring it up on deck, and with the violin in his hand, he followed her to the bows.

Over lunch Wu Tu exclaimed:

"Play the song of the girl who was buried in the Great Wall—you play and I'll sing it."

"I can't play."

"Of course you can. Maid the Seventh said you play very well."

The old pander-woman began to beat Wu Tu over the head with her chopsticks, so that she hurried through the meal, cleared the table and washed the boilers; and when she returned the young husband was playing on the violin and she began to sing. She sang very well, and the new instrument sounded clear over the river.

At night they were still singing. The young husband played, and sometimes his wife would join in the chorus. A lamp-shade cut out of red paper flooded the room with a red light, so that there seemed to be a wedding. The man had never felt happier. He thought he was enjoying a New Year celebration, and his heart was blossoming. But their happiness was interrupted by some drunken soldiers who heard the voices and came clambering on the boat.

"Who is that singing?" they shouted, their thick voices sounding as though they came from mouths filled with walnuts. "Well, what's your name, eh? I'll give you five hundred."

The music stopped suddenly. The drunken soldiers began to kick the boat with their feet, making a dull noise. Then they tried to remove the awning, but they could not find the seams.

"Pretending to be deaf, eh? Pretending to be dumb? Who the hell is enjoying himself here? I'm not afraid of anyone—I'm not afraid of the Emperor. Am I afraid of the Emperor?"

Then stones began to beat on the awning, and there were loud oaths directed against the ancestors of the people living inside the boat. They were panic-stricken. The old panderwoman hurriedly dimmed the lights and pushed open the awning; at the same time the husband crawled into the afterhold, dragging the violin with him. After a while he heard the soldiers entering the cabin, shouting, roaring, kissing Maid the Seventh, kissing Wu Tu, even kissing the old pander-woman. He heard them saying: "Well, who was it? Who was singing and playing here? Go on—get him!"

The pander did not dare to speak, and Maid the Seventh had quite lost her presence of mind. Then the soldiers began to rate them loudly:

"Get him, you whore! Go and get that tortoise to play for us! I'll give you a thousand. Even the first hero of the world, Ch'ou Meng-teh, couldn't be so generous. I'll give you a thousand red potatoes—that's what I'll give you. Go on—drag him out, or I'll burn the boat over your heads. Quickly, there! Don't make your old father angry."

"We were just having a family party . . ."

"God strike you dumb, old whore. You're too old—we don't want to touch you. Go and tell that violin player that we want him to come out. Damn it, I want to sing myself." He stood up, and made a movement as though he was going to search the hold. The old woman was so frightened that she opened her mouth wide open, and could not shut it again. The young wife saw that the situation was growing ugly, pulled at the drunken soldier's hand and put it against her full breasts. The drunkard understood this, and sat down again. "Yes, yes," he murmured, "your father can afford it, he'll sleep here to-night, don't you worry."

He lay down on the left side of Maid the Seventh. The other lay down on her right.

To the young man, hiding in the after-hold, it seemed that the cabin had suddenly grown quieter, and he called out quietly to the old pander-woman through the wall. She heard him, and since she had been deeply insulted by the soldiers, she crawled towards him. The young husband still had no idea what had happened.

"What happened?" he asked.

"Some soldiers from the camp—drunk like cats. They'll leave soon."

"They'll have to! I forgot to tell you that a man with a square face came to-day—he looked like a high official. He said he was coming to-night, and we mustn't receive guests."

"A man with large boots and a voice like a gong?"

"Yes, yes, that's him! And he has a large gold ring on his finger."

"That's the water sheriff all right. When did he come?"

"This morning. He stayed quite a long time—and he ate some chestnuts."

"Did he say anything?"

"He said he was sure to come, and he asked me to see that there were no other guests. He said he was going to give me a drink."

The old woman thought for a moment. Was it possible

that the water-sheriff wanted to pass a night here himself? Was it possible that he wanted someone old, like herself? She could not make it out. She went back stealthily into the cabin, pulled out her tongue at the two soldiers and suddenly returned to the after-hold.

"Well, what shall we do?" he asked.

She shook her head.

"Have they gone yet?" he demanded.

"No, they're sleeping."

"Sleep——"

She could not see his face in the dim light, but she understood his tone, and she said: "Brother, let us go ashore and enjoy ourselves. They're showing a fine play at the 'Three Gods Palace'." But he did not reply.

When the soldiers left at last, the women chattered in the cabin, recalling every detail of the drunken soldiers. Meanwhile the husband remained in the after-hold; and he refused to come out. The old woman called twice, but there was no answer, and she had no idea why his temper had suddenly been aroused. She examined the four bank-notes carefully. She could tell true bank-notes from false. They were all right. She showed them to Maid the Seventh, placing them in the light; and afterwards she held them to her nose and smelled them, remarking that they must have come from the Mahommedan butcher-shop, for they smelled of beef-fat.

Wu Tu went to the after-hold.

"Brother, come out now. They have gone away. Let us sing and do things . . ."

There was no reply. For a short while he had been plucking the strings of the violin gently, but now even these sounds ceased.

Now they were all silent. Outside in the street, they heard the sound of celebrations, gongs were being beaten, drums could be heard and trumpets were blowing in celebration of a wedding. Guests were coming to offer congratulations, they were entertained at feasts and theatrical shows. All night long there would be sounds of celebration.

The young wife went to her husband in the after-hold. Shortly afterwards she returned.

"How is he?" asked the old pander.

Maid the Seventh shook her head and sighed.

They thought the sheriff would not come, and so they went to bed, the old woman, Wu Tu and Maid the Seventh remaining in the cabin, while the husband remained in the hold. At midnight, the police came, led by the sheriff. A solemn stillness held the air, as though even the crows and the hedge-sparrows were hushed to silence. Four policemen watched at the bow, while the sheriff and a single police officer entered the cabin. The old woman turned up the lamps. She knew there was nothing serious. Maid the Seventh sat in bed, her dress spread out over her shoulders. She called him "your honour," and ordered Wu Tu to serve tea. She was dreaming of plucking strawberries in the country.

The young husband was shaken out of his sleep by the old woman. Seeing the sheriff, and seeing an illustrious stranger in black uniform, he was dazed to speechlessness and had no idea what had happened.

"Who is he?" the police officer said.

"Maid the Seventh's man, newly come up from the country," the sheriff replied.

"Your honour," Maid the Seventh interrupted, "he only came yesterday."

The officer looked at the man, and then at the woman, but he said nothing; he knew that what the sheriff said was true. He searched at random here and there in the cabin, till his eyes lit on the small container full of chestnuts. The sheriff took out a handful of chestnuts and thrust them into the large pocket of the officer's uniform. The officer laughed.

Shortly afterwards they went to search the other boats.

The old woman was pulling down the awning, when a policeman returned, saying:

"Old woman, tell Maid the Seventh that the policeman is shortly returning to examine her more carefully. Do you understand?"

"Will he come soon?"

"As soon as the search is over."

"Are you sure?"

"Have I ever cheated you?"

The husband was surprised to notice the old woman's joy, for he saw no reason why the officer should carry out a second examination of Maid the Seventh. But now, seeing Maid the Seventh in bed, he was again out of temper. He was willing to make peace, and willing to talk with her on the side of the bed. But instead of speaking, he sat there perfectly motionless.

The old woman understood him. She understood his desire, and she even understood his innocence. And so she said only: "The officer is returning soon."

The young wife bit her lip. She was speechless and lost in thought for a long while.

In the morning the man rose early, intending to return. Silent, saying nothing, he slipped into his sandals and searched in his pocket for the tobacco pouch. When he was quite ready, he sat down at the side of the low bed, and looked as though he would speak, though he could not.

"You promised the sheriff you would have lunch with him, didn't you?" his wife asked.

He made no reply.

"He is going to give a feast especially for you."

Again there was no reply.

"And take you to the theatre, and give you the kind of meat dumplings you like."

Again there was no reply; he was determined to go.

Maid the Seventh did not know what to do. She went out

and stood for a while facing the bows. When she returned, she fumbled in her pockets and took out the bank-notes the soldier had given her the previous night, counted them, rolled them into a ball and thrust them into his left hand. He was silent. Maid the Seventh thought he wanted more money, and turned to the old woman, saying: "Where are those three notes I gave you?" The old woman gave them to her, and these, too, were thrust into his palm.

But the young husband shook his head and threw the notes on the floor, covering his face with his hands and crying like a child. Wu Tu and the old woman disappeared into the after-hold. Wu Tu was frightened. She thought it was strange that a grown man should cry. She looked up at the rafters, where the two-stringed violin was hanging, and suddenly she wanted to sing; she knew that she would not be able to sing.

When the sheriff came to invite his guests to a feast, there was only the old woman and Wu Tu on board. He asked them what happened, and learned that the young wife and her husband had returned to the country, setting out early in the morning.

The Yellow Chickens

FORMERLY he was a farmer, but when the Revolution came, he followed the occupation of a cook-boy whose sole duty was to keep the fire burning, carry water and carry heavy burdens during the march. He was six feet tall, with long legs, long arms, and unusually long nose and a heavy beard which grew like tangled weeds and now spread in all directions, for it was frequently cut, and this fact alone prevented it from hanging straight down. On the strength of this beard, one might have imagined him at least a general or even a lieutenant-general; and in fact many people have been known to reach high command because of some peculiar physical characteristic. But Hui Ming was a cook-boy, who tended the fires, and he had never received any high appointment on account of his beard.

He belonged to the Thirty-third Company of the Forty-seventh Regiment, which, you remember, took part in the severe fighting on the borders of Kweichow and Hunan when the People's Army was marching north against Yuan Shih-kai. Now ten years had passed, but he was still a cook-boy. He did all that cook-boys should do, and he received in all a cook-boy's wages. But of the army which once marched north, there remained only Hui Ming and the silken banner among those who had taken part in the glorious defeat of the enemy. He had wrapped the banner carefully round his body in memory of his past glory; but no one paid any attention to him, not even the divisional commander, and this was perhaps because he was mild and humble, did his job well, and remained always essentially a good man. People who are good are apt to be fooled. When he was fooled, Hui Ming found no reason to be angry; he never lost his temper, and he knew that he would be a cook-boy to the end of his days.

In every army there are soldiers who are very short—and

these soldiers are the cleverest, and behave like monkeys. Hui Ming was tall, and in the company of the dwarfs he always appeared still more stupid. The dwarfs started it, the rest followed suit, and Hui Ming gradually came to know the torments which are reserved for the fools of the world. And instead of becoming wiser to their tricks, he became stupider and stupider. He resembled one of those large-leafed willow trees which neither the winds nor the rains nor the frost nor the parched summers ever ruin; but instead it seems as though the extremes of climate only foster its growth. He would pay no attention to their tricks, but instead he dreamed of a great expanse of forest on the frontier, where people lived outside the jurisdiction of army laws and where there were no decorations, no lieutenants, no money, no stupid tricks and no bad people at all. It started long ago. The Governor, General Chai-Ye, had spoken of the immense forests on the frontiers of China where they would be garrisoned to protect the country, cultivating the untilled earth, producing food and assuming tasks of tremendous responsibility.

Hui Ming dreamed of all this. He knew there would be New Year festivals, and many other festivals, there would be sentries and frontier-posts and fighting and tobacco, but it would be very different from the army. If someone had asked him why this kind of life appeared to him more enjoyable than promotion or money-making, he would not have been able to answer. The silken banner was still folded round his waist. Some day, he thought, it will be of use. And when this day comes, I will know exactly what to do with it.

Perhaps, too, the banner had something to do with the fact that he was regarded as a fool, and gradually he seemed to grow aware of the fact, and nowadays he rarely talked about the banner except to himself.

One day the Thirty-third Company was transferred to Huanchow, where it was to take part against the army of a counter-revolutionary general. Hui Ming received the news of his transfer as he received all other news. He had ten years' experience in the army, and during that ten years there had been nothing but continual wars. The soldiers died and the half-wits were promoted. Confucius said: "Gentlemen should not chop meat with their own hands," but Hui Ming had never read Confucius and he had no understanding of satire. The wars were not fought in order that common sympathy should be allowed to spread over the country, nor were they fought in order to unify the Party or remove the capital elsewhere—they were fought for no reason at all, or rather they were fought because a divisional commander said: "Advance against the enemy, and you will receive three months' pay." Just that, nothing more.

They reached the front, and Hui Ming was still a cook-boy. Everything was ready—the three pairs of sandals he had already woven, the ropes, the tin bowls and the bundles of tobacco leaves. He had even obtained a really good flint for lighting fires. Obviously the war would be beginning soon. Heavy ammunition carriages trundled by, the wheels fastened deep in the mud; and Hui Ming, like the other soldiers enjoyed yelling at the pitiable horses stumbling forward with their loads. He himself had carried a load of no less than a hundred and sixty pounds on his shoulders, but he was always singing, and when he was not singing, you could hear his high-pitched voice above the others.

The flanks were not yet joined. The Thirty-third Company was stationed on a hillside. As usual Hui Ming carried water, washed the cabbages, boiled the rice, and if ever the commanding officer made some pointed remark about him, he would only smile and ask when the fighting would begin. He did not ask *why* there should be any fighting at all—whether to save the country, deprive some war-lord of his ill-gotten gains or to join a revolution—and the fact that he did not ask such questions showed that he was not so stupid as some people thought.

For three days they had been stationed near the front. Nothing had happened: everything was quiet. After his labours of the day, he would be tired out at night and he would fall on a heap of straw and drop sound asleep. But afterwards he would awake. "Perhaps the guards have received their orders? Perhaps there is a night raid? Perhaps they have already started fighting?" He would shudder, get up from the straw and crawl away. He would notice a sentry standing on a hillock or walking to and fro with his rifle on his shoulder. He would cough in order to attract the sentry's attention—everyone knew his cough—and sometimes the sentry would say: "Give the pass-word," and Hui Ming, though he never forgot the pass-word, would always answer "Cook-boy Hui Ming." This was his own pass-word which he kept to with great strictness. He would advance slowly towards the sentry.

"Well, how is it—any fighting?"

"Nothing yet," the sentry invariably replied.

"I thought I heard rifle shots."

"You must have been dreaming."

"No, I was awake."

The sentry would laugh. "Ghost words!" he would exclaim, and then they would be silent for a while, while Hui Ming pricked up his ears and listened attentively in the distance.

"Listen, listen, did you hear anything?" Hui Ming would ask, and if there was no answer he would whisper persistently: "I suspect there is something doing. I heard a horse neighing."

"That's your own breath," the sentry would reply, but even then Hui Ming would continue talking—about the number of soldiers killed, or some anecdote or other from the wars. He would not crawl back to his bed until he could draw further reply; and feeling cold, he would gaze up at the sky, where nothing had changed.

He did not dislike the wars, for they brought him weariness

and hunger and sometimes excitement. He was even secretly delighted by the confusion, the ridiculous panic and the lamentable disorder of a rout. He hoped the war would begin soon, while the weather held and the men were cheerful. He remembered the previous year in West Hupei. It was June and the dead lay everywhere, red ants creeping over their bodies, their heads purple and swollen to the size of pumpkins, and their bellies swollen and their intestines leaping through the skin. He did not like looking at the dead; and now the days were growing hotter, and soon it would be exactly like last June. But to his amazement nothing happened, the armies were not ordered forward and there even seemed to be prospects of peace.

It was all very irksome. They were just waiting. No decision had been reached, and June was coming on and they would soon be in the middle of the hot weather. For Hui Ming this was particularly terrible, since he believed that every war would bring him nearer to the garrison on the frontier. Nowadays he was asking everyone he met about the opening of hostilities. He was as much concerned as if he had been promoted to major. But no one could give an answer, and it looked as though they would stay there right through the month of June. Five days had passed, and there was still no news. On the sixth day it was just the same.

Those dull days made him indifferent to the occurrences of the night, and he would talk less and less often to the sentry when he awoke at midnight. During these days his whole attention was occupied by a small village, where no soldiers were stationed, since the topographical nature of the terrain made its defence unnecessary. The villagers had removed into the mountains, but now that the situation was improving. they were gradually returning to their farms, and sometimes they would bring baskets of eggs along the village paths and wait for the soldiers to come and buy from them.

Because he was cook-boy Hui Ming was allowed out of

the camp before the fires were lit in the morning, and he often went to the village in order to buy things for his company or in order to talk with some old village men. Moreover, there was a certain kind of native tobacco which could be bought in the village. This tobacco had perfectly golden leaves and tasted good. And when he returned from the village, he always found his carefully-guarded three bundles of leaf safe among his stores. And there was wine in the village, old wine taken out of the cellars, and though he drank little, a small cup would make him feel as happy as a king. And everybody wanted to talk to him about his beard, and sometimes he would boast of how General Chai-Ye had been seen with his own eyes four or five times, though in fact Hui Ming had only seen him twice, and he would talk about the spirit and complexion of the great man, and then he would remember the banner. At this point he would meditate for a while and look craftily into the other man's face. And then, noticing that the man possessed a pair of honest eyes, he would smile and slowly unwrap the banner from his waist. "This is what he gave us. He said: 'Be brave and unfurl the flag from the castle walls.' His exact words. 'Unfurl the flag from the castle walls'—that's what he said." Saying this, he would take out his pipe and begin to smoke leisurely. If it was not that he was afraid of being punished by the captain, he would have unfurled the flag on the hillock just outside the village. And all the while he thought of the place on the frontier.

One day a villager gave him a hen, and he brought her back to the camp, remembering the words of the villager who said: "Every day she will lay an egg." He put the hen in an old wooden bullet-case, and on the second day she really produced an egg. He fed her on rice, and waited expectantly for the second egg, and when on the third day a second egg appeared, he made signs to the hen as though to say: "I really admire you. Carry on the good work." Every day there was an egg, and every day he carried the hen down in his arms to the village so that one of the cocks could cover her. Now a new interest entered his life, and he forgot the war.

He began to care for the hen with the gentle cunning of a mother, and when he discussed her with others, he would resemble a mother praising her own children. He dreamed of twenty or thirty chickens chirping at his feet. Awakening at midnight, he listened attentively—not for gunshots but for the sound of wild-cats coming to capture his eggs. And soon there really were twenty eggs, and he began to find ways and means by which the eggs might be hatched, and he no longer said: "Hen, I admire you," but "Please, hen, be patient." He was very polite to the hen.

Twenty days passed and at the end of this period all the chickens had broken out of their shells into the sunlight. Their chirps and their milky yellow fur made him madly delighted. If only he could be sent to the frontier and take these chickens with him! And now all day soldiers would come along to inspect his chickens, and sometimes they would ask to be allowed to keep one. To these requests, he always inclined, but on condition that though they belonged to the other, he should still look after them. He made a different mark on each chicken, and fed every one alike. When the day was fine, he would pour the chickens and the hen out of their wooden box, letting them play about in the camp, while he stood to one side, half-dressed, his pipe in his mouth. Or else he would take them all down to the village, so that the original owner of the hen could see them; and when the villager paid them compliments, he would expand gloriously, the short pipe in his mouth while he murmured:

"It's all due to your hen—so intelligent—so clever."

So they shared the glory between them.

There were times when Hui Ming was so overcome that tears dropped from the corners of his eyes, and sometimes the villager would say:

"Is it true that there is going to be no fighting?"

"H'm—well—we haven't received any orders."

"Nothing?"

"Perhaps we shall have to fight later."

"And then what will happen?" the villager would ask, thinking only about the chickens.

"Oh, don't worry," Hui Ming would answer, showing the special marks which had been painted on each chicken. "They belong to the company, you understand? If we have to fight, I'll take them to the front. They won't be frightened. You don't believe me? Well, once I brought a cat with me, and it spent two months in the trenches with us—a black cat."

"I thought cats were afraid of gun-fire."

"That's where you are wrong—they are just like men."

"Perhaps so. I've heard that in foreign lands they even set the dogs to help in the fighting."

"Well, that's a good idea. Dogs are more clever than men. I've seen with my own eyes a dog as big as a calf pulling a cart."

And so they talked, and all the while it was as though Hui Ming was becoming more and more out of sympathy with his life as a soldier, and more and more in love with the chickens.

One day, after Hui Ming had returned from one of these conversations in the village, he sat pondering and smoking his pipe beside the box of chickens, imagining that they had grown and were flying among the trees round the camp and even fighting one another. At that moment someone came with some news—he had heard it from the captain's lips that they would retreat during the night.

Hui Ming ran up to him.

"You must be lying," he shouted.

The man brushed Hui Ming away and went on to another part of the camp. Hui Ming went straight to the captain's tent.

"Captain, is it true?"

"Is what true?"

"I heard them saying . . ."

The captain remained silent. Panting as though he had been running, Hui Ming looked over the captain's shoulder and saw people packing up their things. He nodded happily and ran back to his quarters.

The generals of the opposing armies had made peace between them. They had divided the province between them, they had agreed to withdraw their troops and henceforward the slogans which had been so assiduously employed no longer had any meaning. The world was at peace. Hui Ming's possessions had increased by a wooden box and a family of chickens. And when the army moved off, the cookboy moved with them, carrying his chickens and the three bundles of tobacco leaf which had remained untouched. There was no blood, no maimed bodies, no intestines waving over the battlefield; and all the sad and noble expectations of the soldiers had come to nothing.

At the front Hui Ming had been a cook-boy. He still remained a cook-boy. There were no more wars, and the garrison on the frontier, with the silken banner waving over it, faded into the distance. He fed his chickens, tended them carefully and thought of his tobacco leaves. There was enough for forty more days. He was perfectly happy. June had come and gone. He looked down and smiled happily at the chickens.

San-San

YANG's mill lay at the entrance of a long winding valley, where the stream, turning sharply, suddenly grew more rapid; and over the mill-race a stone mill had been built, and from ancient times this had been known as Yang's mill. Looking up from the mill you saw the houses and white walls of the village peppered with the green of trees; and looking down you saw innumerable strips of tussocky fields, resembling so many steamed dumplings. Along the stream the farmers erected bamboo water-wheels, for all the world like round golden gongs. And all day and all night you heard the soft moaning of the wheels.

Yang's mill was the only mill in the neighbourhood. All the rice in the village was hulled and ground there. Every day people came there, carrying their stores of grain which they poured into the stone troughs, and then the sluice-gate would be opened, the water would pour down over the wheel and the screaming stone-roller would crush the grain to powder. Meanwhile the mill-owner chatted pleasantly to the neighbours, all the while preparing the winnowing-fans and the sieves. Then he would throw a white cloth over his head and follow the roller as it drove in circles over the grain, and with a long broom he swept the grain brimming over from the trough. And this is how the grain became white rice.

When the grain was ground and sifted, when the rice and the chaff had been carried away, the owner of the mill stood covered in dust, like a boiled dumpling covered with bean flour. Yet she enjoyed the life, and being far more prosperous than the other villagers, she was the object of the envy of all.

Old Yang, the mill-owner, died ten years ago, leaving the mill to his wife and his daughter, San-san. But though her father had died when she was five, it made little difference to San-san—she still fished in the stream, ate eggs and busied herself with the rice and the grain. She remembered her father as a strange object, always covered in white dust, and now, when she looked at her mother, tirelessly running after the wheel with a bottle of persimmon oil in her hand to grease the iron shaft of the roller, or sitting quietly in a corner shaking the sieves, it seemed to her that her mother resembled her father, and nothing had changed. In summer San-san sat quietly in a draught, cooling herself, making little cages of corn-straw; in winter she crouched over the fire, cracked chestnuts roasted amid ashes, and purred with the cat. Or else, with a trumpet of rushes which a customer had once given her, she marched round the house, imitating the monks in their ceremonies. The roofs and walls of the house were green rattans, there were sunflowers and dates growing in the garden. San-san would wander among the trees, hardly distinguishable from them in her green dresses, and sometimes she would throw corn to the fowls or chase the savage cocks till at last, frantic with their crowing, her mother begged for mercy.

Above the mill lay a small pond shaded with trees, which the sun never penetrated in summer. There were white ducks, and the fish were fatter there than elsewhere. According to local custom, water near the house was a part of the house-owner's property, and after the mill-dike was built, there was an agreement among the villagers not to poison the stream or cast nets there. So the fish grew abundantly. If a stranger came to fish in the pool, San-san would shout after him: "You can't fish in our pool—you must go downstream." Sometimes a stranger would throw out his line, pretending not to have heard her, smiling at her and smoking his pipe; and this so enraged San-san that she would call out to her mother:

"Nian, Nian! Come and look! There's a silly person catching our fish! Come and break his rod, Nian! Quickly!"

And usually her mother said:

"San-san, there are so many fish, let him catch them.

Fish can walk, you know. All the fish in the great lord's pond have come here, because they like our water."

Thinking of fish that could walk, San-san remembered her dream of a large fish which once leapt out of the river and ate some ducks; and she would close her eyes tight and gaze accusingly at the man, counting up the number of fish he had caught, and afterwards she would relate everything that had happened and tell her mother the number of fishes.

Sometimes the fish were so large that the rod would be broken. Then San-san was glad, and it was her turn to laugh at the angler, for it seemed as thought the fish were friendly to her even when her mother did nothing. And she would run back to her mother, laughing happily, and they would both laugh together.

Sometimes, too, the angler was a friend, who never forgot to say: "San-san, may I fish?"

"Fish are everywhere," she would answer. "They are not fed by us. Yes, please fish!"

Afterwards she would sit on a little stool by his side, eagerly watching the fish as they took the bait, and she would relate the story of the man whose rod was broken. Before he left, this friend of hers would give her some of the fish. As she watched them being cut up by her mother, she would remove the white bladders and stamp on them with her feet, delighted at the sound which resembled the explosion of fire-crackers. When at last the fish were washed and salted, San-san hurried to fetch some thread and hang them up in the sun; when guests came, these fish, dressed with red peppers, would be set on the table. Her mother would say, remembering the man with the broken line: "This is San-san's fish." San-san would laugh, saying to herself: "Yes, the cowboys would have caught them if I had not been watching."

And so she grew up, surrounded by clouds of chaff, and in the village everyone wanted her as a daughter-in-law, for they knew that her dowry would be the stone-mill. She was now fifteen. It was already time to think of marriage. Yet her mother remembered the words of a sorcerer and refused to contemplate her daughter's marriage. And now, as in other days, they would wash their faces in the stream after supper and look at the setting sun—so the days were spent. Sometimes they heard gongs and drums in the village announcing a wedding, and she would say: "Nian, Nian, take me there, please!" and her words were both a command and a request. If there was no reason to refuse, her mother would accompany her. Returning late, pockets filled with filberts and walnuts, having dropped into a house for a cup of honey tea, they were perfectly happy if the moon was up; and if it was dark, they would light a bundle of pine-wood which crackled in the night. Sometimes they would visit the castle of the great lord, who owned all the property in the neighbourhood, and then they would be accompanied by a servant bearing a torch or a lantern when they returned to the mill. But more interesting still was to walk home by lantern-light on a rainy night. On such nights San-san dreamed that she was walking along a stream by the light of a little red-paper lantern. And it seemed to her that only the fish knew this.

One evening, when San-san was returning to the mill, she noticed two dim figures standing in the dusk under a tree. One held a stick in his hand and seemed about to cast a line. Thinking he was still another fish-thief, she cried: "You can't fish here! These fish are owned by somebody!"

A voice answered: "What nonsense! As though the fish had owners! Does the water own them?"

"It's only the mill-girl, and she's joking," another voice interrupted.

Presently she heard the voice of the other man saying: "Come here, San-san, all your fish have disappeared."

San-san was alarmed at the thought that someone with an apparently familiar voice was joking with her, and she ran up, hoping to get a glimpse of the man in order to report his effrontery to her mother. Then she noticed that it was the bailiff from the great lord's house, and he was accompanied by a young man she had never seen before—a young man with a crutch. The bailiff laughed. He knew San-san well, and San-san knew him. He roared after her:

"What's happened to the fish, eh? Why do they breed so well by your house?"

She said nothing, but bent her head low and smiled. She could still see the white trousers and white shoes of the young man, who appeared to have come from the city.

"She is really very clever and pretty—not bad," the young man said.

"The village beauty—that's what she is," the bailiff answered, and the stranger laughed.

She knew he was laughing at her. Indignantly, she thought to herself: "Oh you townsmen, you are even afraid of dogs. I wonder you are not ashamed of yourself laughing at others when you are even afraid of dogs." And thinking that she had spoken aloud and been heard by the man, she thought of running away. The bailiff was well-acquainted with her shyness, and murmured:

"San-san, don't go away. Is your mother in?"

"No, she went to the village to listen to the singing."

"Why don't you go and join her?"

"I don't want to."

The bailiff laughed out aloud.

"It's quite clear—you were afraid someone would come and steal your fishes, so you stayed behind."

Raising her head slowly, San-san looked at the stranger. He was very pale. She thought she had seen him before. Perhaps he was an actor who played the female part in a Chinese drama, and he had come down from the stage with the white powder still on his face.

"Is this your house?" he asked, noticing that she was no longer timid.

"Why not?"

"Aren't you afraid of being pushed into the stream?" the young man asked after a while.

"Hei!" she pressed her little lips together, cast a severe glance at him, and cried out sharply: "Look out! The dog's coming! He'll frighten you and push you into the stream and you'll be carried away!" Then, still laughing, she ran away, thinking how amusing it would be if he were carried away by the stream.

A little while later, when it was growing darker, she saw two white figures walking among the trees. She followed them. She overheard them talking about someone in the city, about draining a river, and about a certain school which was to be founded by the bureau of education. She was amused because they did not know they were being followed. Then she heard the bailiff talking about the mill, and how good her mother was, and she felt happier. The townsman was saying:

"The girl is really very good-looking. I suppose, according to the country custom, she will soon be married——"

The bailiff laughed.

"Do you want her? I could arrange with the lord to make the match between you. But you know—the mill will belong to the son-in-law."

San-san spat on the ground and pressed her fingers to her ears. It was unbelievable! They were still talking, though their voices were indistinct now. The bailiff was saying:

"When you become the owner of the mill, you'll have fresh eggs every day—and so many other things."

Once more they burst out laughing.

She would not follow them any more. She sat down on a rock near the stream, her face burning. "Oh, so you want to marry me! Well, I won't! And even if the hens lay twenty eggs a day, I shan't give you any!" The cool wind fanned her face and the whispering stream reminded her of falling into the water, and once more she was happy.

She went in search of her mother who was returning from the village.

"It's so strange," her mother said. "He has to lie day and night in the corridor and let the wind blow over him . . . They say his face is white like a girl's, and he's always smiling . . . No, he can't be a relative of the lord's . . . That's quite impossible, and the lord treats him so respectfully . . . Oh, he could have so many wives if he wanted!" And she went on in a lower voice: "He lies in bed all day long, taking sweet medicine. It's so strange. I don't know what diseases the townspeople suffer from—not the same as ours. I know they have many names for diseases, for they like to be ill, and as for us—we have only a few names, like malaria and fever, and that's all we can afford to have. Oh, but he is so handsome!"

"Have you really seen the pale-faced man?" San-san asked.

"No, I've never seen him—I've only heard about him in the village."

"Then how could you talk so much without having seen him?" San-san asked herself.

She decided to keep it a secret. Once, when they were coming to the pool, she said: "Nian, Nian, have you seen the lord's bailiff?" but there was no reply, for her mother was preoccupied with other things; and this was one more reason why San-san decided to keep the secret to herself.

The next day, when she was walking through the village, the mother met the pale stranger near the lord's gate. The bailiff was also there. The bailiff told her they had taken a walk to the mill and met San-san, and the stranger pointed out that the mother possessed an extraordinary resemblance to San-san, adding that the child was so sweet and clever that she must be a great happiness to her mother. All this delighted and at the same time confused the old woman, and when she returned, she asked San-san whether she had seen the stranger.

"Try to remember, San-san," her mother insisted. "It was late in the evening, at dusk——"

"Yes, I remember. Two men. One was the bailiff and the other was the stranger. What about them?"

"Nothing. I met them to-day. The stranger from the town looks just like a girl," the mother said, laughing and thinking of something else. "They want me to send them eggs," she added. "I want you to take twenty eggs there this afternoon."

"Who is going to take the eggs?" San-san asked, remembering the conversation she had overheard between them. "Nian, Nian, I think they are bad men!"

"Why?"

It was a long time before she answered: "I heard them talking. They want the great lord to be matchmaker, so that the pale-faced man can marry me."

Instead of taking this seriously, the mother burst out laughing. San-san prepared to run away.

"It's nothing," her mother said. "Just talking for fun. Why should it make you angry? The lord is the master of the whole village, isn't he? He'll scold them . . ."

San-san burst out laughing.

On the next day her mother wanted her to take the eggs to the lord's house. San-san shook her head and pursed her lips. There was nothing for it—the old woman went alone. All that day San-san played near the pool, watching the white ducks in the sunlight or lying in a cool bamboo chair near the stream, idly gazing, listening to the drone of the waterwheels, and suddenly she heard a voice saying: "Where has San-san got to? Why doesn't she come out?" It was the pale-faced man, sitting by the pool, quietly angling, but instead of a rod he was using the bailiff's long pipe.

It was curious that he should be using a pipe, yet he seemed to have caught thousands of fishes, and she was about to jump up and tell her mother, when suddenly the bailiff appeared by her side. They were talking quietly together.

The sky was full of red clouds. They were still talking, and she had no idea what to do.

"We have come to buy some eggs," the bailiff said at last. "We'll give you any price you like."

The townsman was waving his hands like an actor.

"Tell her we'll give her all the gold she wants."

"I won't sell them," San-san answered, frightened. "I don't want your money. Go and take your gold nuggets away—we don't want them here!" A little later she added: "I'd rather feed shrimps with my eggs than sell them to you. Take your gold away—we don't want it here!"

Then suddenly the strangest things began to happen. A great hound, pure white, leapt out of the house, barked at them and threw itself upon them, so that they were pushed into the water. The stream rippled. The bailiff's bare skull was floating on the surface of the stream, while the townsman's long hair was all entangled among the willow roots. San-san burst out laughing. The two men were catching fishes with their bare hands . . .

"Wake up, San-san!" It was her mother's voice calling from the kitchen. "I've taken the eggs to the house. The stranger was very kind to me. Go and look at yourself in the mirror. Your face has gone all red with sleeping."

Another day, when eggs were being taken to the lord's house, San-san accompanied her mother. They went in the afternoon. The stranger was lying on a bamboo chair in the courtyard, looking up at the doves swooping in the air. The bailiff was away. San-san was too shy to approach the man and gave instructions to her mother to go up to the stranger, saying: "I've brought the eggs, sir." It was all very confusing. San-san stood outside the moongate. As in a dream, she saw the pale-faced man stand up and sit down again. They were talking about the weather. From time to time her mother turned her head and looked in the direction of San-san, and at last the townsman noticed it and said: "Is your daughter there, too?"

There was no escape for it. San-san had just decided to run when she noticed the bailiff standing squarely behind her. She had no idea how long he had been standing there. He took her by the hand and led her into the little garden, where she stood close to her mother with her eyes turned in every direction but the direction in which she was expected to look.

Then strange things began to happen. There came from the house a woman wearing a white dress and a white cap, a woman who resembled a man, who placed a little tube in the stranger's mouth and grasped his hand. She held his hand for a long while, and taking something which resembled a pen from her pocket, she wrote some characters on a slip of paper. The stranger asked: "How many beans?" "The same as yesterday," the white-robed figure replied. San-san and her mother thought the stranger asked: "How many beans?" because the words sounded similar, and both burst out laughing.

"Dear sister," said the stranger to the white-robed figure. "You have hardly any friends here. You ought to make friends with these kind people here. They live in a very beautiful mill, with a waterwheel . . ."

At last it was time to go. The nurse accompanied them, and all the while San-san gazed at the white cap and laughed silently, till they reached the edge of the lord's fields and the nurse turned away. They walked through a bamboo grove. San-san placed the empty basket on her head to look like the fishermen.

After a while she said: "Nian, do you like that woman?"

"Which woman?"

"The girl with the white cap and the pink-and-white cheeks."

"I thought she looked very nice indeed——"

San-san was puzzled.

"How can you call her nice when she is as long as a long cucumber?"

"Well, she has attended school. Didn't you see her write?"

San-san thought for a moment. "It is all right for men to write," she said at last, "but for a girl it's disgusting."

They began to walk more quickly. The dusk was coming on, but they were already tired and sat down on a long stone under the maple trees. San-san removed the bamboo basket from her head and smoothed down her hair with her fingers, and all the while she was wondering why the face of the town-dweller was the colour of camelias.

"They're so ugly," she murmured at last.

"Yes, they're so ugly," her mother sighed.

One day there came to the mill an old woman who knew all the gossip of the village, and while San-san sat in a corner stringing hemp into knots, the gossip began to talk to her mother about the affairs in the lord's house. Such curious affairs! Take that young stranger from the town . . .

"Some people say she's just a hired woman to look after him, and they pay her so many ounces of silver, but I don't think it's true," the gossip went on. "As sure as I'm here, it's his concubine."

San-san's mother grew pale.

"I'm sure it's not a concubine," she objected quietly.

"Well, why not?" the old gossip objected.

"I tell you . . ."

"Show me facts . . ."

"I can't show you facts, but I am sure it is not!"

It was time for San-san's hair to be washed. The water was boiling; the old woman had gone away.

"How strange you are, Nian," San-san said, unloosening her hair. Why did you talk such nonsense to the old woman?"

Her mother said nothing; her lips were tight-closed and she was thinking of many things, and sighing gently.

A few days later the nurse came to the mill. San-san's mother did everything to make her visit enjoyable, bustling here and there on quick little errands, and once she even thought of killing a hen but she wondered whether she dared invite so elegant a person to dinner. San-san took the guest to the waterwheels, where she plucked marigolds and fished for carp. The nurse caught many fish, but refused to take them home with her, though she was delighted with everything in the house and made a little speech about the pumpkin seeds "which tasted so good." San-san's mother was overjoyed and pressed her to take home a handful of raw seeds.

Then the stranger and the bailiff came again, fishing and returning home with many presents, and a few days later the stranger came with the nurse, bringing presents of bottled sweets and other things, refusing the two live hens which were offered them and begging that the hens should be allowed to remain alive so that they could lay eggs. Nevertheless the old woman persisted, and it was only when the stranger said that he would be pleased if they were killed the next time he came that she allowed them to go free.

From this time onward the mill seemed to have changed. All day mother and daughter spoke about the city, which they had never visited; and they imagined that the city was full of people like the woman in white and the man with a white face, and they imagined people perpetually dressed like the brides of the village in colourful silks, surrounded by servants, and there were special servants sitting all day at the gates to receive cards and there were other servants continually peeling lotos seeds and preparing birds' nest soup to eat. Innumerable wide streets, innumerable carriages and horses. San-san believed in a real city where all these things were possible, but her mother could only imagine a great span of buildings, hundreds of times larger than the lord's castle, but still extraordinarily similar to the castle with its innumerable courtyards. And so they would talk about the city late into the night, dreaming of the future, and sometimes her mother would dream that San-san was already a bride, and in her turn San-san would dream of her mother growing old and weary with the years. These country people, who drew their happiness from their daily lives, lost nothing by their dreams and indeed gained by them; and it seemed that they were even happier in their dreams.

San-san always made scenes when her mother asked her to carry eggs to the lord's house. She would rebuke her mother for not combing her hair—the hair-plait was not smooth—she must change to a new dress, and at the last moment she would say she was unwilling to go. Then her mother would cry a little with vexation, and they would go off together, while her mother spoke tenderly of how the white-capped woman nursed the pale stranger, and looking into San-san's eyes, she would see the same tenderness there. Afterwards they were silent.

Once again the bailiff came to the mill. San-san was busy plucking marigolds near the waterwheels, but when she returned she saw the bailiff deep in conversation with her mother. He looked up and smiled at her.

"Why do you come so rarely to the lord's house?" he asked.

"Why should I go?" San-san answered, gazing at the marigolds in her hand.

"Your friends are waiting for you there," the bailiff answered.

"I have no friends."

"You must have some friends!"

"If you say so!"

"San-san, tell me, how old are you this year. Were you born in the dragon year?"

San-san looked at her mother, more puzzled than ever. What was this man trying to do?

"Don't worry," the bailiff went on. "I know all about your birthday, because your mother has just been telling me. You were born on April 17th, isn't that so?"

San-san thought: "It is nothing to do with you. April 17th or May 18th—it's all the same, and I don't care a straw whether you come to kneel before me on my birthday." She made a sour mouth at her mother. She had plucked the marigolds for her, but now she refused to give them to her. Then she ran out into the garden, after first laying the flowers near the silent stone mill, and decided to make water-flowers by throwing pebbles in the stream.

The bailiff came out of the house with her mother. San-san pretended to be watching two oxen fighting in a distant field. The bailiff stopped and called after her, but she paid no attention to him; and he went away, laughing softly to himself.

Afterwards her mother called to her:

"San-san, there is something I must tell you."

San-san paid no attention to her.

"What is the matter?" her mother asked. "Are you angry with someone?"

"No," San-san whispered, but she could almost have wept.

It was two days before there was peace between them.

Autumn came. The days passed slowly; the ripe ears of corn in the fields were bending in the sun and the rain. Already the new grain was being stored in the barns, already the early ears were being plucked and hulled. Now came the time for weddings, and sometimes when there was nothing else to do San-san would accompany her mother in an apron of onion-blue to a marriage in a country house. They were always loaded with presents. It was during a wedding that they met the woman in a white cap again. She had little to do besides nursing and she had come here to see the wedding presents displayed before all the villagers.

At once she asked San-san why she had not come to visit the lord's house.

Like all country-women faced with such a question San-san said nothing, but gazed up at the nurse's face, noticing that it had become thinner and yellower than ever, and she laughed a little. Then the nurse began to talk to her mother, saying that the invalid was still unwell, a doctor had been summoned from the city and he had advised the invalid to seek a change of air. They were going soon to a distant place, but they would always regret not being able to see the mill and the two women who lived there.

She said, too, that she had sent a message to the mill asking them to come over, but there was no reply. She would liked to have fished in the stream, but the weather was too hot, and noticing San-san's new apron, she asked:

"What a really pretty apron you have! Did your mother make it for you?"

San-san smiled.

"We countrywomen," her mother said, "have no use for good things. We just put on what we have got." San-san thought her mother was telling an untruth. "It's been made up three times," she said in a low voice.

The nurse smiled: "You must be very happy, and still more happy to have such a daughter."

"It's nothing," the mother answered. "Our happiness cannot be compared with the happiness of the city dwellers."

When a great pile of wedding gifts was being carried into the room, San-san ran away to see it more closely, and the nurse took the opportunity of saying:

"When your daughter is married, she will have an even better dowry."

"We are poor," the mother said, "and perhaps no one will marry my maid."

Overhearing these words, San-san decided not to come back to the nurse.

Meanwhile the nurse was inviting the mother to visit the stranger, and perhaps the mother would have accepted but she discovered that her hands were empty, and she would be ashamed to enter the great gate with empty hands. And so she declined, but promised to come some days later.

When they reached the mill, they were both talking about the bride and how she had put powder on her face, and they spoke about the nurse, whose face had become yellower and darker in the autumn sun; and suddenly the mother remembered her promise to see the stranger in the lord's house. At first San-san refused. Then, because it was something so very simple, and would do no harm to anybody, she agreed. And then, having once agreed, she was determined to visit the house the very next day. And because the woman in white had said she might visit the mill, they decided to forestall her by going early in the morning. They would bring the guests home and accompany them back to the house in the evening. Yes, they would return early, kill the hens and prepare the feast.

So they went out early in the morning, carrying the basket of eggs, passing over bridges and through bamboo groves, climbing small hills. The roads were still wet with dew. Fireflies were still shining in the long grass. And seeing the child walking in front of her, slim as a bamboo shoot, knocking down the grass at her feet with a stripped bough, her mother recalled the bailiff's words and still could not understand what they meant. Yes, San-san was growing quickly. The nurse had said something about it, and she remembered the wedding. Well, they had placed the phoenix crown trimmed with pearls on the head of the bride . . . so many presents, goldfish, golden spoons . . . a bed covered with flowers . . . silver apricots . . ."

"What are you dreaming about?" San-san asked tenderly at her side.

"Eh? I was thinking . . . perhaps it is too late for me to go to the city . . ."

"Nian, do you want to go to the city?"

"No . . . but you'll go."

"I don't want to go."

They were silent for a while.

"Nian, Nian, why did you say I ought to go to the city?"

"Child, we won't go. We'll stay here. We have the mill. Is that all right?"

Soon they came to the lord's house surrounded with a park

of elms and parasol trees. When they passed through the gate, they saw some people standing under some elms. Perhaps something had happened; perhaps they were guests who had been invited; or perhaps there was some other reason. It was not strange to them that there should be people there, and so they walked slowly towards the front of the house.

"Perhaps a yamen official has come," San-san suggested. "Nian, you ought to go first and see what has happened." Absent-mindedly, her mother said there might be something wrong, and she put down her basket of eggs and walked slowly on.

San-san met a woman with a baby coming down the steps. Seeing the eggs, the woman said: "Who are you bringing them for?"

San-san said nothing, but her hands strayed to the cloud-shaped cloth buttons of her onion-blue apron, and she lowered her head.

"Where is your mother?" the woman asked.

"Over there," San-san said, pointing.

"A man has just died," the woman went on.

"Who is it?"

"A young man who came to stay with the lord a month ago. He was suffering from a disease and hoped to cure himself in the country. How could we know he would die?"

San-san's heart leaped. At that moment her mother came hurrying back, having also heard the news. She said nothing when she caught sight of San-san and pulled her towards the gate, muttering: "Dead, dead . . . Who would have known he was going to die?"

San-san paused and looked up at her mother.

"Nian, is the white-faced man dead?"

"They say so."

"Then we ought to go back."

Immediately they decided to turn back and see what had happened. San-san wanted to see the woman in white. The gate was wide open. They heard many voices, the country people were talking about the nurse and saying she was the invalid's wife, and many other things which proved that they knew nothing about what had happened in the lord's house. San-san could bear it no longer. She tugged at her mother's sleeves and whispered: "Let's go!"

They walked back in silence to the stream, hurrying because in the distance they could see the grain-chandlers waiting with their stores of grain. San-san looked down into the clear stream, feeling that she had lost something. The stone-roller was beginning to grind the rice, and because the axles were screaming, her mother was looking everywhere for the oil-bottle. San-san could see it hanging behind the door, but she said nothing. She was gazing into the stream. She tried to recall the name of the thing that was lost, but though she tried for a long time, she never found this name.

Under Moonlight

On the eighth night of the moon, the moon was half full and hung in the sky at an early hour. Down at the foot of the long range of mountains which drove up from the south and lay along the border of the province, there were stockades where there had settled the remnants of a people long neglected by mankind and forgotten by history. They had been living in this corner of the world for many, many years, speaking a language of their own, following their own customs and dreaming their own dreams. These fortified villages were surrounded by thick pines and firs, with vast plains below; and viewed from the blue stone castle on the top of the mountain, when the whole earth was dominated by the evening and delicately illuminated in the moonlight, these villages resembled graceful poems filled with harmonious colours. Inside the villages, among the woods and fields, among the heaps of newly-reaped straw, near the unpainted wooden granaries and at all other places there were flickering fires. And wandering in the villages you would see these joyous flames, hear faint voices and catch glimpses of human figures in the light of the bonfires. From the main road there would come the clear tinkling of horses' bells and the more calm, solemn sound of the large bronze bells which dangled from the necks of the oxen. In the homes of the farmers as they left their fields and of the small merchants returning from market, there would be congenial faces waiting at the doors of their homes, and in the kitchens there would be prepared steaming-hot suppers and wine heated in earthenware pots.

In the soft, evening air, fanned by a gentle breeze there hung the heavy smells of paddy stooks, ripe mountain fruits, beetles and the vapours of the earth. Everything was maturing and bringing to its appointed fullness all that had been brought forth by the sunlight, the rains and the dews of summer. A festive mood was spreading over all.

The soft clear moonlight cut the clean outline of the castle whose shadow lay across the slope like the shadow of a giant. And by the opening in the castle wall facing the moon stood No Yu, the only son of the chieftain of the village. Gazing at the moon, this boy, who was named after the god of plagues who protected him, smiled as he pondered the bitterness and happiness of life.

". . . Human life is worth living, for everything in it is enjoyable; the war between men and the war of hearts are both enjoyable. Small wonder there has been a story of a hero who chased after the sun and moon. But still more enjoyable it would be if the sun and moon could be bidden to stop at any place we pleased."

And this was the story he had been told:

"The first tribesman, discontented with worldly good fortune and all that he had obtained by force and intelligence, armed with greedy desire and the gifts of great power, desired to chase after the sun and to search for the moon. His desire was to subdue the god who controlled them and to force them to slow down their courses among those who were granted the world's blessings and to accelerate it among those who had lost their hearts for love and had been emaciated by distress and despair. At last he caught up with the sun, but scorched by its heat, he died of thirst in the great pool of the west. The sun and moon knew full well that this was a human desire, one among the desires of the ten thousand creatures; and they paid no attention to it. The gods were just. They had no prejudices. Man was not the sole master of the world, and the sun and moon did not exist for man only. The sun gave heat and power to all living creatures; the moon, to whom all the insects desired to sing, made use of their songs and her silvery light to draw all things into peace. Since then, the sun and the moon as nonchalantly as ever had continued to pour their light over the world, observing the joys and despairs of human life, beholding the fair as they turned ugly and observing the ugly who were called fair. But human beings were driving forward too quickly. Man was superior to all creatures in intelligence, and more immoral than anything under the sun. And since neither the sun nor the moon could punish men with severe cold or terrible heat, they took counsel of the god in whose charge had been placed the fate of human hearts and devised a way by which men could be punished through their feelings, since they lived on their feelings: the happy should feel their days too short and the sorrowful should feel their days too long."

There are some who maintain that this punishment was devised at a conference between the moon and the devils who appear at night; and these people say that this incident tells of the prowess of the moon and has nothing to do with the sun. However, when people found that time passed too slowly or too swiftly, they would curse the sun and exclaim: "Oh, sun, get thee away!" According to the explanation of the natives, the reason why they hated the sun and did not hate the moon, was because the divinity of man was gradually giving way to evil. Another reason why all creatures adored the moon and man especially cursed the sun lay in the fact that moonlight is softer and has a more peaceful light, and gives mankind the cold light of intelligence instead of a direct and intimidating heat. And therefore those who travelled and worked by night, and all lovers, preferred the moon to the sun. Of all human beings only robbers and thieves hated the moonlight, and among the natives of the place there were no robbers, and so their names were unknown to them.

At this moment the chieftain's twenty-one-year-old son, endowed with superb physique in addition to another blessing from a different source, smiled knowingly at the moon in full contentment; and it seemed to him that the moon was smiling back at him. Beside him lay a heap of white,

This was a young girl, who had laid her pretty head of dishevelled hair against his thighs, and she was sleeping quietly and peacefully, as if lying on a pillow. Her small pointed face resembled bleached marble in the moonlight, or the moonlight itself. Her dark hair was like fine yarn spun out of the wintry night by fairies hiding in caves. Her eyes, her nose, her ears, her little mouth which was the source of happiness, and those round, small and mysterious dimples which the country folk describe as "nests of kisses" —all these were of divine workmanship. Her smile, her glance, a movement of her head and everything else of hers possessed a divinity. She, who had been created by gods and demons, should be accorded the treatment which is reserved only for gods and demons, lest she be wronged.

She lay quietly beside him, clothed entirely in white clothes which covered her tall, round, supple and fragrant body. And in the memory of the young man her body appeared to have been carved from mingled white jade, milk cream, delicious fruits and sweet flowers. They had come here in the daytime. She had sung in the sun, and towards evening she had fallen asleep, but soon she would wake up for the new moon.

A stream of cool light poured down on them, gently stroking the whole body of the sleeping girl. Along the slopes a composite symphony of clear sounds was being performed by various insects. The moon seemed to be standing in the air; it was a long time since it had moved.

Happiness made the young man sigh.

He lowered his head, kissed the hair spun out of the black night and drew nearer to the demon's work.

From afar there came the sound of singing and a reed pipe. Nearby fireflies were hovering around the castle with their little torches, so that they seemed to be guiding fairies among the castle walls.

No Yu, who was known as the most celebrated singer among the youths of the place, began to sing; and lest he

might disturb the girl or the fireflies, he sang in a low voice:
> *A dragon should be hidden in the clouds,*
> *And you should be hidden in my heart.*

The girl was dreaming deeply, but in her dream she turned her head slowly and replied:
> *My soul is like a flag,*
> *And your sweet songs are like a soft breeze.*

He thought she had awakened, but listening on, he found that she had turned her head to the moon and was still dreaming. And so he continued singing:
> *People say that I have a poison in my song,*
> *But every song is but a shen of wine, only enough*
> > *for a day's intoxication;*
> *Of your honeyed words,*
> *A single one will sweeten my heart for a whole year.*

With her eyes still closed in her dream, the girl replied:
> *Neither of the wintry wind nor of the sea gales*
> *Can this flag stand the blows.*
> *O blow lightly, blow gently.*
> *(Blow, spring wind, sweet gentle spring wind)*
> *Blow open the flowers, and do not sweep them low.*

By this time it occurred to the young chieftain that his songs might be a cradle in which to rest her soul, and he continued singing:
> *With their wings birds fly into the sky,*
> *Without wings I fly into your heart.*
> *I shall not ask where Paradise is,*
> *For I am sitting at its gate.*

And the girl answered:
> *My body needs the strongest arms,*
> *And my soul needs the sweetest songs.*

Now No Yu began to think, groping for words in his brain like a jeweller trying to pick jewels from his bag. No Yu's bag was full of glittering pearls and rare stones, and just because their number was too large, he was somewhat at a loss to choose among them and was slightly embarrassed. He felt that while the gods had created beauty and love themselves, it devolved upon human beings to create the compliments needed for the divine workmanship; and it was beyond the powers of common men to find suitable words to express this beauty in all its glory, or to describe the powers of love without losing the original emotion.

"This girl deserves the love of Lung Chu to adorn her body, and Lung Chu's poems and songs to decorate her beauty." Thinking in this way, he felt a little ashamed. He faltered and dared not continue singing.

His songs had become the cradle for the girl to sleep in, and this was why she had again fallen into her dreams after half waking up. But when the singing ceased, she awoke.

Seeing her awake, he closed his eyes and pretended to be still sleeping. The girl had slept from sunset until this time, and had perfectly restored her spirits. Seeing that he was still leaning asleep against the wall, and fearing that the stone wall might be too cold, she took her white cape and spread it over him. Then she lay against him, recalling now the red clouds which filled the sky when she fell asleep and seeing the crescent moon overhead; and she began singing gently, as a mother sings a lullaby to her baby:

In sleep the shining light served to cover me.
Waking, I use the moon as my lantern.

The chieftain's only son burst out laughing. Four shining eyes were fixed upon each other, and at the corners of their mouths each was smiling. In this smile they had recorded all that they had done in the daytime. Both seemed to feel shy at their memories of the past, and they pressed one another and exchanged a new smile. And seeing the paleness of moonlight on each other's face, they looked up at the crescent moon hanging in the sky.

Then, from a distant farm where a sorcerer was performing sacrifice to the earth and the gods, there came the sound of horns, gongs and drumbeats. Following these jubilant sounds to their origin, they turned their eyes into the distance, over the hills and towards the river.

"Without boats we cannot cross the river, and without love we cannot live through this life."

"I can never be drowned in this small river, but I will drown myself in your little mouth."

Their true minds were still written in smiles, and in those mysterious symbols, and yet each saw clearly what was in the other's smile. The white shimmering waters and the thin vapours of the long river in the distance, a river which resembled in its winding courses a running belt, had somehow increased the warmth of their hearts.

The girl spoke of the songs she had heard in her dream and of which she had sung; and she thought that they were both dreaming even then. When the young chieftain explained what had happened, they laughed for a long while.

The girl was as naïve as a spring breeze and as happy as a kitten. The long sleep had restored her from the fatigue of the day. Now, in the moonlight, she resembled a fish in the rapid streams. Meanwhile they talked nonsense and gave rein to their boundless fancies, employing all the foolish words which lovers employ in their dreams, and in the fervour of young love.

The young chieftain said:

"Don't talk! Let me mind a single word to praise the beauty of your eyebrows and your hair!"

"What if I talk! Will it interfere with your flattery? Oh, a talented person shows his talent even in his flattery!"

"The gods do not talk. When you are silent, you are like . . ."

"I prefer to be human. You yourself have mentioned the happiness of being human in your songs! Let us be human, and let us be happy."

"I am of the opinion that you resemble the sisters of the

Lady Fairy Ho. I would prefer you to be a little bit duller than those two elder sisters of yours, so that there might be words to depict your nobility."

"You once told me you wished your hound to be nimbler."

"That's true, for then it would be easier for me to find you in the mountains, and besides, it would be safer if I wished it to carry a letter for me."

"When you wish me duller, you are wishing that the 'antelope' should be duller, too—I would not be able to escape when you urge your hound to bite me!"

"Good music is often repeated. Will you be so kind as to repeat your words."

"Very well. I remember that you wished the antelope was duller."

"That was because when the antelope becomes duller and less nimble on her feet, my hound can chase her down and catch her as a present to you. It is when you are duller that I shall have words enough to praise you!"

"You have splendid words in your mouth, but now tell me about your feelings. If lies are more beautiful than truth, I shall still listen to your lies."

"You have invaded my heart as the night has invaded the earth."

"But when the moon rises, the darkness only invades a small portion of the earth?"

"The moon cannot reach the heart."

"If so, then I must have given you my darkness."

"What you have given me is light, a dazzling light, which pricks and oppresses me like sunbeams. Oh, you stupefy me. You make me so humble."

"Yet your heart remains clear. In choosing your flattering words, you only prove the clarity of your heart."

"Clear water does not breed fish and a pure heart holds no flowery words."

"The flow of a river is endless, and the words of the heart

can never be exhausted. Stop talking! A mouth is not made for talking only!"

At this moment their lips found another use, and they remained silent for a short while. Their two hearts beat together, and they gazed at the long range of mountains, at the river and the villages and the fields under the moonlight, as though in a dream. The notes of the reed-pipe semed to have become moistened in the moonlight, and more solemn. In the watch-tower at the corner of the village the drum was being beaten a second time. The girl suddenly remembered something. She held the youth's clever head in her two hands, printed many kisses on his eyes, his eyebrows, his nose and his mouth, then shook her head at him and sighed helplessly. Then she raised her hands and fell on her knees before him and smoothed down her dishevelled hair. At that moment she intended to rise and leave him.

The young chieftain understood this and embraced her, preventing her from rising.

"Even the fireflies know how to play with their torches. Why are you hurrying away? Where are you going?"

"A shooting star knows where to come and where to go. And I, too, have my own place."

"Treasures should be kept in the treasury, and you should be kept in the home of the man who loves you."

"Beautiful things need no home: the shooting stars, the flowers fading, fireflies and the blue-headed, red-billed, green-winged mango-birds, who sing best of all birds—none of these have a home. Who has ever seen a caged phoenix? Who can bind the moonlight?"

"Even lions need their consorts. Even the gods would approve if I kept you in my home."

"What is approved of the gods is often disapproved by man."

"My father will allow me to do this, because he loves me."

"But my father loves me, too, and should he know about it he would treat me accordingly. If I were bound with ropes and sunk deep in the earth's eye, whose bottom cannot be reached even by forty-eight hempen ropes linked together, still when I am dead I should have no means to come to you, and even if I should live in dreams, still I would not be able to find you."

What the girl said was true, for according to the custom of the tribe a girl was allowed only to love her first lover and to marry the second. If she violated the tradition she would be tied to a mill-stone and flung into a deep pool or thrown into a pit. The custom had come down from ancient times. There was a time in the past when this tribe, like other tribes, imagined virgins as evil. The chieftains were the more enlightened among them, and the sorcerers lived repressed lives, and so they undertook to enjoy the *jus primu noctu* of the girls, and thus gradually they learned to enjoy the virgins. The first man, therefore, could deprive a girl of her chastity, but he could not have her love for ever. If he should marry the girl, he would suffer an evil fate. The superstition had gradually lost its original meaning, but tradition preserved the ancient ordinances of the tribe, and they were obeyed by all the tribesmen. For this reason young lovers did not expect to dream long over their first loves. "Sweet flowers do not blossom for long, the shining moon is not round for ever and the stars do not always shine." So they would sing of their first love with sadness and melancholy. When the day of parting came, they often experienced the feeling of: "The orchids will not open their buds again, nor will happiness return," and so they fled away together. But there were others who threw themselves silently, hand in hand, into the yawning crater of a volcano which had been extinct for thousands of years. And there were still others who risked marriage and later lost the girls they loved and saw them being thrown into the pit.

It was impossible to abolish this custom, and as soon as they came of age, girls were allowed complete liberty. Strangers found it quite easy to enjoy these girls, and the more sensible girls chose a man at haphazard and then sought marriage with the men they loved. Any sensible man, madly in love with a girl and knowing her still a virgin, thought nothing of allowing her to sleep with a stranger. Yet these fiendish customs were not approved by the gods, and there were youthful people who were apt to act in accordance with the will of the gods and against traditional customs. There were still girls who delighted in offering themselves wholly to the boys they loved; and there were still boys who desired to possess the girls' chastity and love them for ever. Though a cruel law was attached to the custom, there were occasions when young people sacrificed themselves to the law.

When the girl first encountered the chieftain's only son, it was spring and the wild yellow plum-flowers were blossoming. She was conquered by his tender songs and his exceedingly powerful limbs; and they had loved one another with a perfectly pure love. Because they loved feverishly and with suppressed passion, they did not seem to have thought of marriage; and it occurred to neither of them to follow the time-honoured tradition of suffering chastity to be deflowered by another in order that they should marry afterwards.

But when autumn came, everything was ripening, the fruits on the trees were falling to the ground, grain was being stored in the barns, the autumn hens were hatching their eggs, and Nature, to decorate the earth which had been quivering and hustling for a whole year, painted the sky glorious with colours and made clear the streams and torrents, and the air was warm and sweet, and the earth carpeted with yellow flowers, and cloudlike colours touched the trees and grasses. Everything was put in order, and soon it became man's turn to undergo the proper transformations.

Autumn ripened everything, and now ripened the love of the two lovers.

As usual, they had met on the afternoon by the old castle. Together they had plucked innumerable wild flowers and scattered them on the large blue stone where they sat side by side. The sloping hills were coloured with a myriad of flowers in full bloom, and here and there the little butterflies were flitting, and appeared to be telling every flower the current news. Looking down the slopes, all that met their eyes was tranquil and enchanting. From the long mountain ridges came the voices of the grass cutters, while down in the village they heard the sounds of axes, someone was building a stable for a new-born calf. In the fields below, the gleaners and threshers were loud in their jokes and quarrels. Moving across the pure sky, white clouds slipped past, and there were flocks of wild geese in formation, followed a little while later by more.

These two young people had eaten mountain fruits when hungry, and drunk spring water when thirsty, and they had taken words and smiles to feed their souls. They had sung a thousand songs and spoken ten thousand words on all the sweet things that the sunlight touches.

But when the sun began to sink at last, they felt something lacking and inexpressible in their lives, and when dusk was drawing near, the mooing of the calves on the slopes sent their hearts shivering.

The will of the gods was raised against the traditional customs, and so at that time they could no longer tolerate the devilish restrictions which were placed on human beings. It may be wise to be rational, but it is also useless. And so they lost their powers of reason and utterly surrendered themselves, and now in a new way they realised the strength of their love for one another, and finally achieved the satisfaction of exchanging one soul for another, and keeping it deep in their hearts. At last they trembled and fainted, became dumb and grew silent. Happiness had exhausted them in a single moment: they fell asleep.

The man awoke first, and in thinking of his changing

happiness, he forgot the future. The girl, for the very reason of being a girl instinctively realised the penalty that would be demanded of them for disobeying the traditions; and this was why she had never even imagined that the young chieftain would ask her into his home. At their age, indeed, they were too young to live anywhere except in the Garden of Eden and they were unfit to live in "a world which thinks only of to-morrows."

However, they had reached the age when they should have been amenable to the customs of the place where they grew up and of the tribe they belonged to.

"Is love something aloof from the world?" This new meditation threw the young chieftain into a silence as dumbfounded as a stone under the moon.

Seeing him silent, the girl knew he was tormented, and in a feigned happy voice she called to him tenderly and earnestly beseeched him to be merry, now that they had reason to be merry:

You, who sing so sweetly,
Pray that your voice shall break open the white
clouds in the sky.
Let the moon fall when she has to fall;
Yet now she must ride overhead.

And it was true that there was a thin cloud veiling the face of the moon, dimming all things around. Their hearts were heavy with forebodings.

The chieftain's only son raised his voice:

I cannot live without the sun.
It is death to live without you.
I have no wish to be Emperor or King,
And would rather be your slave for ever.

The girl said:
"This world permits marriage but forbids our loving."
"There should be another world for us to live in. Let us go into the far away, to the place where the sun rises."

"Will you not want your oxen, your horses, your orchards, your fields, your gowns of fox-fur and your cushions of tiger-skin?"

"With you by my side, I want nothing else. You are everything—you are my light and my heat, my spring waters, my fruits and all the ten thousand things. In order to be near you always, I must go from the world."

Thinking of all the places they knew, there was not one where they could take refuge. In the south lay the great country of the Hans, who would kill them as aborigines. No, he dared not go south. To the west lay an endless range of deserted mountains occupied by tigers, leopards and other fierce animals. He dared not go west. To the north lay the tribesmen's territory, where every village kept the fiendish law, and they had the right to deal as they pleased with exiles. Only to the east lay the place where the sun and the moon rise, and since the sun was righteous and without prejudice, it was reasonable to believe that the place must be one of peace and justice.

But now an old legend began to revive in the memory of the young chieftain—the sun had scorched the first tribesmen to death. Ever since this story had come into existence none of the tribesmen had ventured to go east and live a life no longer ruled by traditional laws. The tribesmen possessed an ancient song in which human desire, a desire which contained all the significance of life and which each man who wanted to live must possess, was interpreted in terms of death, indicating that the greed for life could only be satisfied in death. Death alone, which overcame all things, alone could overcome Fate. There was no world of pure justice on earth, but there was such a world in the air and under the ground; and the spaces of Heaven were limited, while the underworld was boundlessly wide. And this the tribesmen believed more readily, for they had never heard of a dead man being revived, nor heard that the dead filled the halls of the underworld. So every tribesman believed in an eternal life, and so there often occurred cases of solitary suicide or even double suicide, and these would occur whenever lovers feared that they would be unable to find one another afterwards.

No Yu thought of the other world and smiled happily. He asked the girl whether she would travel to that place where people go and never return. And she, after a moment of meditation, raised her head and looked at the moon which had reappeared among the clouds.

Everywhere the water flows,
Everywhere the fire burns,
And as the moon shines in all places,
So will I go where my love reaches.

And saying this, she laid herself against his breast, closed her eyes and awaited the kiss that would determine her death. Then No Yu drew out a knife, and from a hole in the jewelled handle he took out a small poisonous pill as large as a wood-oil seed. He put it in his mouth, and as it dissolved he kissed the girl and drew the poison into her mouth. Gladly they swallowed the medicine which would join their lives, and smiling they lay down on the blue stone bed covered with wild flowers, which had already withered, waiting for the poison to take effect.

The moon faded away behind the clouds.

The White Kid

THERE are men who find beauty in listening to the rain and the wind; there are fools who find beauty in listening to children crying at night and the reeds rustling in the wind, and all this is said to be poetry, but still more poetical are the voices of the tribeswomen which drive men to intoxication and despair. Men who have heard their voices think nothing of bloodshed; and so it has happened throughout recorded history. I could tell you fifty stories about Miao girls who were ugly, though they conquered the most handsome men with their sweet singing. I could tell you fifty more stories about the girls, with long brows and fair faces, so delicate and handsome that they were almost like goddesses and how they captured the princes of the tribes. But it would be better to tell you the story of Melchin and Pao-tzu. Melchin means "bewitching as gold," and Pao-tzu means "the leopard." They were two lovers who had fallen in love in admiration of each other's songs. Their passion was so great that they determined to meet in the caves at night, according to the custom of the country, and there offer themselves in marriage.

It was the custom of the tribe for the lover to bring to the cave a perfectly white kid as a present to the betrothed, exchanging the white unspotted kid for the virgin red blood of the girl. According to the story which is often told, Pao-tzu woke up late the next morning. He had forgotten to meet the beloved, and he had forgotten the kid. He ran to the caves, where Melchin had been waiting the whole night, and found her frozen to death, her heart wanting the warmth of a man. Then Pao-tzu (according to the story) killed himself with a dagger, or according to another story, he killed himself some time later, for he heard Melchin singing and could not find her.

But the truth is quite otherwise. Those who were present say that they found a poem written on the sandy floor of the cave—a poem written by Pao-tzu before he died, expiating the promise he had broken, for he came late to the cave. He found Melchin dead with a dagger in her breast; he took the dagger from her and plunged it into his own side and then fell down dead. As to why Pao-tzu, the most faithful of all lovers, should have been faithless to his bride, we would have to ask the white kid, for it was through the kid that he died. Even nowadays the lovers of the tribe still offer a white kid to maidens, saying that it was descended from the kid which Pao-tzu offered to Melchin; yet no one knows whether the kid which was offered in the cave was male or female. I heard the story as it actually occurred from the bandit Wu Lao-ru, who was himself descended from the man who took the kid from the cave—and the same man who had been Pao-tzu's instructor in feats of physical prowess. This is the story:

Melchin was standing on the southern slopes of the valley, Pao-tzu on the northern slopes, and they were singing from morning to night. The hill, now known as the Hill of Songs, was then known as the Hill of Flowering Chrysanthemums, for in those days it was bright yellow in autumn. When the contest was ended, Melchin confessed that she had been defeated by the boy, and therefore she would offer herself to him and he would dispose of her as he pleased. She sang:

The red leaves follow the September winds of autumn,
I will be made a woman only by you . . .

Hearing this song, Pao-tzu knew that he had achieved victory: he knew he had conquered the heart of the most beautiful girl in the village, and so he sang:

You whose songs are known to be the sweetest,
Pray go to the treasure caves of the yellow village.
The large stars gaze at one another in the sky . . .

Melchin answered:

*My darling, the wind, I have only to follow your words,
I desire only that your heart should be as bright as
the sun,
And therefore you will melt me in your sun's heat,
And do not suffer yourself to be laughed at for being
faithless,
And do not forget that you have asked for my body . . .*

To this Pao-tzu replied:

*Be still and secret, my heart, sovereign goddess of
beauty,
My sweet eyes bear witness to my faith,
Even though it rains knives when the time comes
I shall come to you . . .*

It was growing dark. The mountain of the wild boars then, as now, was shaded with its purple mists. In the sky a few red clouds flowered, watching the sun go down. This was the time when wood-cutters returned home, when the cattle and sheep returned to pens and byres. Pao-tzu bade farewell to Melchin and hurried home to the village, where he hoped to find a new-born kid which he would offer to Melchin in the cave. And Melchin also went home.

She changed her clothes, rubbed fragrant oils over her young body, and painted her face with powder, did up her hair before a large bronze mirror and threw a silk kerchief sixteen feet long around her head. When all this was done, she set out for Treasure Cave, taking with her a long-necked calabash full of honey-wine, an embroidered purse filled with copper coins and a fine steel knife.

To-day, Treasure Cave is still the same. Then, as now the floor was dry, covered with a fine white powdery sand, and there was a bed and benches made out of stone. There was even a fireplace and a natural hole through which one could look out at the stars. But one thing has changed—lovers no longer come here to worship each other; they come to worship the images of Melchin and Pao-tzu engraved in gold, before which candles are kept burning. The old ways are dying, and perhaps this is because the passions of the race are fading away, and men love cattle and sheep and gold and silver and many vain empty things more than they love youth. In our materialistic age the singing of songs is no longer held to be the highest wisdom. It would have been better if they had left the cave exactly as it was, so that lovers could steal there at night, but this is a digression.

Melchin came, wearing her new scented gown and waiting for Pao-tzu. She sat waiting on the edge of the bed, which was made of an enormous blue stone. On this bed she would become a bride. There was straw scattered over the bed, and a straw pillow, and lying on the straw, having hung the white calabash on an iron nail and placed the embroidered purse by the pillow, she waited in the darkness for the appearance of her young lover. Starlight dimly penetrated the opening in the cave. She gazed into the starlight expecting to see his huge shoulders appear.

Softly she sang songs to amuse herself, songs which praised the prowess of the leopard in the mountains, songs which praised the beauty of the leopard among men. She caressed herself with her hands, and smelt herself, noticing that her skin was as soft and smooth as silk and her smell was fragrant. She took the kerchief from her head, loosened her hair and watched it spreading like the darkest night to cover her whole body. She was the most beautiful of all the girls of the tribe, and Pao-tzu must have been lucky indeed to possess that white body of hers.

Her whole body was soft and full and round, and yet she was slender as a willow. Her mouth was small, and her round face was decorated with a noble nose, a pointed chin and a pair of long brows. It was as though her mother had carved her on the model of the Fairy Lady Ho. And in an hour, or two hours, she would offer herself stripped to the skin to her lover: accepting the bitter heat and the fiery energy of the man, she would become his bride.

To-day this beauty has gone. The maidens of the Flowery Kerchief tribe are no longer so beautiful, and the word "love" itself will never recapture the purity of ancient times. In order to explain her feelings at the time, it is not possible to use modern, fashionable words, for she did not sigh or speak in monologues and she only hoped that Pao-tzu would come quickly. She knew that the leopard would bite, but she was willing to be eaten.

But where had the leopard gone?

Pao-tzu possessed no white kid in his home, and therefore he went to the old village guardian to buy one. Carrying four strings of brass cash, sufficient for a female kid with spotless white fur, he entered the guardian's gate and at once declared that he wanted to buy a kid.

The constable knew what was happening.

"You handsome boy," the guardian said, "from what family comes the girl who will be your bride?"

"Your eyes, my uncle, can see who is to be Pao-tzu's bride."

"Only the goddess of camellias is fit to be your wife. Only the fairy of Great Ghost Cave could make love to you. But tell me—who is she, that I may offer her my felicitations?"

"People say that Pao-tzu is handsome, but before his bride he is a grain of dust. I simply cannot speak of myself and her in the same breath. To-night I shall be a man, and how shall I speak the words of my heart? I have come to ask you for one of your white kids to offer in exchange for virgin blood."

The village guardian was an old man, a prophet and one who is skilled in the art of delineating the future from physiognomy. He was surprised to hear Pao-tzu speaking of blood, and the words suggesting a fatal augury, he said: "You are not looking well, my son."

"My uncle, how should I expect to look as I usually look on a night like this?"

"Come under the lamplight and let me see."

Pao-tzu obeyed and turned his face towards the large oil-lamp. The guardian examined him and nodded in silence.

"My uncle, you know so much, will you tell me the omens?"

"Knowledge is a sort of pastime for the old: for the young it is useless. Now go to the stables and choose whatever kid you please—and give me no money, and no thanks. I will see you and your bride . . ."

He stopped talking and led Pao-tzu to the stables behind the courtyard. While the guardian held the lamp, Pao-tzu began to search for a white kid. In the stable there were near fifty goats and half of them were kids; but there were none good enough to please him. Those with pure white wool were too large, the smaller ones were unclean.

"Don't look them over so carefully. Take any one you please."

"I am trying to find one . . ."

"Are none of them any use to you?"

"Uncle, how can I offer a kid of impure wool to compare with my bride's chastity?"

"I would prefer you . . . just take any one, and then run to your bride."

"I can't go empty-handed, uncle, and I cannot use any one of your kids, and so I must try to find one somewhere else."

"Don't worry about the kid—it's not important. Hurry along to your bride, and don't keep her waiting. What she wants is not the kid."

"I have made my promise, uncle!"

So Pao-tzu thanked the guardian and went in search of a new kid. The guardian, as he watched him disappearing from the house, sighed heavily. Fate disposed; there was nothing he could do. He could only close the gate and wait for "intelligence of the event." Pao-tzu visited five houses and still could not find the kid he desired, for they were all too big or their wool was impure.

When Pao-tzu came out of the fifth house, the sky was full of stars and it was a time of quietness. "She will not have faith in me," he thought, "unless I fulfil my promise to her. She will not believe me if I tell her that I have searched everywhere for a kid, and yet go to her with empty hands." He decided to search the whole village.

He knocked at the gates of all the houses he knew, and when the gates were opened, he would say in a gentle voice that he wanted a new kid. He was known to all for his physical strength and for his beauty, and when they heard that he wanted a kid to present to his bride, everyone desired to assist him. They regarded it as a happy omen to search patiently and earnestly in their stables. But he looked at all the kids, and found none that satisfied him.

He had not forgotten that Melchin was anxiously waiting for him, and her request that the first stars should see them together still lingered in his ears. He had promised that he would bring her a young kid. But there were no purely white kids in the village, and he decided to go to another village half a league distant. Looking at the sky, he saw the stars and it seemed still early. And so, following the familiar causeways among the ricefields, he made haste to the other village. He had not gone more than a quarter of a mile when he heard a bleat in the grass. The cry was very faint and feeble. At once he recognised the bleating of a kid, and listened intently. Another low bleat could be heard. He felt sure that the kid had fallen into a deep pit by the wayside, and perhaps it had been there all day, bleating for the dam, crying desperately in the dark.

By starlight Pao-tzu opened a way through the wild grass and saw the pit. He heard the grass moving, the kid bleating again: he was intoxicated with joy. He knew there could be no water in the pit, for the weather had been fine; and when he slipped down into the pit, he found that it was no deeper than his waist and the ground at the bottom was dry and hard. The kid must have known someone was approaching, for it cried out. Pao-tzu saw that it was new-born, no more than ten days old, and it had broken one of its forelegs in dropping down the well—probably because the goat-herd drove the goats carelessly.

Seeing that the kid had been hurt, Pao-tzu lifted it tenderly and walked along the road leading to the Treasure Cave. The kid was still bleating feebly. He knew it was suffering, and it occurred to him to return to the guardian and ask for some salves. It would not be too late.

When he arrived at the guardian's house and knocked, the old man, sleepless with despair over the boy's fate, thought that bad news was on its way. He enquired from behind the gate.

"It's your nephew, uncle. I have found the kid, but I think it is hurt—the leg is broken, and I have brought it to you in the hope that you can cure it."

"Why haven't you gone to your bride? It is midnight. Leave the kid and don't stay a second longer."

"But I am sure my bride will like this kid. I cannot see its colour, but I am sure it is pure white. And it is soft like my bride . . ."

The guardian could not have been more impatient or more alarmed, for listening to the young man singing the praises of the kid which he had found by pure chance, he wondered what had happened to Melchin. He drew the bar and pulled the bar and drew the gate open. A beam of lamplight fell on the kid huddled in Pao-tzu's arms and for the first time Pao-tzu saw the colour of the wool. The kid was whiter than the snows of Ta-li. He lifted it to his face and kissed it.

"What on earth are you doing? Have you forgotten that you have a bride?"

"I have not forgotten. Oh, make haste—heal the kid, rub salves on it, then I shall hurry to meet my bride."

The guardian only shook his head and examined the kid tenderly in the lamplight. In the lamplight the kid ceased bleating, closed its eyes and seemed to sigh.

A few moments later Pao-tzu was walking along the road which leads to the Treasure Cave with the kid comfortably asleep in his arms. Soon he would be telling Melchin how heaven had rewarded him. Walking with vigorous strides, he climbed the hill without stopping, passing over many high cliffs, leaping many raging torrents, till he came to the Treasure Cave. When he reached the opening of the cave, it was nearly dawn. The sky was full of stars, and the opening was silver in the starlight.

"Melchin!" he called gently.

He stepped inside. A strange smell came to his nostrils. He knew that it was the smell of blood. He was stupefied, threw the kid to the ground and ran inside.

At first he could not see clearly, then he noticed that Melchin was lying on the bed, the smell of blood coming from her. Pao-tzu fell towards the bed, put his hands on her forehead, touched her face, caressed her mouth. Her lips were still faintly warm.

"Melchin!"

He called to her many times. At last he heard a weak voice answering his call.

"What have you done to yourself?" he asked.

He heard her low breathing which seemed to come, not from her mouth, but from deep down in her throat. Then she turned towards him, trying in vain to lift herself up, and in a low, broken voice, she said:

"Is it you who sang to me in the daytime?"

"Yes, my heart! I would sing sad songs by day, and at night I would sing you songs of joy. Soon I shall be your bridegroom ... Why are you like this?"

"Why?"

"Yes—why? What have you done?"

"Are you the faithless one, the perfect one—but no one is perfect, and even the most beautiful and handsome have a defect. You lied to me. You promised you would come!"

"No, my heart! It is only because I did not want to break my promise to you that I am late. All night I searched for the white kid and by luck I found it. I have found the kid, but I have lost the person I love. O Heaven, how have I been faithless?"

Melchin was dying, but she knew now that Pao-tzu was late because he had been searching for the kid. She knew she had made a mistake in thrusting the knife into her own breast. She asked Pao-tzu to lift her up: she asked him to lay her head on his breast and to press his lips on her forehead.

"I am dying . . ." she said. "I was waiting for you . . . I saw the day break, and thought I was cheated . . . I put the knife to my breast . . . You wanted my blood, now it is given to you . . . O draw the knife out, and let me die!"

Pao-tzu wept silently as he listened to her speaking of her own death. After a moment, he felt her breasts and found them sticky with blood; and between the breasts lay the handle of the knife. His heard turned cold and he shuddered.

"Pao-tzu," she said, "why do you never fulfil your promises? You said that you belonged to me—your whole body belonged to me. Then obey my order. Take out the knife, so that I shall no longer suffer."

Still Pao-tzu kept silent.

A moment later she said: "I understand now. I believe you. Bring me the kid and let me see it."

He laid her gently on the bed and went in search of the kid. Unintentionally he had thrown it to the ground, so that it lay there half dead, and now lay there panting quickly. The sky had turned entirely white. Cocks were crowing. He heard the water-wheels revolving in the distance. Nothing in the valley had changed.

He carried the kid into the cave and placed it near her breast.

"Pao-tzu, help me—let me kiss the kid."

He held her up and lifted her hand until it rested on the snow-white fleece of the kid. "It is a pity that it should have been hurt . . . Take it away now . . . Draw out the knife, and do not cry . . . I know you love me, and therefore I have no reason to complain . . . O God, what are you doing?"

Pao-tzu was exposing his own breast. He pulled at the knife which was buried deep within her, so deep that he was compelled to use great force, and as soon as the knife was released, a fountain of blood sprang out, splashing him like rain. Pao-tzu thrust the bloody knife in his breast. Melchin watched him and died smiling.

When day had broken, the guardian of the village, accompanied by some of the villagers climbed up the cliffs to the cave. They found the two bodies, a half-dead kid and a poem written with a twig in the sand. The guardian learnt the song by heart and carried the kid in his arms down the cliffside. To-day, the women of the village no longer have passions like these. They can still forgive men, they can still suffer for men, they can still sing their burning and fiery songs, but never again has there been a woman who behaved like Melchin.

Three Men and a Girl

WE marched for four days until we reached the town. The weather was curious, for it turned fine at the moment when we came in sight of the town, and though there are many people who swear at the sun and many others who laugh at it, believing that the sun is there only to harass us, we were not displeased, for we had come to take over garrison duty in the town of X——. The former garrison had left, and we were coming to fill the vacancy and continue all the nonsense that had fallen to their lot.

At sunset, when a red glow filled the sky and shone on our men, a battalion of us went into camp, while another battalion, which had accompanied us on the journey, lodged in the small inns and in the houses of the people, for the next day they would move forward to another town fifty *li* away. Different places had been assigned to different companies. We knew that our company flag should be flying over the Yang Family Temple, but no one knew where the temple lay. We could only ask the soldiers of other companies, and their answers only confused us.

There were, in fact, two Yang Family Temples, and the one we found after a long search did not seem to be the right one, for it was pathetically small and fallen into ruins. Our captain was irritated and he refused to move an inch further. "Since this is a Yang Family Temple, and no one lives here, let us rest our feet here and meanwhile we can send out some soldiers to make enquiries." We had been marching all day. Some of the soldiers were resting in houses, washing their feet in large wooden bowls or hastening into kitchens with salt-fish in their hands; the rest were tired and already sleeping. We were the vagabonds, for we had wandered through the streets of the town without finding anywhere to rest. Now at last, as darkness came on, and we had found somewhere to rest our feet, none of us cared where we were; we piled up our guns in the courtyard and we sat down beside the stone lions and unloosened our clothes.

A young bugler found a gourd full of spirits, and hid in a corner greedily consuming the wine. A few soldiers who saw him tried to steal the gourd from him. Soon the gourd was broken and the wine began to trickle on the ground. The bugler cursed and flew after the robbers.

Hearing the noise, the Captain suddenly remembered that the bugler could be extremely useful: he could call up the headquarters by a bugle-call. The bugler thereupon stood beside one of the stone lions, touching the lion with one hand and holding the bugle in the other, and the sad notes of the bugle blared across the sunset sky in search of our headquarters. It was an extraordinarily touching sight—the bugler, the setting sun, the pale smoke rising from the cooking-pots and floating over the roofs of the houses, the young women standing under distant eaves as they looked on with mingled surprise and curiosity, wearing newly starched clothes of moon-blue, embroidered aprons and with children in their arms.

Soon afterwards came the reply from the regimental headquarters stationed on a hilltop temple. The Captain ordered the bugler to enquire whether we were occupying the proper sight selected for us, but the answer appeared to be quite unsatisfactory to the Captain, for once more the bugler was ordered to send a message of enquiry abroad.

From the southern end of the street two white dogs appeared; they were very sleek, and resembled twins. It was clear that they had learnt that something was happening in front of the temple, and they were determined to discover what it was.

There arose in our breasts a great desire for the dogs. Wherever we were, the sight of a fat dog filled us with unquenchable and bloodthirsty hunger. But something else also drew our attention: a girl was calling in a soft voice, "Ah-pao"—"white dog." The dogs gazed at us for a moment with a thoughtful air, as though they knew this was no place for them, and then they turned and walked slowly home.

And then something else happened. We had been marching all day without rest; and the bugler, instead of resting, had been summoned to make a bugle call four times. Suddenly, as he stood beside the stone lion, he fell to the ground with such force that he twisted his foot and injured the tendons. It was clear that it would be a long time before he could walk again.

This bugler was a friend of mine. We were brought up in the same village, we spent our summers swimming in the same river, we would pass whole days together gathering mushrooms in the forest. Now it was my duty to look after him. I wondered what future lay in store for him, for he was only twenty. Unexpectedly the Captain did not dismiss him, but what was clear was that he would always remain a mugelr. He would have no opportunity of entering the officers' training corps to secure better prospects, and he would never be able to join in battle, and he would never be able to climb over walls in order to meet the local girls at midnight. An accident had deprived him of all that made life worth living, and there was no remedy in sight.

Because we came from the same village, I took special care of the man. I was then a sergeant, and since I had power only over my platoon, I placed him in my own quarters. Though hurt, he still had to rise early in the morning under a pale sky, put on his uniform, make everything shipshape, stand on the stone staircase leading to the temple and blow the *reveillé*. Ten minutes later he had to blow the roll-call. At eight o'clock there was the drill-call, and at ten there was the call summoning the men to a brief rest. And there were many other calls. We were not drilled in the towns, but the bugler was still compelled to blow the call, and every time he blew on the bugle, I would have to go to his help. Or, if I was busy, I would send the cook-boy to help him.

We all hoped he would soon recover. The surgeon at garrison headquarters even guaranteed a speedy recovery. His legs were pressed between splints of fir, massaged, burnt with caustic medicines. Days passed, and there was no change. We were all disappointed, but the boy himself seemed to be more hopeful than anyone else.

He told himself that he would recover, that in two months he would no longer need to wear the splints of fir, and that he would run after the hares in the fields. The surgeon laughed, for he knew that there was little enough hope, even though it was necessary according to medical decorum that he should promise the most fantastic things to others.

Two months passed by, and the young man was still bedridden. The wounds were no longer swollen, he was no longer in danger of bloodpoisoning, there was no putrefaction, but he was fast becoming an absolute cripple. He could never perform his duties without the help of others, and he still stayed in my quarters. An intimate friendship grew up between us.

It was a quiet town, but compared with some of the small cities on the frontiers of Hunan it had a character all its own. There were only four streets with a watch-tower in the centre. There were chemists' shops. wine-shops, opium-dens and gambling houses. So I spent my days with the bugler, and we would go through the streets together and share our wine and our fortunes at gambling.

Although he was not improving his position, he was still as happy as any young soldier can be, he shared in all the enjoyments of a soldier, and if he wanted to go to places where women lived, no one would dare to offend him. When he played cards, no one cheated him. When he blew on his bugle, he was as good as ever. And everyone who knew his misfortune tried to help him.

But somehow his character was changing. A bugler should always have a great passion for his bugle, in the morning he should climb over the hills and play on it until it sings with the brightest tunes, and at night he should blow the bugle under the moon and listen to the echoes of distant buglers. At festivals the buglers of all the companies walked in procession to the market, wearing bright new uniforms, openly displaying themselves. Luck might come to them—a girl with a white forehead and dark eyes might see them, and fall in love with them. Moreover, he was given a great amount of freedom and he might be seen sauntering up some distant hills followed by children who would gaze at him with awe; and so there would arise a great friendship between them.

None of these things could happen to the bugler. He could do his duty, but nothing more. He had been so active before, and now he became sad and melancholy as though something had shrivelled up in his soul. He was maimed. The Captain would publicly refer to him as "the cripple." Yes, and behind his back, many others called him "the crippled bugler." For the sake of convenience, because it was easier to distinguish him from other buglers, he was called by these names—names which were employed even by the cook-boys as they talked about him in low voices.

For a while he still performed his duties perfectly, standing outside the temple or on the stone stairway, but afterwards when we enrolled a young assistant, the bugler no longer performed his duty so well.

We would go to the same bean-curd shop every day, sitting there on long wooden benches and gazing at the shopkeeper as he ground the bean-curd flour or made the beancurds. Afterwards there was a shop where letters could be posted, a magnificent shop where there were a lot of paintings and many scrolls written in letters of gold on gold-spotted paper. The two white dogs we saw when we first came to the village belonged to this shop. All day they crouched in front of the gate, and whenever they saw an acquaintance they would stand up and play for a while; but when anyone called to them they would disappear into the courtyard, where there was always a goldfish bowl.

We could hardly stay in the shop all day for the sake of a single bowl of bean-curd. And we did not stay there because we desired the friendship of the proprietor. No, we came for something else. We were two soldiers, one maimed, the other a sergeant with a certain proprietory right over some of the soldiers: he could call the roll-call, he possessed certain privileges, he resembled a future officer, he could swear at the cook-boy and call him whatever names he pleased, but as soon as he left the platoon he was nobody at all. A sergeant! There were ten or twelve in each company, thirty-six to a battalion, and more than a hundred to each regiment. His badges were only signs of his servitude. Soldiers could do many things which were forbidden to sergeants. There is nothing more pathetic than a mere sergeant. I did not come to the bean-curd shop as a sergeant, but as someone who had arrogated to himself all the privileges of a private. And though we never refused the bowl of bean-curd which the proprietor always offered to us free, we did not come for the sake of the milk, but because we admired the dogs and the mistress of the dogs.

I have never seen anyone so beautiful. I have seen girl students and the concubines of generals, and though the students filled me with awe, and grew up into young buffaloes, the concubines were always prostitutes, and neither pleased me. But this girl was more beautiful than anything I had ever imagined.

We were amenable to army laws as well as to the laws of our own desire. We dared not behave wildly in the town. And so we came each day to the shop of the bean-curd merchant, talking with the young proprietor, helping him with the mill-stone or wrapping the curds in paper; and all the time we were only thinking of seeing the girl as she came out. Our hearts would beat wildly and our blood would rush to our foreheads the moment we saw her white skirt appearing near the goldfish bowl. And all day we planned how we could buy food for the dogs, and so win her favour. At first the dogs appeared to be perfectly conscious of our evil intentions, and after smelling our proffered gifts, they would move away. But when the proprietor of the bean-curd shop threw our gifts across the street, they glanced up at him and seeming to realise that there was no poison because they were proffered by a friend, they began to eat it up.

I suppose there are people who will wonder why we continued with our hopeless quest, for even if we were befriended by the dogs, it was impossible for us to achieve the friendship of their mistress. The master of the house belonged to the local gentry. He was president of the chamber of commerce, and he was the banker to the army. Frequently he would offer banquets to the more prosperous members of our community, the regimental commander, the battalion commanders, the adjutants, the army judge, the cashier, they were all present. Occasionally we would see the paymaster and the battalion secretary calling at his house for a drink or playing mahjong.

We asked the proprietor of the bean-curd shop, and he told us that the girl was the president's youngest daughter—she was only fifteen. Although we knew it was hopeless, we felt happy only to look at her, and even if we failed to see her, we were comforted whenever we heard her voice calling the dogs into the house. We gazed for hours at the bowl of goldfish, in the hope of seeing the hem of a skirt which told us that she was playing about in the courtyard.

At last the dogs became our friends. They would cross the street cautiously and play with us. We hated them and loved them, for just at the moment when we were getting on splendidly, a single call from the other side of the street would bring them running to their mistress's side. They were so tame, and so thoughtful! No dogs were ever on such good terms with soldiers, for usually dogs make a practice of attacking soldiers.

The proprietor of the bean-curd shop was young, silent, stolid and strong. All day he worked cheerfully; at night he closed the shutters and went to sleep. He cared for nothing except his shop and went nowhere except on business. At first I did not even know when he took his meals, and when he went out to buy beans for the curd. Although he spoke rarely, if a customer asked about anything, he would always reply; and his answers were always satisfactory.

Once we invited him to a drink. Just as I was about to pay, I discovered that he had paid already. The second time he was more punctilious and allowed us to pay.

We only knew that he came from somewhere in the country. Now and then country relatives would come up to see him; and from them we derived the notion that his family was certainly not poor. Business was good; he told us that he sent all his money back to the country. And when I asked him when he was going to marry, he only laughed. He knew a few songs which he sang quite charmingly, and certainly he sang better than the people in the barracks. He was good, too, at chess. He was illiterate, but he could read a few characters like "chariot," "horse," "minister," "noble." He never made up accounts, but all the debits and credits were remembered in his capacious mind. He treated us as friends, neither watching over us carefully nor flattering us. Although we had come only to see the girl, it is quite certain that we should not have come so often if he had been less agreeable.

Sometimes we would use rough, silly words in talking about the girl, or we would behave ridiculously towards the dogs. The young shopkeeper always smiled, seeing no malice in our actions. I would say:

"What are you smiling about? Isn't she beautiful? Don't you think her two dogs are happier than we are?" Usually there was no answer. And if he answered it was only with a frank, open smile of almost girlish bashfulness. Sometimes this smile of his would make me querulous, and I would burst out with some remarks as these:

"Still smiling? Why, you fellows from the country know

nothing about beauty. You like women with big breasts and big hips—she-pigs—buffaloes—something you can use. You fellows know nothing about beauty!"

Sometimes the bugler said: "I would like to become a poodle!" and he would annoy the young shopkeeper by persistently questioning him on the subject of whether he, too, would like to become a poodle. At such moments the shopkeeper would only work still harder at the grind-stone, and all the time he would be smiling. We tried to understand the meaning of the smile, but we always failed.

We were perfectly content. We amused ourselves in the shop, we drank bean-curd milk, we watched out for the girl, and sometimes we went to the parade ground to see the executions. Every fifth day there was a fair and on such days a number of bandits brought in from the surrounding countryside would be selected at regimental headquarters for execution in the market place. If our company was chosen to guard the prisoners, we would set a platoon of soldiers over them and the bugler would walk at the head of the procession, blowing his bugle. As soon as we reached the field, the ranks would move forward at the double, and there would be played on the bugle the tune which is reserved for summoning the soldiers to fight at close quarters. Afterwards the troops would withdraw to the barracks, marching slowly through the streets and sounding the "triumph-call." The crippled bugler no longer took part in these ceremonies. And the guards selected for the execution were now chosen solely from the bodyguard of the regimental commander, the same bodyguard which protected him when we went out in the country after the bandits. The privilege of beheading the criminals was also reserved to them. For ourselves, we were only spectators of the tragic and magnificent procession with all its blood-curdling comedy. I, too, was no longer allowed to lead my soldiers and the prisoners through the streets; but this was no loss to me, for we could still see the executions and we could stay on the field as long as we liked.

Once we egged-on the shopkeeper to accompany us. When we approached the place of execution, we saw four corpses lying in the field, stripped to the waist and resembling four dead pigs. Many young soldiers were playing about with the bodies, pricking their throats with little bamboo sticks; and there were a few dogs waiting in the distance.

The bugler asked the shopkeeper whether this made him afraid. There was no answer except for the sweet and understanding smile to which we had grown accustomed. It was a part of our life and of our friendship; and seeing this smile, we felt the same kind of perfection as when we heard the girl's voice.

The days passed quickly, for no one could have been more happy. We could hardly believe that six months had passed since we first sat in the bean-curd shop and gazed at the girl. By now we were perfectly familiar with the shop and with the white dogs; and sometimes we were even allowed to take the dogs to the barracks or to the river. We knew now that we would never be able to approach the girl, and so, though we ceased talking nonsense about our love for her, we still came to the shop and helped the shopkeeper as much as possible. To go there was a part of the habitual ritual of our lives. Now we knew how bean-curds were made, we knew the temperatures at which they must be heated, we knew the difference between good bean-curd and bad. We knew the customers, and we would talk to them and they were our friends. If a soldier came to the shop, the proprietor would beg us to give him an extra helping and sometimes he would even refuse to accept pay. Our lives were divided between the proprietor of the shop and the two small white dogs. And sometimes, when we heard the girl calling the dogs, we would succeed in enticing them away from her, so that they ran out of the house as soon as we whistled.

Frequently we noticed the young officers who walked through the inner gate with their heads high in the air, their uniforms very clean and shining, their faces white and red, their chests stuck out, their black riding-boots with spurs falling heavily on the pavement. Seeing them, I only became more thoughtful; but the bugler would suddenly break out in atrocious melancholy, clenching his fists behind their backs, threatening vengeance. Occasionally I heard him talking with the proprietor about things I did not understand.

Once, when we were drinking wine in a small restaurant, I lost my temper with him.

"My friend, my dear brother, you are a cripple!" I shouted at him. "That kind of girl is only fit for battalion commanders. If we looked at ourselves in the water, we would know that we could have no share in such triumphs. What are we worth? Seven dollars a month, and for that we are only good at marching through the mud, saying 'yes, sir,' drilling all day long, sleeping on straw mattresses at night, our mouths only good enough for beef and sour cabbage, our hands only good enough for holding cold rifle butts . . . We are young, but we can never catch up with those handsome battalion commanders with their school education. We are just dogs—lined up for battle. Do you think we have got a chance with a girl like that?"

I was drunk. I did not know how to restrain myself. I was muddle-headedly trying to give him some good advice, and I remember that I kept on referring to his crippled legs, but always with rather elaborate metaphors. We were alone. I do not know why, but he suddenly changed from being quiet-tempered and thoughtful, and became a wild animal. He flung himself at me. We began to fight, tearing at each other's ears. We were both drunk, shouting incoherently, swearing like madmen. This lasted for a long while. At last some soldiers came past the restaurant, and hearing our voices they tried to put an end to the quarrel, and with a great deal of trouble they managed to separate us and bring us back to the camp. We were sick all over the place. At midnight we awoke from a drunken stupor, and feeling thirsty we went out in search of the water-jar. We drank a lot of cold water, faintly remembered what had happened during the evening, and then we wept. Why had we fought like that? What made us hate one another? Why should we have done such a thing? We wept and laughed, put on the new uniforms which had recently been issued to us, and walked out together to look at the declining moon, which resembled the face of a dead man. There were a few shooting stars in the sky. Cocks were crowing. It was April when we came; it was now October.

The next day we were both very ashamed when we saw one another's faces. Some of the men in the company learned of our fight, and there were some who thought that from now on we would be continually fighting; but the incident of the previous night only deepened our affection.

We went to the bean-curd shop as usual. The shop-keeper was surprised when he saw us, for we had clawed each other's faces, and though we would laugh out aloud when we caught sight of each other, we were not particularly pleasant sights. I told the shopkeeper what had happened, explaining how bitterly and stupidly I had insulted my friend, calling him "old cripple" and many other things, until at last we found ourselves struggling on the floor. It was pure luck that we were drunk, and therefore incapable of really hurting one another.

At that moment the girl came and stood by the gate, and the dogs began to prance all round her, putting out their little red tongues and licking her hands. We became silent, gazing silently across the street. She seemed to notice that something had happened between us, and she nodded and smiled in our direction without the least sign of fear, neither did she seem to feel that we might do harm to her. When she smiled, it was exactly as though she knew why we had been fighting together.

I was very melancholy when I thought of this. I knew that she did not care for us. Probably she thought we came here in order to share the business of the bean-curd shop. I noticed that the bugler was also weighed down with cares, thinking of his smashed leg and of his face, which was even more ugly as a result of the fighting than mine. Meanwhile the shopkeeper pretended to be occupied with the shaft of the mill-stone; he seemed to be wondering whether the stone was wearing away, for with his heavy muscular arms as strong as iron he was lifting the stone. This was the third time. Whenever the girl appeared, I would find him working on the stone. And though I meant to ask him about this, I never had the opportunity.

Soon the girl disappeared through the green and gold inner gate. Like a star, like a rainbow, she disappeared, leaving in our hearts a gap of pure brightness. I was about to give the bugler a smile of complete understanding, but he suddenly broke out in a torrent of self-pity: "Brother, my dear brother, you were so right last night—yes, you called me all the right names! We are pigs and dogs! We are toads..."

Because he was so disheartened, I wanted to console him:

"Don't speak like that—it's not the way a man should speak. We have our wills, and through our wills we can succeed at anything we aim at. If you want to, you can become the President of China, a general, anything you please. What does a woman amount to—nothing at all!"

"I know I shall never become President of China," he answered. "All I want is to be a man."

"What is preventing you from being a man? Soon your feet will be healed, and then our Captain will recommend you for entering the officers' training school, and you will earn your position through your ability like all the other students."

"I am worse than a dog. The best thing is to ask the Captain to let me become a regular soldier as soon as my feet are healed. I will drill on the parade ground all day..."

"No, no, you'll get your commission," I said, and I turned round to look at the shopkeeper, for the young man had set the stone mill and was working at the handle again. "The way we are living is just like pushing a mill round—what do you think?"

Hearing these words the proprietor seemed to think that they were not fit to be spoken by someone in my position, nor were they appropriate to his own life, and so he smiled at me, gently and confidingly—only that smile. Suddenly the truth dawned on me. We were all three in love with the girl.

On October the fourteenth I was sent to army headquarters seventy *li* away with some important messages. I remained there a whole day waiting for a reply. It was two more days before I returned to the small town. As soon as I reached the town I handed the documents in at the regimental office, received six dollars for the performance of my duties and I had decided to enquire from the people in the company whether anyone was returning soon to my native village, so that I could send four dollars home for cured meat which we would eat during the winter. Suddenly I saw the bugler. I had no time to tell him of my joy, for he suddenly burst out with the words: "Do you know the girl is dead?"

What was he talking about? I was sure he was talking nonsense. Why should I listen to such demonstrable lies. I sat down and began to change my sandals, and suddenly it occurred to me that after all he might be speaking the truth, I jumped up violently and began to throw a steady rain of questions at him. Yes, it was quite true. I could hear funeral rites being performed in the distance, gongs were being beaten, drums were sounding, a trumpet was playing the tremulous low notes which always accompany funeral processions. With one foot naked, and the other in its sandal, I ran out into the street, pulling the cripple with me. We ran with the speed of firemen running to put out a fire—we ran in the direction of the bean-curd shop, caring neither for the feet of the bugler nor the surprised stares of the passers-by. Even before we arrived, I knew that the sounds of drums and gongs came from the house opposite the bean-curd shop. A chill came over me. I felt as if I had received a heavy blow. The droning of the gongs, and the golden sparks like fireflies before my eyes . . .

At last I sank down on the wooden bench in the shop. I took the bowl of bean-curd milk which my friend offered me and began to drink it. I gazed at the house. People were going through the gate, where white linen cloths of mourning were hanging; and there were many children with their heads swathed in white linen eating vegetables outside the gate. I watched a man burning paper money and little silver paper shoes, which he was stoking with a long stick, his back bent as he stooped over the small fire. The flame blazed upwards, smoke and ashes rose above the high white screen of linen cloth protecting the inner courtyard.

Yes, it was all true, it was all real. My whole body was convulsed. Yet I laughed. I looked at the shopkeeper. He did not seem quite so calm as usual—evidently he, too, had received a heavy blow. He pretended not to see me, and turned his head aside. I looked at the bugler, whose face seemed to me at that moment more terrible than ever. I do not know why I found him so terrible, but I felt that I wanted to strike him over the face. However, I refrained.

I made enquiries and learnt that the girl had committed suicide by swallowing gold on the previous day. We had no idea why she had committed suicide or why she had decided to swallow the gold. Many people die like that, and it is unreasonable that the living should demand explanations. We felt that we had lost something dear to us, something that we had never been able to name until that moment. At first we talked in melancholy tones, but soon afterwards we were laughing. It is difficult to know why we were laughing. It was as though we knew she was only a flower and that none of us would ever possess her. At the moment when the flower faded, we were naturally melancholy; but when we thought of all the flowers that are possessed by rogues and assassins, and of how some are strong and of how others perish at the least sign of frost, then we felt easier in our hearts, and consoled ourselves with the thought that at least we had seen her and loved her.

But when we returned to barracks, we were still grief-stricken. Our lives were completely destroyed. Our hearts would never again leap up wildly at the approach of familiar footsteps, we would never again lose ourselves in our dreams. Always there would be this gap of brightness in our imperfect lives.

In our hearts we knew that whether the girl was alive or dead meant nothing to us. When we left the barracks, what difference would it make? And even if we stayed there all our lives, the lame bugler and the poor sergeant, we would never get nearer to her than the two dogs.

The next morning we arose early. We sat on our beds, gazing silently at one another, and both of us were striving to escape from our memories. We were both liable to take offence at trifles, but this morning our temper knew no bounds.

"Your eyes are swollen, you fool!" I laughed at him, but he made no attempt to reply; he only gazed at me pathetically.

"The trouble with you is that you want to be the chief mourner," I said, and perhaps I was not surprised when he remained silent. It was my privilege to ridicule him to my heart's content, and this I did, until he suddenly turned to me and whispered: "Can the dead be revived?" Even then I persisted in ridiculing him.

When at last we reached the bean-curd shop, we found the shopkeeper sitting on the bench with his head buried in his hands; and when people entered the shop, he simply asked the customers to take whatever they wanted from the shelves. When he noticed us, he looked a little more cheerful, and he smiled as though to conceal his wounds. His smile showed that his mind could still support the strain of the girl's absence.

"What's the matter?"

"She was buried this morning—early!"

"Really?"

"Yes, she was carried out before the sun rose."

"Then why are you looking so miserable?"

"Oh, nothing," he answered, and hurried away to bring us our bowls of milk.

As we sat in the shop gazing at the house, we were filled with melancholy thoughts. After a while the bugler and I left, and we went to play cards in a woman's house. There we discovered that the girl had been buried at a place called Bream Hamlet, two *li* from the town.

When I saw the bugler weighed down with pompous melancholy, I was tempted to beat him, and swear at him. He annoyed me. His utterly cheerless manner was an insult —an insult to my admiring love for the girl. I could not bear to sit and play cards at the same table with him. I returned to barracks alone, lay down on the straw mattress and went to sleep.

That night my friend did not return. He had told me that he would not come back, and I knew that he was spending the night with the woman, so I was not surprised. The next day I had no desire to go out and I remained quietly in the bed. In the afternoon I was feverish, my head ached, I felt sick all over, and I no longer had any desire for food. They boiled some herb medicine for me, which I drank. I was told to wrap myself up in innumerable blankets in order to induce sweating, and it was already twilight when I awoke, my whole body bathed in perspiration.

I rose and went into the garden behind the temple. The rain had ceased, and the sun was setting over the curving roofs, tinging them yellow. The white cloud in the corner of the sky was being baked crimson in the sun's descending furnace. In this dusk, watching the faint banners of kitchen smoke over the roof-tops, listening to cocks crowing and dogs barking, I remembered all that had happened on the day when we arrived. I thought of my friend's fate, our own life, the melancholy that weighed us down, the unanswered questions which seethed in our imaginations. And then I went back to bed. I had no desire to eat or speak, or even to think. I do not know how long I lay with my head swathed in the wadded cotton coverlets. Faintly I heard soldiers playing cards and quarrelling upstairs, and dimly I saw people moving about. I felt as though we were all going forward, we were marching, we were arriving at some strange unknown destination. Past things again returned to my mind, and once again I saw the bugler falling... I woke up with the feeling that someone was lying by my side. I threw away the cover. There seemed to be no light coming from the lamp, but the dim light of the large oil-lantern high up in the hall illuminated a figure sitting motionless beside me.

"Cripple, is it you?"

"Yes."

"Why are you so late?"

He hid his face in the darkness and did not reply. I had no idea what time it was, for I had been asleep. I asked him. He did not seem to have heard my words, he was still sitting there motionless and without a word.

After a while he said:

"Brother, the sentry nearly shot me."

"Didn't you know the pass-word?"

"How could I have known the pass-word?"

"Is it past twelve?"

"No idea."

"Where have you been? Why do you come back at this late hour?"

There was no answer. I found that the kerosene lamp which the soldiers had placed on the rice-box for me was still burning with a low flame. I wanted him to turn it higher. He did not move. For the second time I called to him.

When the lamp-flame burnt brighter, I saw that the bugler was covered with mud, in a terrible state. There were wounds on his face, as though he had been fighting again. I was surprised by his appearance, but I did not know how to cross-question him, and it was impossible to ask him where he had been all day. My thoughts were still confused. It all seemed part of a dream, for only a moment before I was dreaming of how he had fallen to the ground.

"Brother, dear brother, someone has dug open the grave."

"Whose grave?"

"It must have happened a long while ago. I saw it."

There was a tone of persistence in his speech, and I began to grow afraid that he had gone mad.

"Whose grave are you talking about? Where is it? How do you know?"

"How do I know? I heard people say she was buried there, and I wanted to have a look. I went there once—no one had touched it. To-night I went there again. I remembered the way perfectly—the coffin had been taken away."

Either he or I was mad. Suddenly I understood who it was he was referring to, and I jumped up like someone possessed, shouting:

"You have been to her grave, have you? You have been to her grave?"

He was not in the least taken aback.

"Yes," he said quietly. I went to the grave yesterday and again to-day. I didn't mean to do evil! I swear it! The Heavenly King is above my head, and I swear I brought nothing—no spades, nothing. I saw the gravemound yesterday, but to-day it had changed. I swear that it was the same mound, but it was entirely changed. Someone had been at it—someone has dug up her coffin and taken it away!"

As soon as I heard this, there occurred to me the name of a man. I did not say this name aloud, for the image danced quickly through my brain and immediately disappeared again. I had a curious belief that the girl had somehow been revived, she had struggled out of her coffin and perhaps already she was talking with her parents at home. I suspected that her death was only assumed; a man had dug her out in time and saved her life. Then, too, I thought that perhaps my friend had gone insane, and lost his way in the cemetery and mistaken one grave for another. I thought of all these things and I knew that none of them could be true.

In the end I asked him why he went to the grave. He was afraid, he thought I was suspecting him of some crime, and he swore seven oaths and called the gods to witness that he had never had any intention of stealing her body from the grave. He kept on saying that he had not brought any grave-digging tools. He kept on arguing interminably, and when he saw that I was still incredulous, his eyes filled with suspicion and tears. I knew that if I failed to show that I trusted him entirely, he would go mad, try to throttle me and perhaps choke me to death.

My sickness was spirited away by fear. I wondered what to do with him, and with many wild words I consoled his broken heart. He cried. He was no longer so excited; but now that the excitement was over, his tears were still more melancholy. He was afraid to awaken others with his sobs. At last he told me the truth: he had actually thought of taking the girl, for he had heard people saying that a girl who died by swallowing gold might be revived if a man embraced her within seven days. He told me that on the first day, when he went to the graveyard, he had told himself that he would save her only if he heard her cries for help; and on the second day he had decided to take her, even if there were no cries coming from the grave. But when he arrived he found that the earth had been dug up, the coffin lay above the earth and the lid had been removed; and there was nothing at all in the coffin except for a few clothes. No doubt someone else had come a little earlier, he had excavated the grave and carried the body away.

Now he no longer called upon the gods to bear false witness. He began to tell me everything with complete honesty, hiding nothing; and as I listened to him, I could find no more words of consolation, for I still thought that we might both be dreaming. And I thought, too, that if we were not dreaming, then the bugler would repent of everything he had said in the morning, for though it was impossible to restrain a desire like this, it was incredible that he had actually put it into action. And when he repented of having told me all this, he would probably kill me, so that no one would ever hear about it. I became suddenly very alert. He had made his confession—like any woman. Then it occurred to us that there was still another problem, whether we should report the matter or try to forget it entirely. For a while we discussed the matter, and we agreed to do nothing until we had gone to the bean-curd shop early next morning. The bugler was tired out: he had been walking on his crippled legs for a long way, and he had been weeping almost continually since his return. He soon fell asleep. But because I had been sleeping all day, I found it impossible to sleep any more, and I gazed down at the boy's tormented sleeping face and mud-stained body, and then I turned out the lamp and sat by his side till daybreak.

When we reached the bean-curd shop it was already late. The shop was closed. Once again the image that flitted through my mind the previous night returned to me. The door was locked from outside, which showed that he was not staying late in bed. I began to grow afraid. I dragged the bugler away and began to run in the direction of the barracks, and all the while I was explaining to him the thought that had suddenly entered my head. He was still dubious, and soon afterwards he disappeared. When he returned he was more pale than ever. He said he had been to another shop, and there learnt that the proprietor of the bean-curd shop had locked up his shop the previous night and disappeared.

For three days we did not dare to go out. At length we heard that there were rumours all over the battalion headquarters that the grave-mound had been disturbed and the body had been stolen. Then, too, we discovered that her body had been discovered in a cave half a *li* away; and there she lay, naked, perfectly white, safe on a bed of stone, and all over her body someone had strewn the wild blue chrysanthemums of the place. For three days she had lain there, tended by the young man who owned the bean-curd shop.

A few hours later we heard that he had been arrested and brought to garrison headquarters. Soon afterwards he was executed. Even at the last moment before his execution, his mind remained clear; he showed no sign of being bewildered. He asked for nothing—neither food nor drink; he blamed nobody; occasionally he gazed meditatively at his wounded foot.

"Who hurt your foot?" I asked.

He shook his head and as though recalling some amusing story of the past, he smiled softly and briefly, saying:

"It rained during the night. When I carried her away, I almost fell into the coffin."

"Why did you do it?"

He smiled at me, very tenderly. For a while he said nothing, gazing into my face. He seemed to be thinking that perhaps I was still a child, and therefore could have no knowledge of love. And as though he was speaking only to himself, still smiling that slow meditative smile, he said: "She was so beautiful, so beautiful——"

At that moment a soldier appeared and interrupted him.

"You are going to be executed soon," the soldier said. "Are you afraid?"

"What is there to be afraid of? Why should one fear death?"

Questioned in this way, the soldier seemed to become

suddenly shy; but a moment later, in a loud voice, he began threatening the man.

"So you are not afraid of death, you fool! Well, in a few minutes, we're going to hack off your head!"

Once again the man smiled softly to himself. And his smile seemed to be saying: "Who is the real fool?"

I remember that smile. It has remained fresh in my memory for ten years.

Time passed. We no longer went to the bean-curd shop, drinking milk on the long wooden bench. Hardly anything has changed. The bugler is still a bugler in the Forty-seventh Company, he is still lame, and he never speaks about the things that happened when we were young. He is innocent of any crime, but he is perpetually weighed down by melancholy. As for myself, I am the father of three sons, and when the present Captain surrenders his post, I shall take over the command. But I, too, am oppressed with grief. I find it difficult to talk to the young, because I am always thinking about the things that happened in the past.

Lung Chu

I

It was as though the parents of the Lang Chia tribe had carved and gilded the Buddha of the Heavenly King, and so handed down to posterity a model of beauty for their sons. Lung Chu, the son of the chieftain, was seventeen years old, and the most beautiful of all the sons of the tribe. He was as strong as a lion and as tender as a lamb; the ideal of all the youths of the place, the most gifted, the most wise. He was so beautiful that a sorcerer had once, in a fit of jealousy, attempted to cut off his nose, but finally he acknowledged the youth's beauty and paid homage to his charms.

In all the tribes—the Lang Chia, Black Dame, Lo-lo, Flowery Kerchief and Long Foot—it was agreed that Lung Chu was as bright as the sun and as fresh as a flower. But Lung Chu himself was annoyed by this endless flattery. He had seen his own beauty in the pools, he had gazed at himself in copper mirrors, and he knew that he was not overpraised. But what had happened? His own beauty kept him apart from the girls.

It was not their fault that they did not dare to love him. No woman can treat a god as an equal, or make feverish love to him, or shed tears and blood for him. Women are timid creatures; they can love handsome men, but it is impossible for them to love one as beautiful as the sun.

Though Lung Chu was beautiful, he possessed no pride in his beauty. All the Miaos[1] who lived in the neighbourhood of Green Rock would have sworn to this statement. They said the chieftain's son had never ill-treated man or beast,

---

[1] The Miaos are the aboriginal inhabitants of China. Ssu-ma Ch'ien's famous history of China records the defeat of the Miao tribes of Huang Ti, the Yellow Emperor, while the *Shu Ching* or Book of History, one of the Five Canons of the Confucian Classics, records the rebellion of the Miao people and their submission to the Emperor Shun. The Miao people have their own culture, but apparently nearly all the written records have been lost. They survive in the mountainous regions of Yunnan, Kweichow and Hunan.

and had never been discourteous to the aged or to women. Whenever there was a quarrel between young men and old, the old had only to say: "You are not like Lung Chu, who treats our white hairs with respect," for the young to bow gracefully and admit their shame. Women would say that if their sons were as beautiful as Lung Chu they would sell themselves to Kiangsi cloth-merchants in order that the sons should have money to spend. Young virgins asked nothing better than a husband who resembled Lung Chu, while married women would quarrel with their husbands, saying: "You're not handsome like Lung Chu. There is no reason why you should make me suffer. If you were like the prince, I would be like a cow or a horse and slave for you." Everyone admired Lung Chu, yet he was the most lonely man of his tribe. They say a lion is a truly solitary animal, but he was not so solitary as Lung Chu, for no girl dared stand before him, swaying her body a little and smiling at him with eyes half closed, nor had any maiden ever thrown him a purse she had embroidered. No girl had interwoven his name and hers in the odes they sang at the beginning of a new year. Yet it happened that his attendants and slaves, because they were young and strong, and because they were close to Lung Chu, were privileged to enjoy the small mouths and long arms of the women of the tribe.

"Oh, lonely prince, Heaven must help you, for you cannot help yourself."

He would have given everything he possessed if only a young girl would come and sing for him, and then present him with all the young ardour of her chaste body lying among furs. But this never happened, and people said that the caves of the Ch'i Liang mountains would close before ever he possessed a girl. So he spent his days in lonely rides over the mountains, and in hunting, and four years passed, and it was still the same, except that he was perhaps even more beautiful now. The years had added strength to his body; he was more vigorous. Hair had grown in places where hair should grow, muscle had grown in places where muscle should grow, and his heart was now completely prepared to love and be loved. Meanwhile the caves in the Ch'i Liang mountains had not closed, and his whole future lay before him.

It was the custom for the young people of the Lang Chia tribe to be betrothed during the singing festivals. They would sing to one another, and in the end the girls would offer themselves to the men whose singing they preferred. On fine days, early in the morning or late at dusk, the singing festivals would be held in deep valleys or at the river's edge, and the girls would be perfumed and delicately powdered, and they would wear colourful silks and flowers. It was considered a shame for a man to be unable to sing, and no girl could obtain a husband without the gift of a song. Neither money nor beauty nor lineage were sufficient to obtain a bride; it was necessary to pour out one's heart in passionate song before one could obtain the beloved; and it was immaterial whether the song was melancholy or gay, weak or strong, angry or joyful. What mattered was the intensity of a passion expressed in singing, and it was believed that those who could not sing well of their love were incapable of passion, or even of leading good lives.

It would seem that Lung Chu was deficient in the power of singing to the beloved, but in fact he was the best singer in the place. His songs were exemplars. The rhythms of his songs were so famous that lovers followed them. Everyone knew his voice, and no woman dared to join him in song. And this was one more reason why he was deprived of the love of young girls: his songs were altogether too good, too perfect.

Many came to him for advice in singing. His servants, and the youths of the place, would congregate round him. When strong emotion choked them, when they were at a loss to understand their feelings. When their songs were exhausted, they would beg for his instruction; and having received it, they would sing to their girls and later they would disappear into the caves where their vows were fulfilled. Many learnt his songs by heart, but among them there was not a single girl. The attendants of the prince were all boys. There is a saying among the tribesmen: "Only a lion can understand his loneliness."

II

It was now autumn. the ninth month. The corn was being threshed, the oil-nuts had been gathered, the potatoes dug out of the earth and stored in cellars, the winter hens began to sit on their eggs and the chickens were coming. For many days it had been warm. The girls hurried to the hills to gather grass, carrying with them long scythes and wicker baskets. On the slopes of the hills and in the caves, voices could be heard singing. In the caves the youths lay side by side on beds made of straw and wild flowers.

At such times Lung Chu was more lonely than ever. Though it was the best time of the year for shooting pigeons, he dared not go out for fear of coming upon the lovers in the grass. Since there was nothing else to do, he would spend the whole day grinding his knife on a whetstone, and murmuring:

So shall I stroke the fifteen-year-old girl
So many times in the day.

And he would gaze tenderly at the knife, the same knife with which he skinned leopards, and he ground it with oil so that it became as brilliant as the sun and so sharp that a breath of wind would tear a piece of hair along its blade. Now and then he would look up at the warm sky or listen to the distant singing of the girls—the sky was blue, and against the vast blueness of the sky the wild geese were writing Chinese characters for "eight" and "one"[1]. And seeing them, he did not smile.

He was weary of life. A vast weight settled on his

---

[1] Describing a wedge-formation (λ is the Chinese character for "eight") or single line of file (— is the character for "one").

shoulders. It was inconceivable that the buddhas and holy kings should have allowed him to remain inconsolable—it could only be explained by the shame of the girls, who dared not match his beauty with their own, or by some theory of racial decadence. It was clear that if the women refused to pursue those whom they adored, madly and with all the cunning in their power, the race would decline and at last be no better than the Hans.[1]

The dwarf slave drew near and prostrated himself on the ground, holding the feet of the prince.

Lung Chu continued grinding his knife on the whetstone, and the slave was also silent, stroking the feet of his prince. Listening to the distant music of the lovers, the prince began to speak in a musical yet solemn tone, in which there was mingled a hint of disapproval:

"Slave, slave, why do you disobey me? Why do you behave like this?"

"I am your slave."

"I would prefer you to be a friend."

"My master, my lord, how else should I behave? How should I dare to be an equal to you? And who would be unwilling to be the slave of Lung Chu, the beautiful one, and who would . . ."

Lung Chu stamped his feet, and the slave stood up. When he was on his knees, the slave seemed to have the height of a full-grown man, for his trunk was perfectly proportioned.

"Why are you so melancholy?" Lung Chu asked, seeing that the slave was weeping.

"If you have found me melancholy, this day of mine is worth living."

"You are so clever."

"If my master approves, a dunce may become a genius."

"I was referring to your absolutely unnecessary cleverness —this cleverness which puts sublime nonsense into your lips. Come now, what has happened?"

[1] The Hans are the descendants of pure Chinese stock.

It was not till then that the dwarf came to the point. Distressed beyond words, angry, frowning and fawning alternately, he began to stamp his feet in imitation of Lung Chu. An onlooker might have thought he had drunk poison or an insect had bitten his navel, but it was clear to Lung Chu that his distress could only arise from a loss in gambling or an unfortunate love affair.

Lung Chu said nothing.

"My master, my lord," the dwarf continued. "I can conceal not a straw of my affairs from your eyes. Your servant is being tormented by a woman."

"Fie upon you! Who would torment you—you with your flattering songs?"

"My master, my lord, love has turned your servant into a songless bird."

"Men become cleverer in love."

"Oh yes, they seem to be a little cleverer than usual, but before a still cleverer person I find myself as stupid as a pig."

Lung Chu bent his brows. A worried expression appeared on his face, and looking at the short legs of the dwarf, he said:

"Is it that which spoiled your love?"

"No, she has not yet seen me. But if she had known that I was the slave of the incomparably beautiful prince Lung Chu, she would long ago have led me to Yellow Tiger Cave and I would have had pleasure with her."

"You have been too clumsy with her?"

"Master, I swear it is not true! She could not measure my stature through my voice. But I am sure that she has taken the measure of my heart's stature through my songs."

"You are a fool! If you had really been bitten by the pangs of love, you would not talk like this."

"My master, my lord," the dwarf complained sorrowfully, shaking his large head, "how else shall I behave? Before the beauty of my master even a dead man sings praises. I was prostrated by love, but now my courage returns. I shall sing to her again, and if I am again defeated, I shall not say that I am the slave of the master, lest others laugh at my master for keeping such a poor slave and the whole tribe is disgraced."

The dwarf was about to go away when Lung Chu pulled him back.

"Tell me about the girl," he said.

The dwarf spoke of her beautiful hair and figure, her voice which resembled fermented rice, mulberries, quinces, the perches in the stream. "Her voice is as sweet as the dog's flesh of Ta-shin, as the jewels of Green Rock, and the——"

The prince saw the desire plainly written on the dwarf's face, for nothing sweeter could be known than the dog's flesh of Ta-shin or the mulberries and quinces of the village, and he decided to see whether the girl was indeed as beautiful as the dwarf said.

They went into the hills together, the prince hiding in a heap of straw, while the dwarf sang aloud according to the instructions of the prince. At first there was no reply. Later they heard a voice rising among the distant bamboos. It was in the sweet tone cultivated by the girls of the Flowery Kerchief tribe.

Lung Chu listened intently to the sounds. At the end of the third verse, there was a pause, when it was required of the other singer to make a reply. Lung Chu told him to make the reply, and then he himself would sing three verses. He would sing of good wine drunk by the best singers, of the nice flesh they would eat, but you, beautiful girl, who do you belong to?

So it was done, and the girl's voice could be heard saying in reply that good girls belonged only to good men, and she sang a song of three verses describing the man she desired, mentioning Lung Chu and two other names—heroes of antiquity. She seemed to be implying that since the singer was not Lung Chu, it was vain for him to hope for her love.

"Oh, Master," the dwarf cried out," she has mentioned your name and put me to shame. I will sing to her that you are my master, and she is fit only to possess his slave."

But since Lung Chu kept silent, he did not sing. Lung Chu's heart was beating wildly. Innumerable women had sung: "You are not Lung Chu and therefore I shall not sleep with you," but this was entirely different, for the girl had shown by her voice that she held Lung Chu in respect.

So he ordered the dwarf to sing four more verses. The first verses were in the form of questions: what was the use of boasting that one could drink much wine when in fact one could only drink less? And since it was impossible for the lowest in the land to obtain the love of the prince, and since watered wine seemed better to her than lees, she should consider herself fortunate in making love to his slave. But the girl answered still more cleverly, saying: Only the maidens of the Black Dame tribe made love to slaves, while the girls of the Flowery Kerchief tribe loved only princes, and she herself was determined to practise singing with the men of the Lang Chia tribe for three years so that some day she might sing with the prince.

"My master," the dwarf said, "she is flattering you, but she is also looking down on me—your slave."

So Lung Chu smiled and said:

"Why don't you sing to her and say: Young girl on the opposite hill, have courage and sing with my master, who is the prince. You said just now that you wanted to disgrace her by saying that I was here."

The dwarf could hardly believe Lung Chu's words. It was absurd to believe that his master had fallen in love with the arrogant girl; and since she had offended his master, and since his master remained unmoved, it was necessary for him to show his anger. And so if he told her that Lung Chu was there, then at least she would be made ashamed.

Seeing him hesitating, Lung Chu made a long low call, signifying to the opponent that the game was not yet over.

"Master," the dwarf said suddenly, "now that you are here I have no more songs."

"Then sing as I tell you. Ask her to come over and see Prince Lung Chu, who is like the rainbow and the sun."

"I dare not."

"Why not? I want to see the kind of girl she is. She looks down upon us and says we are not worthy to be loved by the girls of the Flowery Kerchief tribe."

The dwarf obeyed and a few moments later the girl made her reply, saying that the snipe on the opposite hill need not chirp any more, and the stupid fellow on the opposite hill need not sing any more. He ought to spend three years taking lessons from one of Lung Chu's slaves, and then perhaps he would learn to sing . . .

"How shall I answer?" the dwarf exploded. "She wants me to spend three years taking lessons from Lung Chu's slave! She obviously does not believe that I am the most trusted of all your slaves!"

Then Lung Chu told him the words of a very powerful song. He sang it and for a long time there was no reply from the other side. So he sang the song a second time, and immediately afterwards there came a reply charging him with having stolen the song from Lung Chu's repertoire, adding that it was worth while for all the maidens of the Flowery Kerchief tribe to strew flowers on the path where Lung Chu walked. The dwarf was utterly ashamed, but Lung Chu laughed and began singing in a low resonant voice which could be heard only on the opposite hill, saying that the repetition of a certain commonplace name made him only feel ashamed, and he was the most unhappy of all the men in the tribe; for all other men possessed sweethearts and he alone was deprived of them.

The girl answered some time later, saying she was certain

he was not Prince Lung Chu, who possessed a voice like silver bells and gongs, and the prince himself was so great that the girls of the Flowery Kerchief tribe were fit only to make a cushion under his feet; and therefore she begged him not to laugh at her. The rhythm of her song was perfectly regular and there was an extraordinary modesty in her intonations, and in the words. And so Lung Chu answered with all the powers of his voice, uttering the sweetest words from the purest heart, in the most passionate melody. It seemed that all the sounds of the world ceased in this moment, for the chirping of the birds and the distant singing of the boys and girls were harmonised in the full-throated eagerness of his voice. There was no answering voice from the other side. They waited for a while, but the girl was completely silent.

They were still waiting when the dwarf said: "My master, she has been completely defeated by you. She boasted that she wanted only to sing with the Prince of Lang Chia, but now she knows that even if she sings for thirty years, she will not be good enough." And saying this he burst out singing:

O boastful girl from the Colourful Kerchief tribe,
From now on you will never boast again.
If you are willing to be the bride of the slave of Lung Chu,
He asks you to come and meet his master and your man.

There was still no reply. "Perhaps she has hanged herself out of shame," the dwarf whispered in jest, but Lung Chu looked alarmed and immediately started to run down the banks of the stream. The dwarf followed him, carrying an immense bouquet of wild chrysanthemums and red tulips, preparing to take the part of the bridegroom. He ran so fast that he resembled someone "riding a cloud or tall.

III

"Lion, I have said of you that you will be alone for ever."

These words were written on the tombstone of an anonymous Lang Chia hero.

Lung Chu failed to find the girl. Shortly before he arrived she vanished from the bamboo grove. There were innumerable wild flowers scattered on the earth where she had been. Though there were many young girls and youths lying in the long grass, there was no sign of her; and when he passed, they stood up and bowed gently, conquered by his beauty. So he returned to the bamboo grove and the shed petals on the earth and the heap of dry straw where she had been sitting, feeling all the time like a leopard who has scented blood. But though he felt her presence there, he was filled with a profound melancholy and decided to return home. The sun was setting, small fires were burning and everywhere the cocks were crowing. The dwarf had thrown away his bouquet of flowers and followed his master with his long arms hanging down to his knees, crestfallen. He had sworn that he would embrace her at all costs!

Lung Chu could not sleep. At midnight he climbed the fortress wall, carrying his knife, wearing a leopard skin over his shoulders. He looked into the distance, hearing nothing and seeing nothing except the wild grass fires which kindled and faded here and there on distant hills. The villagers and the whole earth were asleep. The cool moon and the cold dew stirred his sorrowful thoughts, and he looked into the upper air, heaving a sigh. And what made him still more melancholy was the sudden cry of a baby in the night, and it was clear that the baby was crying for milk.

"Meanwhile," he thought, "all fair women are asleep in their nests. The youths are weary of singing and their bodies are weary of labouring, but now they are at rest. But what of the young girl who has awakened my heart? Surely she is not sleeping among her quilts—surely it is not allowed to her to sleep. She should be thinking of the songs sung by the prince she admires. She should be wishing and praying that I might suddenly descend upon her from the air. She should be desiring me only, tortured by the desire to possess me, as though mourning over the death of her love."

Saying this, he drew out his knife and made an oath to Heaven:

"To the great gods and to the great Ancestor, I swear that I shall never lie with any girl unless I can have this girl, even though it means that my line perishes. And if it is true that love is bought at the price of blood, then I swear that I shall cut off this hand of mine unless . . . "

And he returned to the house and fell asleep, still wearing the leopard skin over his shoulder. Presently he dreamed that the girl came towards him, singing gracefully, wearing a white skirt and a white cape, and the skirt was covered with little silver bells. Her hair fell over her shoulders and she resembled the goddess of mercy. She was so marvellous and so divine that he prostrated himself before her, yet she paid no attention to him and passed by. He ran after her and caught her by the skirt; then she turned towards him and smiled. Her smile made him bold. He lifted her in his arms so that her clothes hung down to the ground, and he fled with her into one of the neighbouring caves . . .

The next morning Lung Chu sat on a low stool, musing on the bitterness and misery of the world. The sun came out of a clear sky as he pondered the happiness that remained for him. The dwarf came in, to crouch low at his feet. The dwarf's brows were knitted together. Lung Chu gave him a light kick.

"My master, my lord, were it not that now and then thou didst condescend to kick thy slave, thy dwarf would be incapable of tumbling so gracefully."

"Disgusting thing, you deserve ten slaps in the face."

"No doubt that is due to my stupidity. The dwarf who attends your highness should be ten times cleverer than I."

"Fie upon you, humming-top! What are you pretending

now? How many times have I warned you not to behave like this?"

"My master, my lord, I have only one ambition—to write the history of your miracles."

"I suppose you have lost all your money in gambling and wish to recuperate your losses. You are a genius only in talking nonsense . . ."

"I am a genius only in losing the girl I love."

Lung Chu sighed; perhaps he was weary of the continual flattery of his dwarf, perhaps he was still thinking of the girl. Suddenly he kicked the dwarf again and said:

"Enough of your nonsense! Let us go to the place where the girl was singing—we may yet meet her."

"My master, my lord, this is exactly what I came to see you about. I have discovered all about her. She is the daughter of the chieftain of the Ox Palisade, who is famous for his good daughters and his good wine. There are three daughters, and the youngest is the one who sang to us. But the other two are still more beautiful. Such daughters are all to be enjoyed by men of good fortune—they are all right to rub the back and rub the feet of the prince of Lang Chia. If you want them, master, we can send men to take them over by force."

"Be quiet!" Lung Chu said, slightly offended. "The Prince of Lang Chia is not a robber!"

Saying this, he ran out of the fortress in the direction of the Ox Palisade, followed at a distance by the dwarf who was standing on his head. The most extraordinary thoughts were passing through the prince's head. It occurred to him that if the youngest of the daughters could sing to him, then the elder daughters must already be ripe peaches. He paid no attention to the dwarf who kept tumbling and saying:

"My lord, my master, not so fast! Caged birds cannot fly away! What is the use of hurrying, my master?"

Though he heard these words Lung Chu paid no attention

to them and hurried in the direction of Ox Palisade. Approaching his destination, he felt warm and at the same time he remembered that he would need the dwarf's assistance, and so he rested on a green stone under an elm. Two arrow-shots away lay the stone gateway to the Ox Palisade, and nearby lay a huge well from which fresh water brimmed and melted into a silver thread of stream, crystal-clear. And near the well a young girl with a thick queue, her head lowered and her back turned towards him, was washing vegetables. A little yellow flower was set in the upper part of the queue. Lung Chu gazed at her, hoping against hope that he might be able to see her face, but she did not turn round and meanwhile the dwarf came running up, gasping like a seal. He had not seen the girl; he had seen only Lung Chu. And thinking that Lung Chu was about to enter the palisade, he shouted:

"My master, my lord, don't go in there! The dogs are like leopards! Of course you are a lion of the mountains, my lord, but even so you shouldn't let the dogs bark at you and become a laughing stock to the Flowery Kerchief tribe!"

Lung Chu had no time to stop the dwarf, and he knew that the words were heard by the girl. She chuckled, raised her head and turned to see who was there.

At first sight, everything became clear. There was no need to demand his name. She knew he was Lung Chu, who had sung to her and found her at last. And the prince also knew who she was.

Now Lung Chu, whose eyes did not blink when gazing at the sun, who possessed at all times the most perfect dignity, whose heart-beats remained unchanged even when he was confronted with a tiger, suddenly felt on looking at her that he had become completely ridiculous. The dwarf saw that his master was quite beside himself; and seeing the girl beside the well, he knew at once what had happened. He knew that this was the girl whom his master had defeated in singing, and he knew that she had recognised the prince.

Standing there giggling, he made a foolish gesture and began pointing at the girl, while the other hand was held over his open mouth.

"Stupid dolt!" Lung Chu whispered into his ear. "What are you playing at?"

The dwarf coughed, and though she paid no attention to him, he began speaking in his most musical voice:

"The slave of the prince of Lang Chia yesterday committed a wrong and has now come to apologise in the presence of his master. The unpardonable fault will remain unpardonable for ever, for I have led to you the one whose singing you admire above all others."

"A crow who flies with a phoenix is better than a golden pheasant," the girl replied.

"But if the crow is accompanied by no phoenix," the dwarf replied, "someone will want to pluck his feathers."

Lung Chu pulled at his ears, and the dwarf realised once again that he had been speaking out of turn, and he hurriedly begged for pardon, bowing with his hands joined together. The girl began laughing.

"My master, my lord, the kindest master and the kindest lord in the world," the dwarf went on, noticing that she had turned her head, "you have done wrong!"

"How have I done wrong?" Lung Chu demanded.

"There is no need for you to bestow upon me gold or silver, for everyone knows the depths of your generosity; nor is there any need for you to punish your slave, for everyone knows that your temper is perfectly controlled. But why is it that you don't order your slave to carry away the girl's basket, so that you can talk with her?"

And without waiting for Lung Chu to speak or the girl to finish washing, he took the basket, hung it on his bent elbow, winked and went away.

After a long pause Lung Chu walked to the well.

Ten days later, with thirty oxen and thirty jars of wine as a present to the betrothed, Lung Chu became the son-in-law of the chieftain of the Ox Palisade.

The Lovers

SECRETARY Huan came to this village in the hope of curing his nervous depression.

One afternoon, when he was taking supper under the trees in the courtyard, and he was looking with a troubled gaze at the fried chicken which had been served up in blood, he suddenly heard voices shouting outside: "Hey! Come along! Come along! We have just caught a couple of them!" and he heard all the villagers scampering down the street, as though something really serious had happened. Although Secretary Huan had no desire to be an onlooker, he put down his rice-bowl, and with the chopsticks still in his hand, he wandered into the street.

People were running in all directions, and all the while they were shouting: "Down by the Pao-tao hill—yes, down by the Pao-tao hill—come along quickly—before they are sent to the judge's court."

Secretary Huan was puzzled. He had no idea what had happened. And suddenly thinking that two wild boars had been caught, he hurried forward, caught up in a stream of villagers climbing along the footpaths he had never walked before. Suddenly turning a corner, he came in sight of a crowd which filled a small hollow among the hills, but the crowd was so thick that it was impossible for him to see what had happened. He had been thinking only of wild boars . . . But in the centre of the crowd there was only two country people, a man and a woman, tied together with ropes; and he noticed that the villagers were more interested in his own appearance—his hair, his leather shoes, his woollen trousers with their knife-edge creases—than in the two young people they had captured.

He could not help looking at the captives tenderly. They were so young, and the girl was weeping silently, and there was a wreath of wild flowers on her hair. Secretary Huan was still puzzled. Someone began to tell him that a forester, passing over the southern hills, had found them lying side by side on a heap of straw. It was terrible! It was an affront to the village! The judge would have to be summoned, and there would be a trial—the judge wearing a pair of black spectacles and sitting at a desk covered with a red cloth. Some of the village women approached the couple and scratched their noses to show their disapproval, and they seemed to be saying: "It is outrageous! Just because of the fine weather——" And there were old men who shook their heads wisely, having forgotten the eagerness of their own youth, and they seemed to be saying: "Really, morality must be preserved. Where the devil is the world coming to?"

The evening wind was fanning his face, and there came to him from the mountains the music of flutes. Looking up, Secretary Huan noticed the pink glow of the clouds, and suddenly he thought there could be no harm in asking the man who was tied with ropes and whose head was bent low as though meditating, where he came from.

And this man who had been captured heard a gentle voice questioning him; it did not sound like a judge's voice, and he raised his head to look at him, having noticed previously only the bright leather shoes and the narrow creases of a strange pair of trousers. He knew that this man with the foreign appearance had pity on him. He shook his head a little, as though to express his sense of an injustice committed, and then smiled pathetically.

"Where do you come from? Do you come from these parts?"

"No, of course he doesn't!" someone interrupted.

Well, then, what about the girl? It was quite clear that she did not come from this village, for she dressed differently. He looked at the girl again. She was so young, hardly twenty. She wore linen clothes, blue-moon coloured, very clean and starched. Her face was pink, she was tall and apparently well-bred. There was no doubt that her figure and her manners had nothing in common with those of countrywomen. And it seemed to Secretary Huan that she was weeping because she was afraid, and not because she was ashamed.

Thinking that they may have run away from their families, he began to have a great pity for them, and he decided he would do everything possible to arrange their escape. But he knew no one in the village, he did not even know the magistrate's name, and his host had departed for the city. And suddenly it occurred to him that these villagers had no love for interfering strangers, and he might even make matters worse. He was thinking in this way when someone began to make a speech.

"That's what I say! They ought to be taken to the village magistrate's office and whipped with thorn-branches, and they ought to be stripped to the skin—both of them!"

It was a man with a large red nose and a face full of pimples. He had shouldered his way through the crowd, stroked the girl's face with his large, hairy hand, and made his speech. It looked as though he was quite prepared to whip the couple himself, but at that moment someone plucked at his girdle and pointed to the townsman in their midst.

Meanwhile there were some women who were highly offended by the actions of the couple, but though they supported the whipping, they had no desire to see them stripped. But the children were delighted. At the words "whipped with thorn-branches" they had given little whoops of excitement and gone out in search of them everywhere. They delighted in seeing thieves or wild dogs or wild cats being beaten, for they themselves were often beaten by their fathers with ox-goads.

Secretary Huan was still puzzled and at a loss what to do. Suddenly there appeared in the crowd a man who resembled a soldier who had risen from the ranks. He was called

"Captain" by the crowd, which eagerly surrounded him and related the story of the young couple found in the hay. Huan realised that this man possessed some power in the village, and he kept silent, wondering at the turn of events.

Now the Captain knit his brows and gazed solemnly at the crowd with the expression of a general reviewing his troops. Then he caught sight of Huan, and since the crowd was pressing near and it was necessary to show these townsmen the importance of the local militia, the Captain shouted: "Stand back there!" so suddenly that the crowd almost burst out laughing. Then the Captain turned to the victims, and began to brush the boy's face with a straw of dog-tail grass which he had picked up by the roadside. When he spoke, his voice resembled the tone of a custom's official speaking to passengers:

"Where d'ye come from, eh?"

There was a short pause. The boy who had been found in the hay looked up and saw a red mole on the Captain's face, near the ear.

"I come from Jao Shang."

The Captain seemed to be quite content with the answer and turned to the girl.

"What's your surname?"

She did not answer, but raised her head and looked into his face. Then she looked at Secretary Huan and bent her head low again, seemingly from shyness, staring at her feet. Her shoes could only have been worn by a rich country girl, for they were embroidered with double phoenixes. Some rascal in the crowd was talking about her feet. In the same rather mincing tones the Captain continued:

"Come on! Speak out! Where d'ye come from? If ye don't answer, I'll have you sent to the district offices!"

Usually the country folk stand in awe of officials; and because they were afraid of officials they would sometimes press a case firmly, in the hope that it would be tried by officials and so they would frighten their enemies. And there are countrymen who are so terrified that their hair stands up on their heads at the mere thought of "going to the district offices."

But the girl showed no fear. She was still tied to the man and she could do nothing, and so she kept silent.

Suddenly Secretary Huan heard a voice in the crowd shouting: "Beat them! Beat them!" It was the old way—the country folk afraid of officials, having no respect for anything except the extreme punishments supplied by the cangue, the whipping board and split bamboos. And someone suggested that they should find a large mill-stone, tie it round them and throw them into a pool.

Meanwhile the victims remained silent and unafraid. Indeed, their lack of fear clearly troubled the Captain. He even repeated the threats of the country people in an even more severe tone:

"Well, that's what they say—d'ye hear? You've violated the customary laws, d'ye hear? You have done something against them and so their judgment is quite proper and legal, and even the great office-holders in the city can't go against them."

"I came from Jao Shang to visit a relative at Huan P'o," the girl said in a low voice, shaking her head a little.

"Then the man began to speak, timidly and gently:

"We were going to Huan P'o together."

"Escaping, eh?"

"No—just going the same way," the girl answered.

Everyone roared with laughter, for if they were "going the same way," and not "escaping," it suggested that they had only met by chance.

The forester, who had first found the couple, came back running from the village office, having searched everywhere for the Captain in vain. Now that he had found the Captain he was delighted. He saluted, winked, and began to explain, smiling, that he had discovered these shameless people doing a thing which—and in broad daylight, too—

was—well, h'm—ought to be stoned to death, Cap'n. And hearing this the Captain became more determined than ever, and he really believed that they deserved death by stoning, but before the punishment took place it was necessary to investigate the family histories of the accused, for it might be necessary to fine them thirty dollars as well, and perhaps he could order that a cow should be impounded from the victim's family, and perhaps—well—an official can always benefit from such things. So he asked innumerable questions about the man's family and seemed indeed to grow kinder as he went on.

The Captain laughed proudly. Now he knew everything: he knew about the man's house, his wealth, his position, the names of the members of the family. And it was at this point that the man made an unexpected confession. He said he was the girl's husband, they were newly-married, and they were on their way to see the girl's father at Huan P'o, and the sun was shining and they rested on the hay and the birds were singing and the mountain flowers were so fragrant in the wind and there was so much sweetness in the air——

Hearing all this the people still insisted on exemplary punishment, the bachelors and spinsters because they were envious of the couple, and those who were married because "they must uphold morality. Huan took the Captain by the arm and began to talk with him. He wanted above everything that the Captain should set them free. The Captain looked at him suspiciously, caught sight of his Kuomintang badge on the lapel of his coat, thought for a moment that he might be talking to an interpreter for foreigners because he wore western clothes, and in order to show that he was not himself a countryman, he laughed aloud and held out his hand—but Secretary Huan for some reason refused to take it. So the Captain rubbed his hand against his legs, and a crafty look appeared on his face.

"No, yer honour—quite impossible. We can't release' em!"

"Well, why not?"

"We have to punish 'em. Haven't they offended against the whole village?"

"Well, just let them apologise. No punishment."

"Hey! What's he talking about? This is our affair!" shouted the man with the red nose, and the others roared their agreement. And when Secretary Huan turned and searched for the man in the crowd, the red nose had bobbed down and disappeared.

Now people came up to support Secretary Huan, and they begged the Captain to show mercy to the victims. Among these people there were women who were terrified by the presence of the townsman in their midst, and there were some who knew the position which Secretary Huan held and they whispered into the ears of the Captain, who nodded, realising now that it was impossible to get any money from the couple. But in order to maintain his own self-respect in the face of the villagers, he said:

"Quite right, yer honour! But you know—it's a question for the villagers themselves to decide. They must go to the militia office."

"I'll go and see the officer in charge."

"Of course, of course. That's the best thing. Let's go at once. But don't let the villagers say anything——"

Huan saw through his trick. It was clear that the Captain wanted to place the responsibility on his head.

The crowd made way for them, the victims were taken along, there were negotiations at the militia office and soon the young people were released. The Captain simpered up to the girl:

"Ain't yer ungrateful. You ought to pay thanks to his honour. Ain't he released yer?"

The girl was removing the wreath of flowers which some-one had thrown over her head as a practical joke, but hearing the Captain's words she saluted him gravely with joined hands, still holding the wreath in her fingers. Her husband saluted in the same way.

The Captain went on his way, and Huan followed the young couple as they passed through the courtyard, for they would have been jeered at by the crowd if he had not accompanied them. They walked in silence. It was getting late. The man said they would be in time for supper at Huan P'o, for it was only three miles and they could walk there easily by starlight. He looked up at the sky, where several stars were twinkling. It was a beautiful evening, the mountains coloured violet, and the dusk slowly invading the earth.

"You should go now," said Huan. "They won't make any more trouble for you."

"I'll come and call on you sometime, sir," the countryman answered.

"May God bless you, sir," the girl said, and they went away.

Standing by the bridge at the foot of the mountains, it seemed to Secretary Huan, enjoying the fragrance of the wind, that it would be good to have some memento of this strange event. He thought of the wreath of flowers in the girl's hand, and he shouted after them:

"Wait a moment! Please leave me the flowers—just drop them on the ground."

He heard the girl laughing and watched her as she put the flowers on a rock by the roadside. They waited for a while. They seemed to be expecting him to take the flowers from the rock. But since he did not go, the man came back and offered him the flowers.

When they had disappeared at last through a bamboo grove, he sat down near the stone bridge and buried his face in the fading wreath of spring flowers.

The Fourteenth Moon

ON the fourteenth night there was a moon, and perhaps if there had been no moon Tzu-kao would not have had the courage to do that which was so extraordinary to him and so ordinary to others.

Tzu-kao lived in Coin Alley, and after supper he always sauntered along the bank. The weather was hot and the river had dried up, so that the slightest breeze brought the foul air into the streets. And bathed in this evil-smelling air, he walked slowly with his head drooping, and sometimes he would gaze at the passers-by and the rickshaws and the white moon hanging overhead. There came to him, as though from some indigestion, a faint sorrow which he did nothing to alleviate. Two women passed close to him, and their scent lingered in the air long after they had gone. It seemed to him that the scent remained for him, since there was no one else in the street at the time.

He turned round. Two figures in white were disappearing down Coin Alley.

"Prostitutes," he murmured, but he could not have told the difference between those who are prostitutes and those who are not prostitutes; and perhaps there is no very great difference. They both want money: they are both prepared to sacrifice something to the acquisition of money, and a man who thinks earnestly over the ways in which he has secured the love of women must come to the conclusion that there is little difference between them. Even the contempt which we may feel for a prostitute, since she so eagerly and so openly proclaims her desire, fades away in time. And perhaps it is true that all women, or at least nine out of ten of them, are shamelessly devoid of shame.

"Yes, they are quite shameful, but the others are no less shameful."

This is what Tzu-kao was thinking, but in a little while he began to think that he, too, was shameful.

"They have so many charming ways, they are the source of so many pleasures—and there are so many women in the world. I am ashamed because there is not even one who accepts my love, and then again I am ashamed because I am so cowardly that I am tender to them only in my dreams."

A little while later he thought: "I must be a rascal and chase after them. It is the only way. And even if they are prostitutes, surely it is still love?" But already the two women had disappeared down Coin Alley, and there remained only their lingering scent in the air.

The moon was whiter now, and there were several stars. It was one of those nights which seem to have been made specially for lovers—the wind, neither too hot nor too cold, neither too strong nor too soft. The summer was nearly over. Tzu-kao returned to his lodging-house and his dreams.

"Is she coming?" Tzu-kao asked with a forced smile, seeing the lodging-house boy thrusting his head round the door.

The boy appeared to be peculiarly mysterious to-night. He smiled. It was one of those smiles which are worth more than ten sentences.

"Is she coming?" he repeated.

Again there was only a smile. Tzu-kao felt shy before the boy. He was ashamed of himself, and so he lowered his head and gazed at the book again.

"Boiled water, sir?"

"Yes, please."

But even when the jug had been filled, the boy remained in the room, as though there was something he wanted to say. He gazed round the room, his eyes wandering easily. He saw the iron bed, where the beddings had recently been changed; the books usually heaped on the bed had disappeared. It seemed to the boy that the room smelt more fragrant than ever before. Even the bookshelf had been put in order, and all the newspapers were neatly folded in squares. The oil-burning stove, which usually stood on the desk and with which he boiled his milk, had been hidden away.

Tzu-kao grew utterly weary of him—the little sharp face continually peering round the room, as though it expected to find something still more unusual. The boy went to the door, and already one foot was outside the door, when Tzu-kao heard himself saying:

"Isn't she coming?"

"Oh, she's coming all right."

The boy burst out laughing. He was so accustomed to these errands, but it was curious that he should make such an errand for Tzu-kao. He had imagined that Tzu-kao was a virgin, and he wondered how Tzu-kao would behave. And all the while Tzu-kao imagined that the boy was ridiculing him because he looked so young. Best to pretend that it was all perfectly natural, and if the thing should ever happen again and the boy was once more sent out on an errand, he was determined that he would show a sophisticated and experienced air. Suddenly the boy burst out laughing, and said:

"Are you married, sir?"

This was Tzu-kao's opportunity.

"My dear boy, of course I am! In fact it was two years ago——"

The boy believed him and went away, suitably impressed. Tzu-kao laughed silently, musing over the curious interlude with the boy and feeling sorry for himself. But the girl had not come.

He went into the courtyard. It was cooler there, and there was a light wind. "The roundness of the moon and the roundness of the lovers," he murmured, but he could not remember the poem in which the lines occurred. He may even have improvised them himself. But whether the lines were written by Tao Yuan-ming or by Li Po—it was all the same to him, for they suited the night perfectly.

THE FOURTEENTH MOON

The moon hung a little to the west, high in the sky. It was not yet ten o'clock. The fourteenth moon was not the roundest—the roundness of lovers was more round than anything in the world. He heard the thin sounds of a trumpet and drums beating from the direction of the river. He knew it came from the blind singers. He raised his head. There was only one star, and the Milky Way was still not clear in the heavens. Tendrils and leaves hanging from the melon frame were swinging in the cool air, casting shaky shadows on the ground. It was a night of "cool wind and bright moon."

"If she comes, we will sit in the little courtyard and talk about nothing at all—random things, the kind of things that lovers talk."

And if the woman was not entirely vulgar, why should they not pretend to be lovers? And perhaps even if she was vulgar? But what could he say? It would be terrible if they remained silent. He could hardly ask her name, and certainly it was better if neither knew the other's name. Causelessly she would come and go; causelessly they would meet and part. And perhaps each would retain "a shadow in the heart" by which they would remember their happiness. Best of all, if she came and was perfectly silent, silent perhaps for an hour like friends who have no need to speak and nothing to say. But perhaps they might be happier still as they talked throughout the short night, embracing each other under the moon.

"Yes, it will be like a play," he thought, but he was worried at the prospect of long waiting.

It began to be quite cold. Returning to his room, thinking of how he should receive his guest, he was more ill-at-ease than an official searching for his name in the lists of the examination.

"Sir, she has come," the lodging-house boy called in an extremely low voice, and shortly afterwards a young girl was pushed through the doorway.

There was no need for him to blush: it was not broad daylight, and the lamp was shining. In this light her cheeks were green, like a sunset, and he felt his cheeks burning.

"How is she?" The boy dared not enter the room, and asked from outside.

"You can go now," Tzu-kao answered the boy, and remembering that he must show the civility of a host, he said to the girl: "Sit down, please."

She sat down timidly, shrinking a little like a mouse at the sight of a man: she seemed to be trying to make her body occupy less and less space. As Tzu-kao had imagined, neither said anything. Tzu-kao would have been worried if the woman had been accomplished at her trade, but already the defensive and offensive had changed sides, and it was he, Tzu-kao, who was accomplished. It was a terrible strain to keep silent. As last he opened his second line of attack.

"Have a cup of tea?" he asked, pouring it out.

She nodded, but she did not immediately take the proferred teacup. Slowly, after a great length of time, her hand was outstretched towards the cup, and she lifted it to her lips.

She wore a bright blue linen coat, a black silk skirt, black shoes, black stockings. He was shy, dared not look in her eyes and gazed only at what lay beneath her shoulders.

She drank the tea and then seemed to remember her reason for coming there. She turned her face towards him. He was still examining her, though timidly, trying to say something but unable to utter a word. He raised his hand to smooth his hair. It was cut short and stood up in disorderly little curls. Though he did not look at her face, he knew she was looking at him; but the more he tried to calm himself, the more tormented he became, and at last he managed to look her in the face. Seeing his head raised, she allowed their eyes to meet, and then turned her glance aside. He looked at her hair, her face, her neck, and then from her shoulders down to her waist, and through her thin clothes he examined her thighs, her legs and her feet. It was as though he was a connoisseur appreciating a marble statue.

This happened for a long while. The girl still remained perfectly silent. She took another sip of tea, and patiently examined the cloud patterns painted on the tea-cup.

Tzu-kao was suddenly troubled at the thought that the girl who was sitting five feet away from him resembled his sister. Judging from her appearance she could not be more than twenty. His sister was fifteen, but the difference was not very great.

The girl was perfectly aware of her duty, and now she stood up and drew close to him. She laid one hand on his shoulder and placed the other round his neck. His heart began beating wildly. He raised his head, and this time she did not avoid his glance. He smiled, and she answered his smile. She inclined her head towards him, and her face touched his, and each felt the heat of the other. His neck itched deliciously when her hair touched him, and unconsciously he put his arm round her waist.

Now Tzu-kao behaved towards the girl in exactly the same way as the hero he had seen in a moving picture, and now for the first time his mouth touched hers. After a while he wept, thinking of his sister. She took out her handkerchief and rubbed the tears from his face, and then she began to kiss the place where the tears had been. And all the while he kept repeating: "I'm so worthless—no woman will ever want me."

"Don't you like me?" she asked gently, laying her cheek against his.

"How can I help liking you? You are so good, and you have made me so sad." There were tears in his eyes and he could not continue talking.

Tzu-kao felt that he had been offered someone purer than any virgin, and in her turn the girl believed that at last she had found a lover. She had offered her body to others, and they had only trampled on her fine feelings. But now she had found a doctor who would heal her wounds.

Such things are quite common in the world, and in the city of Peking no one knows how many such occurrences take place throughout the year. But to Tzu-kao it was not in the least a common occurrence, and though it was not exactly mysterious, it was at least out of the ordinary. She had offered herself to him, but in fact he had offered himself to her: it was she who received, and it was she who filled him with dreams, while the moon sank slowly to the west.

Ta Wang

OUR armies were on the march. Already we had climbed over the steep slopes of Cotton Hill between Szechuan and Kweichow. This immense slope, ten miles up and ten miles down, continued for a whole day, but when we reached the summit, we were rewarded by the sight of distant hills and long stretches of cloud and mist. For ten years I had wondered about the view which could be seen from the castle on the hill-top, and now at last I saw my dreams fulfilled. I remembered that on the borders of Szechuan there were enormous towns, where five thousand head of cattle would be marketed on market day. And then, too, we passed an ancient temple where there were pine trees so large that six men joining hands could not surround them. To the south of the temple lay the Tower of White Bones, and in the pit below, shaped like a shallow well, lay a mound of bleached wrist-bones, and sometimes there were gold and silver bracelets hanging on them, which no one would think of stealing or even touching.

Our army moved on until we came to the headquarters at Lungtang. There we stayed in a theatre-temple. We lived in the boxes of the dress-circle, and this was better than our previous camping place--there were no paper bandages sticking on the walls and the local situation was not so disorderly as at Hweihua, where we had stayed to clear the bandits. We each had a wooden bed and a mattress, and a bamboo shed had been built over the courtyard, so that it was not so hot as it might have been. The town stood across the salt-road between Szechuan and Hunan, and there was a small river, and boats from the Tung-t'ing lake would come here through the North River of West Hunan. There was a good deal of wood-oil export, a post office, some clean and comfortable boarding houses and a red lamp district. There were also big oil stores, dye-houses, distilleries, dispensaries and pawnshops, and a Dragon Cave which was well known for a hundred miles around. All the year round there was a cold stream as cold as ice coming from the immense cave, so cold that even in June no soldier would dare to bathe his hands or feet there for fear that his bones would ache and his limbs become numb. This stream irrigated thousands of acres of fields: there had never been a drought in these parts. Among all the people in our army, from the commander down to the smallest horseboy, I think I was the one who went to the cave most often. Almost every day I visited the place, and I would carry a large calabash and bring back fresh water for my friends.

I was a special-duty clerk in those days. I had little to do. I had only to register the date, the name of the addresser and that of the addressee, and the subject of the document. The documents were divided into three groups—urgent, important and ordinary. At nine o'clock in the evening the books were sent to the chief-of-staff and the commander to be looked over, and then they would be returned to me. Though my position was higher than that of a clerk, yet I was paid only according to the rank of a sergeant. But there were advantages—I no longer had to pay for my food, for this was provided by the adjutant's office, though normally I would have to provide it myself. When I received my pay, I would invite my friends to eat noodles at a restaurant down the street. This would cost two dollars. My great friends were the people in the commander's bodyguard, some of the adjutants and a young messenger-boy.

Our quarters were separated by wooden boards. I occupied the corner at the end of the dress circle, for though my duties were commonplace, no one was allowed to see the documents which were placed in my hands. Next to me were the commander's twelve bodyguards, then came the chief-of-staff, then the commander, then the army judge. On the other side of the theatre there was the office of the courts-martial, the army cashier and the armaments depot, while a company of guards were stationed on the stage. The auditorium was used as a dining-room, partitioned with mattresses of split bamboo and cloth curtains, and sometimes the courts-martial were held there. On all the doors were white paper labels bearing the names of the occupants, and these labels were in my handwriting. Next door to me, in the room belonging to the bodyguards, weapons hung on the walls, but my walls were pasted over with interminable calligraphic exercises. Among them were many sheets of paper bearing the inscription: "Excel Chung and Wang, overcome Tseng and Li," for I knew that among the dead the famous calligraphists were Chung and Wang, while among the living there were Tseng Lung-jan and Li Mei-en. If I could overcome them, I thought I would be the greatest man in the world.

I have said I knew the members of the commander's bodyguard. There were twelve of them, and the one I liked most was their chief, who had once been a bandit, a *tawang*, a real man. He had killed about two hundred people with his own hands, and had had seventeen wives.

Tawang means "a great lord." He was short and had a dark, swarthy face. Except for his piercing eyes, it was impossible to tell from his expression how much energy and courage he possessed. Once in Chenchow during a severe winter someone dared him to jump into the river. He said nothing, immediately stripped to the skin and jumped in. After swimming in the river for about an hour he climbed on the bank and said: "Do you think one could lose one's life in such a little amount of water?" Then again, if someone complained that he had been cheated at poker, the *tawang* would say nothing for a while, but afterwards he would go out and get the money back and throw it down on the table, and then go away without saying a word. The commander of our army had once saved his life; so he descended from the mountains and became the chief bodyguard of our commander, who had himself risen from the ranks. He was paid at a captain's rate of pay, and served his commander faithfully like a slave.

In those days I lived near the *tawang*, and he would come over and talk with me. Whatever I asked him, he answered to my full satisfaction. I learned strange things from him. Though I was accustomed to see the records of all kinds of crimes—arson, murder, rape and so on—it was through him that I came to understand the underlying meaning attached to these things. I discovered the nature of crime, and at the same time I learned why it was that society could not tolerate these things, and how it was that this strong rebellious soul had come into being. Through his candid narration, I learned how dazzling and miraculous are the strange vicissitudes and occurrences of life. He had been captured and sentenced to death as a bandit, he had escaped and at last he had become a *tawang*! There were days when he would sing from old Chinese dramas, and sometimes he would write and paint flowers, but when he was weary of talking he would leap on the table and dance the old dances called "Capturing the three strongholds" and "Fighting at the four gates."

One day, when we were eating in the adjutant's office, somebody mentioned that the Szechuanese army kept a strange prisoner locked up in a temple. She was a famous beauty who had become a bandit chief at the age of eighteen. When she was captured, all the young officers went mad about her, and two young officers fought a duel over her and were killed. When she was taken to the brigadier's headquarters, every officer wanted to have her, but nobody was allowed to take advantage of her arrest. As soon as I heard this, I wanted to see the girl. I was curious; and it seemed, too, that such things were food for my soul. So I laughed and said that I would offer anyone a drink who would let me see the girl. And immediately afterwards forgot about the matter.

One evening, when I was cleaning my lamp-chimney, the

tawang entered suddenly and said: "Brother, follow me and we'll go to a good place. You will soon see what you want to see."

I had no time to question him. He pulled me downstairs, and led me through the courtyard.

We came to a temple where a platoon of the Szechuanese army was stationed. He seemed to be acquainted with them all. He went straight through to the furthermost hall and turned into a courtyard where a woman was sitting beside a palisade.

She was sitting on a vermilion-coloured blanket, with her back to us, sewing nonchalantly under the lamplight.

The *tawang* said: "Sister Jao, Sister Jao, I have brought a little brother to see you!"

The woman turned round. The lamplight was dim, and I saw only her white face and a pair of large eyes. She stood up when she saw me and stepped towards us, and when she came closer I was surprised by the beauty of her figure. Her face could not be called beautiful, but the set of her eyes and brows and the perfection of her figure were really extraordinary. She was in fetters, and the fetters seemed to be wrapped in cloth, so that she moved noiselessly. Separated by the palisade, we interchanged greetings, and then I heard her ask the chief of the commander's bodyguards:

"Brother Liu, Brother Liu, how is it now? You said you would try to do it, didn't you? To-day is the sixteenth."

"I know to-day is the sixteenth," he answered; and the woman spat and closed her lips tight. She appeared dissatisfied and disconcerted. The chief guard was nodding at me and pointing to the woman, but I was looking in the other direction, trying to see all that lay beneath the lamplight. I understood that I was not allowed to stay long, and I said I would go back. The woman asked me to call on her to-morrow. This I promised. The guard accompanied me beyond the gate and grasped my hand, as though he knew there were many mysterious things left unexplained; then he returned to the temple.

I could not believe she was a bandit. I thought there might have been a mistake. I could not forget what we had done at Hweihua.

A night passed. At breakfast the next morning I was told that I ought to invite everyone to a drink. The girl bandit Wang Jao-mei had been executed, and I could go to the bridge and see her whenever I wanted. Somebody, who had witnessed the execution, reported that she said nothing, sitting quite calmly on that vermilion blanket of hers, and did not fall down when her head was cut off. I was astonished. I could not believe she had been killed. I had seen her the previous evening, and she had asked me to call on her. As soon as breakfast was over I ran to the bridge. Her body had been put into a white unpainted coffin; I saw only a few stains of blood and the pale ashes of paper money. I hurried back to see the chief bodyguard. He was lying in bed and silent. I dared not ask him any questions, and returned to work in my own room.

But in a short time I learnt all about the affair from one of the guards.

The girl bandit should have been executed long ago. In spite of her beauty, none of the officers who admired her dared to approach her or apply for her release. Her bad behaviour was known to everyone. She was kept in prison, and she was even treated better than the other prisoners, because they wanted to do everything in their power to find the seventy rifles she had buried away, no one knew where. When the *tawang* heard of this he went to see her often, for he knew the lieutenant of the Szechuanese platoon. As he came to know the woman, he told her that he, too, had sixty rifles buried on the Hunan border, and he would try to bail her out and they would remove the guns and return to their mountain strongholds, living like *tawangs*, free from all restrictions and fears. The woman trusted him; their hands would grope betwen the palisades. But when the soldiers learned of this, they would become querulous at the thought that what none of their officers could obtain was granted to a rank outsider. So the whole platoon stood at the gate, armed to the teeth, prepared to make as much trouble as possible for the *tawang*. But he was perfectly aware of the situation, and when he heard his name being called out, he tightened his belt, took a pistol in each hand and said:

"Brothers, I beg you not to be foolish. The pheasants are flying everywhere in the sky, and it is only luck which brings them down. I am sorry if I have offended you but I beg you to pardon me. Let me pass, for bullets cannot distinguish people like a lamp."

The soldiers knew he was no fool. They knew, too, that several lives would be lost if they refused to let him pass, and they knew that the Szechuanese army had only a company stationed in the place while the Hunan army possessed four battalions, so that a conflict would do them no good. Therefore they gave way and let the *tawang* pass through with the pistols in his hands. Early the next morning Wang Jao-mei was taken out and summarily executed.

He lay in bed for about a week, saying nothing and eating nothing. Then all of a sudden he got up and appeared to be as lively as ever. He came to see me in my room, and as soon as he saw me, he said:

"Jao-mei died for my sake. I have been weeping for seven days. Now I'm all right."

It seemed to me both amusing and pathetic. I had nothing to say, so I held his hand and smiled comfortingly.

Some days later I had a chance to return to Hunan, and I prepared to get a passport and return on a small cargo-boat. Travelling by river, I thought I would see the famous rapids, and see many strange new places. Meanwhile the *tawang* had been making love to a laundress and meant to have her for a concubine. But one day, on his way out of the temple, someone had appealed to the commander, and he learned that there was something irregular in the arrangement, and he had informed the *tawang* that they were guests here, they must obey the rules and this would endanger the army's good reputation.

"I am free to do as I please," the *tawang* said afterwards. "Civilisation allows it, and if the commanding officer refuses me this privilege, well then—I'll resign, go home, summon up my men and play my old game again!"

Since he could not have the woman, he resigned, and the commander promptly gave his permission. The *tawang* decided to leave with me, and our two names were written on the passport. We had fixed on the ship, and we were taking our breakfast, prepared to leave that very afternoon. We were chatting in my room, and he was telling me what had happened before Wang Kao-mei's execution, when the army cashier suddenly sent for him to receive his back-pay. He went down cheerfully, but in less than a minute I heard a whistle and the duty officer calling for a horse. I wondered what had happened. It sounded like an execution. Had a soldier escaped? A moment later I heard somebody shouting. I pushed open the window. I saw the *tawang* standing there in the courtyard, with his arms bound behind his back. The guards' company had been summoned, and the duty officer was asking for his orders. The prisoner would soon be taken out.

The *tawang* raised his lean shoulders and spoke in a loud voice to the people in the galleries.

"Chief-of-Staff, Adjutant-in-Chief, Chief Secretary, Judge —please say something—let me have justice—please beg the commander to spare my life. I have followed him for many years now. I have done nothing wrong. My wife is even now serving his lady in their house. For mercy's sake have mercy on me!"

They all looked at one another, but said nothing. Suddenly the commander came out into the hall. He looked very self-possessed, he held an ivory pipe in his hand and stood under the eaves, graceful and smiling, looking up at the officers who gazed down from the galleries.

"Commander, have mercy on me, do me a favour, don't kill me!"

Then the commander replied:

"Liu Yun-t'ing! None of this nonsense! You are disgracing yourself! A man should die bravely when he has done wrong and deserved his death. That is the custom in our army. We are guests here, yet you violated a woman prisoner at night in gaol. Well, I paid no attention to that, for I thought of your great merits in the years you have served under me. But now again you have done evil. You wanted to seduce someone else's woman, and you wanted to go home to summon up your men! I consider it better to kill you and remove an evil from the place rather than let you go home and commit all those crimes which make you hated by the people. No more nonsense! I'll look after your wife and children! And as for yourself, be brave and be a man!"

Hearing this, the *tawang* did not cry out any more, but smiled at the people in the galleries and appeared to be at ease.

"Good, my commander," he answered. "Commander, thank you for your kindness through the years. Good-bye, brothers, good-bye brother." After a while he added: "Commander, you really must be dreaming. Somebody once tried to bribe me with six thousand dollars to kill you. I refused!"

The commander seemed to be deaf to these words. He ordered the adjutant to fetch the coffin.

The *tawang* was then carried beyond the gates, and was never seen again. I sailed down river that afternoon. Of the two names on my passport, one had been scratched out with a vermilion pen. The passport accompanied me down dangerous rapids, and I handed it in at Paoching five days later at the adjutant's office.

There is little more to relate. General Chang, our commander, was killed by machine-gun fire three years later together with his bodyguard and four sedan-chair bearers as he entered the inner gate of the old examination hall at Chenchow, while trumpets were sounding a welcome. He had been invited by a junior brigadier of his to dinner. A year later, at exactly the same place, this brigadier was murdered by someone sent by the general of another army.

The Rainbow

I

ELEVEN o'clock.

Half an hour ago I returned to my home. On the way I passed under an old archway, which in daytime is filled with the stalls of the street-vendors, but in the clear moonlight it was mysteriously vast and deserted. Suddenly I was struck by the faint fragrance of plum flowers, which made me stare into "nothingness," for the vastness of the archway filled my spirit and the quietness of the place, though possessing neither shape nor substance, possessed an extraordinary heaviness. I stepped slowly towards this "nothingness" and entered a small courtyard, where there was a room with a bright stove and the perfume of plum blossoms. It was like New Year's Eve; crackers were sounding in the crisp air. In absolute loneliness I began to read a strange book. I opened it cautiously. On the very first page I read the words: "We are spirits of flame!"

II

The fire began to blaze. The room was as warm as spring, giving you the desire to put on thinner clothing. The light beneath the orange lamp-shade tinged the walls, the carpets and everything else in the room with an unearthly colour. And there hovered in the air the scent of a sour lemon which lay in a lacquered vermilion dish, shaped like an autumn leaf, which lay near the window.

The window curtains hung low. On these pale brown curtains coloured horses were drawn, and seemed to be galloping. The visitor who enters the room finds himself in a strange state of loneliness, which is afterwards dissipated. Unperceived by her guest, his hostess has entered, her image emerging in the large mirror oposite the stove. A white face with long brows and a smile breathing of spring. In the loose hair over her delicate white ears, blue flowers are waving.

Her fingers are soft and long. When she smoothes her hair with her hands, her smiling face is inclined gently to one side and seems about to disturb the quietness of his mind.

"I am so sorry—have you been waiting long?"

"No, only a short while. And the room is so warm and quiet—it has been a pure enjoyment."

The smiling face disappears. The chair by the stove is moved slightly. The black kitten with the white nose and white paws, lying on the silver-red cushions, is no longer allowed the warmth of the fire and leaps to the ground, yawns in order to demonstrate that he cannot be so unreasonably removed and walks slowly away.

The guest continues to stare round the room. Once again he sees the coloured horses waving on the curtains.

"It is warm in your room—almost like being in a greenhouse."

"Are you hot? You must be wearing too many clothes. I'll open the window for a moment."

He had wanted only to praise the warmth of the place: he had not meant to say it was hot. Now that the windows were being pushed open, he could only be silent.

Snow was flying outside. As soon as the window was opened, cold air rushed in. The window was closed again.

"I am beginning to feel hot, too. I'll go and change my dress."

She left the room for a moment.

He gazed at the coloured horses on the curtains. They seemed to be running and leaping. And then there was this loneliness again. The plum blossoms were fragrant.

She came back wearing a green silk gown, which made her appear thinner.

"Aren't you afraid of the cold—wearing such thin

clothes?" It will be troublesome if you catch a cold. You know, medicines are always bitter . . ."

"I'm not cold at all. The dress is thick enough. It was made seven years ago—I came upon it again in the autumn. I was afraid it would no longer fit me and that I would have to give it away, and then I thought about it, and wondered who I should give it to, and after a while it was given to myself." She warmed her hands before the stove, her small graceful fingers extended towards the fire. Before he could praise her hands they drew away and began to stroke softly the hem of her gown. "I made it myself. I like the soft silk material and the patterned lining. And it's so heavy—so heavy."

"It fits you perfectly. Its heaviness, as you say, contrasts with the graceful slimness of your body." All that he wanted to say dissolved into a smile. His hostess understood, and returned the smile to him.

When the hem was turned up, he saw her long slender legs threaded in mouse-grey stockings. They were like columns, like poplars, like a road leading to a silent green meadow.

Saying nothing, he continued to caress with his eyes her ankles, her smooth calves, the rounded knees. As though perceiving the slight indelicacy of his eyes, and the imaginary roads he was travelling, the hem curved down tightly over her knees. Sighing gently. "How do you like my stockings? The colour is not very pleasing, but the material is really fine." The slender hands were stroking the stockings beneath the gown. They seemed to be saying: "The material is fine—this makes my feet prettier, doesn't it?"

"In hot weather you are much less troubled." But the words meant: "In hot weather you never wear stockings and your feet are still nicer."

The hem curled up again. "Oh much less troubled in hot weather." ("Everyone says my feet are nice-looking, but really they are not nice-looking at all.") "And then fashions are always changing."

"My dear, every nation is squandering millions and millions of dollars on things which are entirely unimportant, so what does it matter whether there is a change in stockings?" (Why do you mind the expense, since it adorns you? An artist in a stocking factory contributes no less to human welfare than an engineer.)

"This is all too deep for me. I just like kicking the sand barefoot when I reach the seashore." (I am not afraid of being gazed at or being kissed, but not everywhere.)

"Then, too, I suppose there are new fashions in bathing costumes." (My darling, you look much more charming when naked.)

Each seemed to be able to understand the voiceless utterances of the other. At that moment she smiled and fell silent. As a rule a wise woman's shyness is a mixture of virtue and desire. So there were encouraging and disapproving elements in her silence and in her smile.

She raised her feet a little. (I know all your silly ideas, but your silliness is not unpleasant!) Then she began to withdraw them a little, for fear he might kiss them. (Enough! Why are you always so silly?)

"You can't imagine how gracefully you walk. Wherever you are, joy and health seem to stream from you." But what he really said was: "Do you prefer climbing hills or walking along the seashore?"

"I prefer the sea, because you feel so free there." But when she opened her mouth, she heard herself saying: "The sea is much more pleasant. The cold, wet sand, the ebb-tide. It's so free, and so nice to be able to walk barefoot."

"I have a passion for sea-shells," he said. "Beauty is so strange."

"So many things are strange! So many things make me humble and adoring." (You are joking! You only think you are humble, you only think you adore. But you are a strange person, for having imagined so many indelicacies, you have done nothing indelicate. You know very well how to protect yourself.)

"But then I always see what others ignore. What I see is unreal, and perhaps even unintelligible to others, and I suppose this is a kind of tragedy." (Do you really want me to treat you so courteously? It seems to me that you are encouraging me to do something else.)

"How much poetry have you written recently?" (A hint of sarcasm in her voice, as though she was saying: "You are writing poetry all day, and your passions are immersed in calligraphy. You are almost entirely remote from life.")

"I have been writing a novel. Prodigiously overworked. It's charming, but not serious. A story of hunting a doe in a snowstorm. What is surprising is that the doe is caught. Like a children's tale, and probably only children will understand it." (You will understand after reading it. You, too, desire beauty and the wilder flights of the soul which occur so often in children's stories. But be careful when you are reading it.)

She seemed to understand him perfectly, for she smiled: "Have you really finished it? Then you must show it to me. Let me try out my childish innocence on your story, for I have no idea whether I still possess this innocence."

"I desire nothing better than to see whether my understanding of human nature deserves the approving seal of your intelligence. Sometimes I would doubt this power of mine, and though others have praised it, I am still uncertain."

She lowered her head (the drooping of the lily) to read the wild story. As she began reading, she feared that he might feel neglected, and so she raised her head and glanced at him tenderly. There were summer clouds and spring rains in her eyes. He said: "Don't look at me—please look at the story. And please don't allow yourself to be offended by anything in it."

"Since you have written it, I must read it slowly."

"Yes, it is a story which can only be understood when read slowly."

"You mean—the story is too deep, or I am too stupid?"

"Neither. I meant the language is uncouth, unfamiliar. Everything that is unfamiliar may be considered dangerous and troublesome."

"Good. Let me see whether I can discover something in it."

She went on reading the story quietly. The guest went on quietly reading the coloured horses on the curtains. They seemed to be galloping and vanishing into the limitless expanse of green reeds.

He seemed to feel a need for continuing imaginary conversations.

——Too beautiful. As a rule a beautiful woman rarely realises how much vexation her beauty causes to others, and how much happiness.

——Really? You are joking! What do you mean by gazing so steadily at my feet? You are artless in appearance, but you are a romantic at heart. I know you once kissed my whole body, but what you said was: "The horses are drawn with gusto and seem to be running away in all directions." What ran away was your heart! You are travelling the same road again. I am ashamed that you should speak in this way, but I am not afraid. Besides, are you sufficiently endowed with a sense of sin?

——This is all perfectly true. I want to kiss your toes, your knees, your legs, all the secret places of your body. You must understand how honest and unselfish are my desires.

——I understand everything except one thing. You are full of imagination, but you do nothing!

There were only two people in the room. Outside the house, there was silence save for the sound of flying snow touching lightly against the window-pane. Occasionally the accumulated snow fell from a pine tree, but the sound was barely audible. The guest imagined he heard the voiceless words communicated between them, but what he actually heard was his own heartbeats.

The fire blazed.

She tapped her toe on the floor while reading, as though to say: "Start from here, please. I am not afraid of you, however mischievous you may be. I know what you are going to do. How silly you will be, and how hurried!"

Her hair was soft and dark; her neck seemed to have been carved from jade or white fat, her eyebrows and her eyes were quite charming. There was a small dimple on her cheek. Her small breasts protruded. The dress was perhaps a little too thick.

At the moment when his eyes kiss her hair, it is soft as silk, and when he kisses her forehead, her eyes are closed slightly. When they kiss her cheeks, a nameless and intoxicating fragrance is exhaled. When they kiss her neck, they seem to be sucking, and they leave a little red mark. When they kiss both her breasts, the dress is decidedly a little too thick. So he says:

"My dear, aren't you feeling hot, so near the stove?"

"I am afraid of the cold but not of the heat," she answers without raising her head, laughing. "I am a cat—a quite pretty Siamese cat—and I do not like to move. Especially when I am near a stove. I can sit here for a whole day without doing or thinking anything." She laughed again—a little musical note which came from her throat.

"How far have you got?"

"I have read to the passage where the doe thinks herself very safe, standing on a lonely ledge of rock where the winds and snows cannot reach. Her eyes are gazing brightly in another direction, but the huntsman is already slowly approaching. He thinks he can hold her by the hind-legs, and he is gazing down at her soft fur, and he seems to be in no hurry . . . It's not imaginatively understood. Beautiful, but unreal."

"Please read on. You may criticise it when you have finished it."

The smile fades as she reads. He knows that she has reached another chapter describing another incident relating to the doe, and showing how similar the creature is to a human being. The tenderness flowing from her eyes and caused by her new love is described as human. There is felt by both of them an unfamiliar and new emotion which mingles with their lives and causes them consternation.

When she shakes her head a second time, the meaning is entirely different from the first. No longer "approval" or "disapproval," but a timid acknowledgment that there may be people outside the house. But only a light snow is falling.

He goes to the window, pulls away a corner of the curtains, cleans the dew from the glass and gazes out. He sees only the pallor of the night, pure and clean. When the curtains fall: "The whiteness which conceals everything has made everything vanish and signifies—the spirits of flame!"

Meanwhile there is about the stove in the room another whiteness, pure and clean, which signifies—chastity.

She places the book on her knees and sighs gently. Her stockings seem to have been removed by the guest; her feet are as white as frost. It seems to her that the guest is saying: "I am not being indecent. I like to look at them, and if you are not offended, I will kiss them with my lips. I want to journey along the road of poplars and bask in the shade and lie beside the well, where grass abounds and white sheep pasture. I will follow the hunter's way, however silly it is, however despicable."

She feels uneasy, draws her feet in and pulls her skirt lower down. She dare not continue to read the story, and so warms her hands over the fire, pretending to be cold. Almost unconsciously she pulls open the furnace door, throws in three lumps of coal and stirs the fire with the bronze poker. "These fires should burn properly. I like the heat so much."

"Finished?"

"No, but tell me—how did you find that doe?"

"Very well, let me warm myself and then I'll tell you. . . . I do not know in what mood I found her. When my fingers touched the smooth fur of her feet, I wondered whether I was touching a living doe or only an image of perfect beauty. I thought of the ancients who depicted women's fingers as soft grasses or as bamboo shoots. Those who have never seen the maternal tenderness in a doe's eyes shining like dew are sure to wonder why I kissed her eyes for so long a time. What was so curious was that she had no thought of escaping while she was near me. She was neither frightened nor afraid. She seemed to be entirely conscious of my intentions, and they were agreeable to her, and there was no need to utter a word. It was I who was discomfited."

"She didn't try to escape?"

"She wished to escape, but she didn't go. Snow was falling outside the cave. She may have desired escape, but that would have been more dangerous than staying with me. Besides, I would have been a fool to let her go. I saw that she could not understand very much of what I was saying, and instead of words I spoke with my hands and my lips, caressing her, calming her. Then I began to hear her sighing . . ."

"Quite impossible."

"Perhaps not with you, but certainly with this deer."

They were silent for a moment.

"Aren't you too hot? I know you are still wearing too many clothes." And he whispered to himself: "Poetry is also a flame. When its life is consumed, there is left only the shadow of blue flames and a little heap of ashes." At this moment he does something to her.

Twenty minutes later he asks again: " Do you still feel cold?" and draws out from a heap of silks a transparent grey shawl which he wraps over her shoulders. "Strange, the horses on the curtain are really moving." But, in fact, at that moment, they seemed to him utterly still.

As she stirs the fire, she says gently: "I am thinking of the doe. Why didn't she escape from him?" But she was saying this only to extricate herself, for the event now belonged to the past.

Silence continued in this room with its orange lamp-shade and the ruddy fire.

The next day she sat beside the stove and read a letter:

"Darling, I must be still dreaming—my body and soul still intoxicated with delight—still kissing your eyes and your heart. You are everything in my dream, and I am possessed of you. What I have found is not only your body, but a halo, a wreath of flowers, a cloud. All the words of poets lose their meaning here. Whiteness is the highest morality, but you are beyond 'morality' now.

"In the Song of Songs it is said: 'Thy navel is like a round goblet that wanteth not liquor.' This was the first time that my lips have touched it, but I had no fear of being drunk. When the fruit is ripe, it signifies that life is ready to give. But life fades slowly, even though no one picks the ripe fruit.

"I have found pieces of china, so smooth and pure that I never thought I would ever again see anything like them. But what I saw with my eyes in the evening was smoother and purer than any of the famous pieces of china I have seen.

"Let me recall to you a painting made by an artist of the Yuan dynasty. Here is a meadow of soft grass, cloudy and silky, and here and there are small mounds and hills. I would give everything to live my whole life in these soft plains. It seemed that I was given an image carved neither of bronze nor of jade, yet it was precious and noble and infinitely rare. The wonder of this sculpture still surprises me. It was pale green in some places, there were two tiny moles in another. These are 'the small cups where warm kisses are kept.' So I desired to live my whole life among these 'cups of kisses.'

"The stalk of a lily is slender, and your neck and shoulders exceedingly resemble a lily. When your beautiful head lay inclined, and the lamplight shone on your forehead and on your long, slender neck, really it seemed to be a lily which has not yet blossomed. Oh, my fingers trembled! I dared not pluck you! And then you smiled, and you were a lily in flower, life moving and streaming within your veins. You were still nobler in your silences. . . . And all this is only abstractions . . . I think of the pale blue lily and the yellow pistils, and your brows bending . . . Darling . . ."

III

The book became a blue flame and vanished into "nothingness." I left the room and found myself again under the old archway; and it seemed that out of all my life only the blue flame had been preserved which, had it lived elsewhere, would have been no more than a heap of ashes, a withered plum flower, a remnant of my life which had lost all colouring and fragrance in these strange times. I remembered the first sentence of the book: *"We are spirits of flame!"*

I have returned to my house. Half-past eleven. The yellow light of the tung-oil lamp covers my table and scatters its faint brilliance over my room. Here and there I see books written by people who lived two thousand years ago, thousands of miles away, books by myself and by unknown contemporaries. A grey mouse stalks among the books where the lamplight fails to penetrate. Its unhurried steps show that it is alive, and yet it has nothing whatsoever to do with these accumulations of lives. How many more books shall I read as I live on? How many more shall I write?

I must rest, but I do not know where I can find rest. I am very tired, still living in a kind of excitation.

The lamp-wick flowers into snuff, a flower that blossoms in the flame. "It will fade and fall only when the fire is consumed. It is a symbol of life." My heart is also burning, I do not know why.

Though the fragrance of the plum-blossom is lost, yet I search for the state of mind from which this fragrance emerged, trying to discover something, as though my life were still worth living if it could be found. Then, in the shadow of the past, I find a yellowness and something withered and dark, which signifies the life of someone else or perhaps the form of another of my dreams; and it is not necessary to enquire which dream it is. I look quietly into the depths, searching for those dark withered leaves of the past, seeing another person's attitudes changing from joy to madness, and I see my own image reflected in the joy and madness of another and in the hesitation between giving and taking, between hatred and love.

Like a beam of sunshine printed on a wall. Like a young heart beating. As though everything in the world had acquired order and significance again.

I conjecture that there must be another book relating how a woman is amazed and blinded in the thin sunshine, in a cool autumn, by her own beautiful figure, her silky black hair, the stain of rouge on her lips, the perfume on her cheeks, the clarity and smoothness of her shoulders and limbs, and those tender cries streaming from her eyes as bright as swimming, and then the contradiction between love and hate when the limbs are melting. Such wonderful lives are lost into sunshine and left behind in the passage of time! All lost, and never to be found; and when you search for it what is left is seen to be dark and withered as well. Is it a flower taken from my own hair or a scrap of paper picked from the roadside? I cannot tell.

When I try to understand the meaning of "life", I see a number of mythological phrases—"passion", "love", "hatred", "giving and taking", "God and the devil", "person", "meeting by chance", "failing to meet through misfortune". Half an hour later these terms resume their significance. I love these abstractions ardently, and while gazing into space I see in life only an embarrassed obstinacy, and the gradual withdrawing of that obstinacy is all that I have gained from the experience called "living". All the other knowledges are helpless here. It is five o'clock in the morning, before dawn.

When I open the door gently, the day is already lengthening. A stream of sunlight, long familiar to me, flows into the room, shining obliquely on white walls. The Burmese wooden ships painted in gold over the bookcase shimmer in the fresh daylight. Everything is new.

But now it is again ten o'clock at night. Clear moonlight. The verandah is flooded with the moon. I open the door and let the moon in. Then there seems to be someone who, following the moonlight, enters the room and stands behind me: "Why do you torment yourself? What do you mean by these symbols of life?" I force a smile. My eyes grow wet with tears. "I am writing the story of Feng-hsien, the fox-goddess who entered a mirror and came to life again because her lover was faithful. I want to revive her through my pen."

The Frontier City

I

From Szechuan there is a highway running east to Hunan. When the road reaches the small mountain city of Ch'a-t'ung, just inside the border of Hunan, it crosses a river; near the river you will find a white pagoda and a small isolated cottage, where there once lived a family which consisted of an old man, a girl and a yellow dog.

A stream winds down the valley. It meanders along for two or three *li* and empties itself in the river, but if you leave the stream and climb the mountain, the city is then only one *li* away, for the creek forms a bent bow and the straight path the string, and there is a slight difference in their lengths. Now this stream is about two hundred feet across, and the bed is made up of large pieces of stone, so that even when it is too deep to touch bottom with a pole, you can still see the fishes swimming in the clear and transparent water. Since the stream lies across the main thoroughfare between Szechuan and Hunan, and lies on the boundary between the two provinces, it might have been thought that a bridge should be built across it; but the landscape was such that it was impossible to build a bridge, and instead there was a square-ended ferry-boat which could hold twenty men or ten horses, and if there were more people to be ferried across, it was necessary to make a double journey. On the prow of the boat a short pole had been erected; an iron ring was fastened to the pole, and through this passed a rope stretched between the banks. And when the boat was drawing close to the bank, the ferry man cried: "Wait, wait awhile," and holding the ring in his hand he would pull the boat to the bank. Then the people walked off the prow with their cattle and whatever else they possessed; and they would climb the hill and disappear.

The boat was public property, and there was no need to pay. But there were some who insisted on paying: they would throw a handful of copper coins on the deck; but the old ferryman always picked them up, one by one, and try to thrust them back in the hand of the giver. He would say in a testy voice:

"I've got my wages, three bushels of rice and seven hundred cash. It's quite enough for my needs. Who would want such a sum as this?"

Nevertheless some people still insisted on paying him for his services. To set his own heart at ease he would accept the money and later he would ask one of his passengers to buy tea or tobacco at Ch'a-t'ung with the money. Then he would hang some fine leaves of native tobacco at his belt, giving it away to whoever seemed in need of it. Or else he would take a few leaves and tie them into the bundles which people carried on their backs, saying: "You know—the best tobacco—the finest quality—take it—it will come in handy for a present."

As for the tea, he brewed it in a big pot on summer days, and served it to thirsty passengers.

Now the ferryman was the old man who lived in the cottage which lay beneath the pagoda. He was seventy years old, and since the age of twenty he had guarded the stream: no one knew how many people he had carried across the stream in those fifty years. He was so old that he ought to have a rest; but Heaven had not yet granted him this august permission. Living quietly and honestly, he never reflected on the significance of his work in the world; and the happiness which gave him his strength, giving him also a complete forgetfulness of death, was the young girl who was his constant companion. Strength came with the dawn and thoughts of death came with the night, but he was unaware of these things. His only friends were the ferryboat and the yellow dog, and his only relative was the child.

Sixteen years ago the child's mother, the only daughter of

the ferryman, had loved a soldier from Ch'a-t'ung, though the old ferryman knew nothing of the affair. When she grew pregnant, the soldier wanted her to run away with him down-river, but elopement was against the military code of the time, and the girl dared not desert her ageing father. They discussed the matter for a long time, the girl lacking all courage to go and the soldier unwilling to ruin his career. At last they decided on suicide. "Though it is impossible for us to live together, no one can prevent us from dying together," the soldier said, and shortly afterwards he poisoned himself. The old ferryman heard of this, but he never addressed a single harsh word to his daughter and pretended the most perfect ignorance of the affair. So they lived on quietly together. The girl, however, felt the most terrible shame for what she had done, and when the baby was born, she drowned herself in the stream. By a miracle the child lived and grew up, and now she was fifteen. The cottage lay between two hills covered thickly with bamboo groves, whose jade-green leaves filled the eyes with interminable bright colour, and so he called her "Green Jade."

Green Jade grew up in the wind and sun, so her skin was black. She saw only green mountains and blue water, so her eyes were clear as crystal. Nature had nursed and educated her, and she was as innocent and agile as a young animal. She was as gentle as a mountain antelope, never took thought of cruelty or sorrow, and she was never angry. Whenever she saw a stranger on the ferryboat paying attention to her, she gazed back at him with bright eyes, as if she could escape into the hills whenever she liked; and then, seeing that he had no dangerous intentions, she would forget about him altogether and play with the water.

In all weathers the ferryman guarded the stream. Whenever a passenger appeared, he pulled at the rope, his back stooping as he brought the boat to the other side. Sometimes when he was tired, he went to sleep on a great rock in the stream, and then Green Jade would jump into the boat whenever people beckoned from the bank without telling her Grandfather that they were there; and she brought them over and said nothing of it to the old man. More often she would accompany her Grandfather and the yellow dog in the boat, and they would work together; and when the boat was approaching the bank and the old Grandfather was shouting: "Wait, wait awhile," and the yellow dog was jumping ashore with the boat-rope between his teeth as though in an effort to prove that he, too, was useful in the world, then it seemed that the whole family was fulfilling its appointed tasks.

Once in a while, when it was warm and there was a gentle wind, they would find themselves without passengers. Then Grandfather and Green Jade would sun themselves on the rock before their cottage, sometimes throwing sticks into the water, so that the dog would leap down the high bank and bring the sticks back to them. Sometimes, too, both Green Jade and the dog opened their ears wide to listen to Grandfather telling stories of the wars that had been waged in the city many years ago. Or else Grandfather and Green Jade would make little flutes of bamboo and play wedding music, but if anyone wanted to cross the river, the old man would put down his flute and follow them into the boat. And always at such moments there would be heard a high-spirited cry from the rock:

"Grandfather, Grandfather, listen! I'll play—and you sing!"

Then Grandfather would sing while the boat crossed the river, his shaky voice trembling with the sounds of the flute in the quiet air; so it seemed that everything became more living, though in fact everything was quieter.

And sometimes the boat would carry calves from Szechuan, or sheep, or a bride's flowery sedan. At such times Green Jade insisted on ferrying them over, and standing on the square-ended prows she would pull at the rope lazily so that the boat would go slow. When the calves and the sheep and the sedan-chair left the boat, she would follow them for a while, never returning until she had stood on top of a neighbouring hill and watched them disappearing in the distance. It was only then that she returned to the boat and brought it under the sheltering eaves of the bank, there mimicking the little bleats of the lambs or the moo-oo of the cows, or else she would pluck some wild flowers and wreath them round her hair in imitation of a bride.

Ch'a-t'ung is only one *li* away from the ferry, and whenever there was shopping to be done—whenever Grandfather wanted wine to celebrate the New Year festival, or whenever there were household goods to be bought—Green Jade would go alone with the yellow dog. Whatever she saw in the shops was deeply impressed in her mind. The bundles of rice noodles, the jars of white sugar, the fire crackers and the red candles so filled her mind that long after she returned she was still talking to Grandfather about them. And she never forget the great junks on the river, which were larger and far more interesting than the little ferry boat on which they spent so much of their lives.

II

Ch'a-t'ung is surrounded by hills and water. On one side the walls of the city crawl up along the hills like a serpent, and on the other side there was a small space between the wall and the river where the junks anchored. These junks carried wood-oil, green salt and painted walking-sticks on their journeys downstream; they brought back cotton yarn, cloth and seafood. Connecting all these docks there is a lane called River Road, where the houses are half on land and half over the water; and it was necessary to build them in this manner because land was scarce and wood was cheap. And whenever the spring torrents rose over the level of the street, the city gates were closed; and then the people in River Road would set up long ladders against their houses and stretching from the roofs to the city walls, and cursing and yelling at the top of their voices, they would take their pots and pans and rice-panniers into the safety of the city, to wait there until the flood waters disappeared and they could come out through the muddy city gate. If the flood happened to be particularly severe, some of the houses would be washed away, and people would gaze at them helplessly from the city wall. The victims said nothing. They had no complaints, and indeed they greeted all natural disasters in the same quiet undemonstrative way. From the city wall they would see the flood-waters spreading in ever widening torrents, while houses, cattle, sheep and even trees floated down in the stream. There would be men quietly waiting in sampans along the dead water near the old custom house; and when a dead log or some animal or other or a broken boat appeared on the turbulent waves, or they heard a woman or a child crying, they would paddle into midstream, catch the object against the side of the sampan and return to shore. Like all the natives of the place they were brave and chivalrous, as well as interested in money. And whether they were rowing out in search of someone who was still alive or something that was quite dead, they would behave with admirable courage and truly earned the applause they received.

The river was once known as the Yu Sui, famous in history, but now it was more commonly known as White Stream. At Chenshow this river meets the Yuan Sui, and joins its own purity to the muddy waters of the greater river. But if you climb towards the source of the White Stream, you will reach the Tayu caves near Nusu, where the water is so pure that you can see the small pebbles and rocks thirty or forty feet below the surface of the water, and when the sun is shining you can even watch the fishes gliding in remote depths and the small red stones which are known in these parts as "flowering cornelians." The fishes seem to be floating in the air. And all along the banks there are great mountains shrouded in slender bamboos, used for making paper; and though the seasons change, the bamboos remain a deep, penetrating and vivid green. The houses near the river are surrounded with peach and apricot groves, so that in spring wherever there were peach-blossoms there were also houses, and wherever there were houses there was wine. You saw the houses by noticing the purple-coloured clothes which were hung out to dry. But when autumn and winter came, the houses stood out against the cliffs and along the riverside, and you would see them shining clear in the distance with their yellow mud walls and black roof-tiles, and they were all perfectly placed in harmony with their surroundings. Travellers who loved poetry or painting would crouch low in the boat for the whole of the thirty day voyage upstream, never tiring of the splendours which Nature continually unfolded to his gaze. There were miracles everywhere, and Nature was never more charming and captivating than along the rivers of Szechuan and Hunan.

The White River has its source in Szechuan. During the spring floods small junks can proceed as far as Hsiushan Mountains, and Ch'a-t'ung was always their last port of call in Hunan. In spring the river was at least half a *li* across, but in autumn and winter, when the floods subsided, there was only a small river two or three hundred feet wide spanning the river bed; the rest was a shore of blue stones. At such times merchandise proceeding from one province to the other would be landed at Ch'a-t'ung and carried by coolies on shoulder-poles of polished pinewood, and imported merchandise would also be carried by human labour in small bundles.

There are only about five hundred families in the city; and there was only a company of soldiers, from the Green Army, to patrol the frontier. Of the citizens, some were landowners and proprietors of oilshops, others were moneylenders to the farmers, mortgaging their oil and rice and cotton crops; and all the families were descendants of the garrison soldiers. There was a revenue office in the little temple which lies along River Road; but the officer himself lived in the city.

The soldiers lived in the yamen which once belonged to the lieutenant-colonel in charge of the defence of the city; but no one ever saw the soldiers, and if it had not been for the bugler who was continually demonstrating his prowess in the streets it would have seemed that the soldiers had no existence at all. On winter days all you can see in the city is cloth and cabbages drying on the doorsteps, and red turnips hanging under the roofs, and little palm-leaf baskets full of chestnuts and hazelnuts also hanging under the roofs, and in odd corners you would find fowls and chickens pecking and chirping in the straw. Now and then you would find a man in a doorway sawing a board or splitting logs with an axe, stacking the firewood into little pagodas. Or you would see a woman talking and working in the sunlight, her back bent over her work, clothed in stiffly-starched blue cloth with a white apron falling from the level of her breast. Everyone lived quietly and meditatively. And this silence increased their conception of the power of dreams. In the city men lived in confident anticipation of love and hate. But what they were thinking about, no one knew.

From the high ground overlooking the city, you could stand at the threshold of your house and enjoy the view of the river and the further bank. Whenever a junk approached the city, you saw the haulers toiling along the bank; and some of them brought from distant cities little sweet-cakes or packets of candies, and the children clamoured after them. As for the grown-ups, if they had hatched a brood of chickens or raised a few pigs, they gave them to these men in exchange for a roll of blue cloth or a jar of good bean sauce, or a good quality chimney for their kerosene lamps. And this was all that concerned the good housewives in the city.

Although the city was so eminently quiet and peaceful, River Road was rather an exception to the general order, for it was there that the traders sought out their contracts with the merchants from East Szechuan. There were hotels and lodging-houses for the merchants, and barber-shops which were real shops, not just wandering chairs. There were restaurants, haderdashers, oil shops, salters, clothing shops. There were shops where you could buy hard-wood pulleys, bamboo rope, pots and pans and kettles for the passing ships, and there were also brokers who acted as employment agents for the seamen. In front of the small eating houses, there were shallow jars filled with trout fried yellow, dressed with beancurd and decorated with red peppers. Nearby there were some vermilion chopsticks in a bamboo holder, and you could sit down at the long table just outside the door and take up the chopsticks in your hands. As you did so, a heavily powdered woman with plucked eyebrows would ask: "Sweet wine? Spirits?" and if you were high-tempered or humorous, or if you cared for the woman, you would probably answer: "Sweet wine? I am not a child! Asking me to drink sweet wine, eh?" At this, she would ladle out pure distilled wine from a large jar with a wooden dipper, pouring it into an earthenware bowl and offering it to the guest.

The grocer sold kerosene and kerosene oil lamps, and candles and paper and incense. Oil shops sold wood-oil. Salt shops stocked the green salt produced from hot springs. Clothing shops sold white yarn, white cloth, cotton and black kerchiefs, which the Hunanese tie round their heads. Ship chandlers' shops sold everything, and you might find an anchor weighing more than a hundred pounds, rusty and rain-soaked and sweated by the sun, standing outside their doors, waiting for a customer's purchase.

The doors of the sailors' employment brokers were open all day long. It was there that the junk owners received hirsute sailors. The junk owners wore delicate silk gowns. Indeed, these places resembled tea-shops, though no tea was sold there; nor was it unusual to find people smoking opium pipes there, though there were no opium dens along the quay. In fact, people came to these brokers' shops in order to enjoy themselves, and wages were never discussed, since all wages along the river were fixed. The "dragon-headed" junk owners would sit in the middle of a crowd of sailors, discussing business conditions in the two provinces, and all the news of the river. Here men would gamble over their shares of profit, but the main business was the buying and selling of junks, and of women.

With the growing rise of the city, prostitutes had come to settle in those houses which hung over the river's edge. They had come to the frontier city either from the surrounding countryside or in the wake of the Szechuanese army. They dressed in artificial silk jackets, wore trousers of chintz, plucked their eyebrows as fine as silk threads and soaked their hair in strong perfumes. Having nothing to do all day, they sat in their doorways making slippers, embroidering the toes with double phoenixes, listening to the junkmen singing as they climbed the masts. At night they performed their duties, deriving an almost perfect happiness from the performance of an honest toil, receiving merchants and sailors by turns.

There is a curious purity in the habits of the frontier people; so it happened that prostitutes would rarely insist on being paid by those who were well known to them, though from strangers they would demand money before closing the doors. Mostly they depended for their living on merchants from Szechuan, but their affections were given freely to the young sailors. If it so happened that a young sailor and a prostitute fell in love, they would bite each other's lips and necks and swear an oath: "After we have separated, we shall be good." For forty or fifty days the sailor and the woman would keep their word, fastening their hearts tightly upon the beloved. And if the man failed to return in time, the woman would grow mad with desire, dreaming of the time when at last the junk lay moored to the quay and her lover stepped unsteadily down the gangway towards her. Or else, growing suspicious, she would dream of him disappearing on some strange errand upstream, having entirely forgotten her. At such times the more gentle ones dreamed of drowning themselves or committing suicide by taking opium, while the harder ones dreamed of murdering their lovers, running towards them as they came from the boat with a kitchen knife in their hands. And though their lives were so different from ours, yet they were so perfectly immersed in their loves and their hates, so soaked with desire and so chilled by neglect, that they forgot everything else. Perhaps their only difference from us was that they were more innocent and more foolish. A short contract, a lifelong marriage, a door closed for a moment—all this trade in human flesh was regarded by them as proper and even respectable, nor did the onlookers feel any contempt for their trade. And since they believed that friendship was worth more than money, and they were perfectly capable of abiding by their promises, it happened that they were often more virtuous than the city-dwellers.

Shun-shun was the dock manager in this city. He had served in the army towards the end of the Ch'ing dynasty; he had been a sergeant in the famous forty-ninth army at the Revolution. Many who were sergeants at the time received posts of distinction, and others were beheaded or dismembered. But thanks to the rheumatism which he had derived from a life of dissipation, he returned to his native city, and with the money he had saved he bought an unpainted junk with six oars, hiring it out to a ruined junk-owner who plied between Ch'a-t'ung and Chengshow. Luck was with him; for nothing happened to the boat, and with the profits he had married a widow with a pale face and ink-black hair, who provided him with a dowry. Soon he was the owner of eight junks and two sons.

He was a broad-minded and happy-go-lucky man, but he was never as rich as the other merchants, for he loved to surround himself with friends and he gave ear to all requests for money. As a soldier, he had known the sufferings of wanderers and the dispossessed. And when any junk-owner, who had lost his ship, came to him for help, he was always willing to help him to the limit of his power; and so too when he met a vagabond soldier or a wandering scholar. The money he made from water he gave as freely as water flows. Though he suffered from rheumatism, he still swam well; and though his gait was not well balanced, his judgment remained unimpaired. The laws governing the river were simple, for they were decided according to well-known rules: when one junk rammed another there were fixed customary dues, and if one junk-owner invaded the purlieus of another, this also was settled according to customary laws. But to govern these cases they needed an old man, wise and famous for integrity. During the autumn the last judge had died, and Shun-shun was named as his successor. He was only fifty, but he was so intelligent, fair-minded and peace-loving, so completely without greed, that no one objected to him on account of his age.

His elder son was now eighteen, and his younger son seventeen. These boys were as sturdy as oxen; they could row, swim and walk long distances, and whatever the city boys did they could do as well. The elder son resembled his father: he was chivalrous and fair-minded, he was open-hearted and paid no attention to trifles, but the younger had more the temperament of his mother and resembled her even in the pallor of his face and the ink-jet hue of his hair. He had no love for conversation, and merely by looking at him you knew he was clever and passionate.

Because they were growing up swiftly now and needed some training, they were sent out on the junks as apprentices. When the junks sailed downstream they would be sent out to live the lives of the common sailors, taking the heaviest oars or leading the haulers, eating the common dishes of the sailors—salted fish, peppers, pickled cabbage—and sleeping on the hard planks of the deck, or of the holds. Or if they were sent upstream by land, they would follow the bales of merchandise for East Szechuan, passing through Dragon Pool and Yuyang and over the roads of the Hsiushan Mountains, wearing only sandals on their feet whatever the weather. They carried short daggers and used them when they had to: drawing them from their sheaths and standing on clear ground, waiting for their enemies. They would fight hand to hand to the finish. The prevailing spirit among the sailors was described by the proverb: "You fight enemies with your knives, and make friends with your knives," and therefore they never lost an opportunity for fighting. Knowledge of their trade, the art of making friends, adaptability to strange surroundings, hardiness with the knife in protecting their names and their fortunes taught the boys the value of courage and instinctive morality, with the result that they came to possess the strength of tigers while at the same time preserving an essentially peaceful attitude towards life, neither proud nor vain. And so it happened that the names of the father and his two sons were respected in the frontier city whenever they were mentioned.

Ever since the children were quite young, the father realised that the elder resembled him; and perhaps for this reason he loved the younger more; because of this hidden preference, he named the elder T'ien Pao, which means "Protected by Heaven," and the younger Nu-sung, which means "Sent by the Plague-god". According to the legends of the place, one who was protected by Heaven might yet suffer ordinary human ills, but one who was protected by the Plague-god was necessarily immune from them. Nu-sung was so handsome that the artless people of Ch'a-t'ung could find no words to describe his beauty, and therefore they called him Yao Yun, after the eldest son of the famous General Yao Fei of the Sun Dynasty. No one had ever seen Yao Yun except on the stage, where he wore a white helmet and white armour, but he was so beautiful that no other words described him.

III

Because on the borders of these two provinces the military authorities were scrupulous in the performance of their duties, protecting the land and concerning themselves only with local affairs, no extraordinary incidents had occurred for many years. Neither land nor water had suffered the impress of war, or the attacks of bandits. Everything was in good order, the people were peaceful and it seemed that except for the death of an ox or the overturning of a junk or family dissensions and griefs they were given over to a reign of continual happiness and content, though the rest of China was in turmoil.

The happiest days of all were those on which there occurred the Dragon-boat festivals, the Mid-Autumn festivals and those which introduced the New Year. These festivals had excited the people for ages, and they were still the most enjoyable days of the year.

During the Dragon-boat festival all the women and children put on new clothes and wrote the character "Wang" on their foreheads with orpiment wine. That day there were great banquets of fish and meat. People lunched in the usual way around eleven o'clock, and afterwards those who lived inside the city walls locked their gates and marched down to the river to see the festival. Those who had acquaintances in River Road would enjoy the race from windows overlooking the river, while others stood at the gates of the Revenue Office or along the docks. The boats started from the long pool downstream and finished just outside the Revenue Office, where the army officers, tax-gatherers and other important officials were waiting. Long before the event, the oarsmen had been in training; they had made little groups among themselves, and each group had selected the strongest and most sturdy youths to practise in the pools. The dragon-boats were not shaped like ordinary river-craft: they were long and narrow, with upcurved ends, striped with vermilion paint. When not in use, they were usually hidden away in dry caves along the river-bank and dragged down in the water when they were needed. Each boat held from twelve to eighteen oarsmen, and there was a leader, a drummer, a man to play the gong. The oarsmen held short paddles which they wielded in time with the drumbeats. The leader sat in the bows, his head swathed in a crimson turban, and he gave commands by continually waving the two small flags he held in his hands. Meanwhile the drummer and the boy who sounded the gong sat amidships, and they beat on their instruments as soon as the boat left the starting-place. And since the speed of the boat depended on the drumbeats there were times when the sound of the drums and of people yelling exactly resembled continual explosions of thunder. Prizes were given in front of the Revenue Office, a roll of red silk and a little silver medal pinned on the turban of one of the members of the crew, for the glory was shared by all. At that moment some soldiers would fire off a round of five hundred crackers in honour of the victorious crew.

As soon as the race was finished, there were always a few army officers who delighted in letting loose on the river some green-headed drakes with long necks to which a multitude of red silk ribbons had been tied. They did this in order to show their delight in the occasion, and to demonstrate their sense of favours received. Then anyone who could swim would dive into the water after the drakes, and whoever caught one owned it henceforward. At such moments the pool was unrecognisable: full of swimmers wildly pursuing the green-headed drakes, until silence came and dusk covered the sky.

Shun-Shun, the dock-manager, had been the best swimmer of them all in his younger days. He had never failed to catch the drakes. By the time Nu-sung was twelve, he could dive into the water without coming up for breath until he was under the drake he wanted, and his father would say cynically: "Now that you can swim like this, there is no reason at all why I should jump into the water." Thereafter he never swam unless it was so save someone from drowning. Even if he had been eighty, he would still have helped the homeless and the wanderers over the earth; and if necessary he would have dived into a fire to save them.

T'ien Pao and Nu-sung were the best swimmers and oarsmen in the city.

The Dragon-boat festival was drawing near; the race would take place on the fifth day of the month. On the first of the month the people living in River Road held a meeting to decide whether their boat should be launched that day. It so happened that T'ien Pao had to go overland with some merchants to Dragon Pool in East Szechuan with a consignment of goods specially made for the festival, with the result that only Nu-sung was left to take part in the race. Sixteen youngsters, as strong as young animals, marched upstream to the cave where the boat lay hidden, carrying joss-sticks, candles, fire-crackers and a drum which was provided with legs, and with a drumhead made of raw cowhide painted over with a vermilion-coloured representation of the celestial sphere. While the candles and joss-sticks were being lit, they drew the boat into the river and sailed downstream. And then when the crackers were fired and the drum was being beaten, the narrow boat shot downstream in the direction of the pool.

All this happened in the morning. During the afternoon another dragon-boat belonging to the fishermen was launched from the other bank; and the two boats began to rehearse for the race. The first sound of the drumbeats coming from the water sent the people into a state of delighted expectation, while the prostitutes living in the houses overlooking the river were immediately caught up in dreams of their distant lovers. Many junks would arrange to arrive in time for the festival, but many more would still be wandering downstream. So there were conflicting emotions among the inhabitants of the small frontier city, and many would be cheered and many others would remain silent, their brows knit together.

When the drumbeats could be heard over the hills, and when they reached the ferry, it was always the yellow dog who noticed them first. He barked and ran round the house, excited beyond measure, and if there were passengers crossing the creek, he would follow them to the east bank and run to the top of a hill and stay there, barking loudly in the direction of the city.

Green Jade was sitting on the big rock in front of the cottage, making mock grasshoppers and centipedes out of palm leaves, when she saw the yellow dog waking from his sleep in the sun. Immediately he began to run about as though possessed, crossing the creek and coming back again still more excited than before. She said, reproachfully, "Dog, dog! What is the meaning of all this? Really you are not allowed to behave so disgracefully". But as soon as she noticed the sound of the drumbeats, she too began to run round the cottage; and she stood on the top of a hill, listening for a long time, while the music of the drumbeats in her ears filled her with recollections of a previous festival.

IV

It happened two years ago. On the Dragon-boat festival, which always takes place on the fifth day of the fifth moon, Grandfather had found someone else to look after the ferry and he had taken Green Jade and the yellow dog to the city to see the race. The banks were crowded with people, and four long red boats were slipping easily through the water. The river was in flood, deep green, and the sky was bright, and the drums were beating merrily. Green Jade was silent, her lips closed tight, her heart filled with unspeakable joy. The banks were crowded, everyone was gazing at the river with wide-open eyes, and soon she found that her Grandfather had disappeared, though the yellow dog remained at her side.

Green Jade could not take her eyes away from the boats, but all the while she was thinking: "Grandfather will return soon," and as it was now a long while since he had disappeared, she began to be troubled. On the previous day Grandfather had asked her whether she would be afraid of seeing the race alone, for there were so many people on the banks. And she had answered: "I'm not afraid of the people at all, but it's not so amusing to go alone". Grandfather pondered this remark for a long while, and at last he remembered an acquaintance who lived in the city. That night he hurried to the city and begged the old fellow to take his place for a day at the ferry, while he himself went to the city with Green Jade. Moreover, since the old man was even lonelier than Grandfather, and possessed neither dog nor child, Grandfather invited him to come over early and take lunch with them and drink orpiment wine. So the old man came, and after lunch Grandfather and Green Jade disappeared in the direction of the city. All the time Grandfather seemed to be preoccupied with thoughts that lay heavy on his mind, and at last he said:

"Green Jade, Green Jade, there are so many people there—it's so crowded! I suppose you wouldn't care to see the race alone?"

"Why not?" Green Jade answered. "But you know—it's not so amusing when you are alone."

But when they reached the river, the red boats took up all her attention, and Grandfather was not so necessary to her enjoyment. The old man said to himself: "It's still very early—there are at least six hours in front of us, and really the old fellow will be lonely. I ought to go back and tell him to come out and enjoy the race."

He said to Green Jade: "It's terribly crowded. Stay here and don't run away. I've got to go and see someone, but I'll come back and take you home."

Green Jade was so immersed in the spectacle of the race that she hardly knew what he was saying. And knowing that the yellow dog offered a better protection that anything he could offer, he went home to watch over his ferry.

When he reached the creek, he found his old friend standing in the shadow of the white pagoda and listening to the distant drumbeats.

Grandfather waved to him to bring the boat over, and soon they were both standing beneath the white pagoda. The old fellow asked Grandfather why he had come back so early, and Grandfather answered that he wanted to take his place so that he could see the race. And he went on: "There's no need for you to come back here, unless you want to. If you see Green Jade, just tell her to come back by herself. And perhaps you might go a little way with her if she is afraid of the dark?" But the old man had no desire to see the race, and preferred drinking with the old ferryman on the rock beside the river. This pleased the old ferryman so much that he immediately brought out his wine-gourd and offered it to his friend. Soon they were drinking and discussing dragon-boat festivals of the past, and it was not long before the old fellow got drunk and lay on the stone and fell asleep.

But Grandfather was also drunk, he could not leave the ferry and therefore it was impossible for him to return to the city. So Green Jade was left to herself, becoming increasingly perturbed as time passed and there was still no sign of her Grandfather.

When the last race was run and the garrison officers had let loose swarms of green-headed drakes on the river, even then Grandfather had not returned. Green Jade thought he might be waiting for her somewhere else, and taking the dog with her, she began to push her way through the crowd in search of him. The sky was darkening, and the soldiers who had come out of the city with benches on their shoulders were now returning, and only a few drakes remained in the pool, and the drake-chasers too were drifting away. The sun was setting in the direction of her home, and dusk was already covering the waters with a veil of fog. And suddenly, watching the changing lights over the water, a terrifying thought occurred to her: "What if Grandfather is dead!"

Then she remembered that Grandfather had told her to stay where she was, and she began to derive assurance from the thought that perhaps he had gone into the city and met an old friend of his, and they had been drinking together, and so he had been unable to return as soon as he had wished. And since this was perfectly possible, and there was no need as yet to run home with the dog, for there was still some light in the sky, she decided to wait patiently on the dock.

Soon the two long boats belonging to the people on the other bank were moored in a small bay and disappeared from sight. Most of the onlookers too had disappeared. In the houses where the prostitutes lived, lamps were being lit, and the girls were beating their small drums and strumming their moon-shaped fiddles. From the other houses came the sounds of talking, of the "finger-game" and all the laughter which arises from a feast. And in the junks moored beneath these houses, tables were being set for dinner and you heard all the sounds of cooking, and the simmering of cabbages and turnips as they were poured into boiling oil. The river was darker now. In all the river there was only a single drake and a solitary swimmer in pursuit of it.

The wind coming down the river was cooler now, and still Green Jade was waiting on the bank. And still she thought that her Grandfather would come for her.

In the houses of the prostitutes the music was growing louder. She heard people talking in the boats below.

"Ching-ting, listen to that girl of yours drinking and singing for the Szechuan merchants. I'll bet you my little finger that it's her voice."

Another sailor answered: "Yes, she is drinking and singing with them all right, but she is still keeping me in her heart. She knows I'm on the junk."

"She gives her body to another and keeps you in her heart, eh? Can you prove it?"

The sailor thought for a moment. "Sure!" he said at last, and he began to whistle a peculiar lilting whistle, and immediately the woman's singing ceased and the two sailors laughed aloud. Then they began to discuss the woman, employing the most vulgar terms. Green Jade was not accustomed to hearing words like these, but she could not move away. One of the sailors went on to say that the father of the woman had been murdered, stabbed by a dagger in sixteen places; and then once more the strange idea that Grandfather might be dead returned to her mind.

The sailors were still talking when the white drake began to approach the shore where Green Jade was standing, and she thought: "I'll catch you if you come nearer." But when the drake was still some distance away from the shore, she heard a man's voice laughing and calling out to one of the sailors in the boat. She was still waiting for the drake to come nearer, but suddenly she noticed that there was a man in the water and he was carrying it; he was treading water and coming slowly towards her. And the sailor shouted over the intervening darkness of water:

"Second Master! Second Master! That's really good! That makes five you have caught to-day."

"He was a cunning little devil, but he's mine now," answered the man in the water.

"You're good at catching drakes, and soon you'll be good at catching the girls," the sailor rejoined.

There was no reply. He was swimming strongly to shore, using his hands and feet, and when he climbed ashore he was dripping with water. It was only when the yellow dog began to bark that he caught sight of Green Jade. Except for the girl, the dockside was deserted.

"Who are you?" he asked.

"I'm Green Jade."

"And who is Green Jade?"

"The granddaughter of the old ferryman at Blue Stream Hills."

"Well, what are you doing here?"

"Waiting for my Grandfather. I must wait for him."

"You *must* wait for him, eh? But where is he? Must have been drinking, and they carried him home."

"Not true. He said he was coming, and he will!"

"You can't wait for him here. Go up to my house. Over there where the lamps are lit. Why not wait for your Grandfather there?"

Green Jade instinctively mistrusted the man, and remembering the conversation of the two sailors, she imagined that she was being invited to accompany him to the house where the women were singing. Green Jade never used swear-words before, but she had grown impatient with long waiting and she really believed that the man was insulting her, and so she said in a low voice:

"You swine! You ought to be beheaded!"

She spoke under her breath, but the man heard her. He guessed her age from her voice, and answered laughingly:

"So you like cursing, eh? Well, if you don't want to go, you can wait here, but don't be surprised if a fish comes out of the water and bites you."

"Even if a fish does bite me, I'll never have anything to do with you!" the girl retorted.

And now the dog, as though he understood that his mistress was being insulted, began to bark. Meanwhile, the man raised the white drake above his head, brandishing it in order to scare the dog away, and then walked off down River Road. The dog began to run after him, as though to revenge itself on the insult, but Green Jade called out:

"Dog, dog! Take care what people you bite!" She meant to remind the dog that there are some people not worth barking at; but the man heard the words and mistook them for a compliment; he laughed merrily and disappeared.

Time passed. It seemed a long time later when a man came along the road, bearing a torch made of old rope from the junks and calling her name. But as he drew near, she failed to recognise him. "The old ferryman has gone home," he said. "He won't be coming back to fetch you, but he sends word by a man who crossed over on the ferry to say that you must go home at once."

Hearing that the man had been sent by her Grandfather, Green Jade had perfect faith in him and obediently followed him homeward. He held the torch and led the way, and sometimes the dog walked in front and sometimes behind, as they followed the city wall towards the ferry. While they walked, Green Jade asked him who told him she was standing beside the river; he answered that it was his young master, and he himself was a labourer belonging to the young master's house and he would have to return to River Road as soon as he had seen her safely home.

"But how did he know I was standing here?" Green Jade asked, puzzled.

"He was hunting the drakes in the river," the man laughed, "and saw you standing there. Out of the kindness of his heart he invited you to take shelter in his house, but you only swore at him."

"But who is he?" she asked, more puzzled than ever now.

"You don't know him?" the man asked in a surprised tone. "He is Nu-sung, the Second Master. They call him Yao Yun sometimes. He has asked me to take you home to your cottage."

Nu-sung, of course, was known everywhere in Ch'a-t'ung, and Green Jade was shocked at the thought that she had spoken to him without civility; and therefore she was ashamed and silent, following the man without a word.

When they had climbed over the hill and looked down at the lamps burning in the cottage, the old ferryman saw the torch which the labouring man was holding, and soon he was pulling the ferryboat across the stream to meet them, and all the while he was calling in his husky voice: "Green Jade, is it you? Is it really you?"

Green Jade said nothing, whispering softly to herself: "No, Grandfather, it is not Green Jade. Green Jade has been gobbled up by one of the fish in the river!"

She sank down in the boat, and the labouring man returned to the city with his torch. And still Grandfather kept asking her:

"Green Jade, why don't you answer me? Are you angry with me?"

Green Jade said nothing, but by the time they were safely across the stream, her anger had evaporated. When she reached the house, she saw another old man lying dead drunk on the floor. But something else, which had nothing at all to do with Grandfather, kept her silent all night.

V

The two years had passed by.

It so happened that during these two years there was never a full moon during the Mid-Autumn festival. Usually during these festivals the young people had spent their time singing under the moon, but since there was no moon the festivals themselves left only a faint impression on Green Jade's mind. However, the New Year's festivals were observed; the soldiers and peasants carried paper lanterns shaped like lions and dragons, and in this way they would welcome the spring on the parade ground, to the sound of tumultuous gongs and drums. Stripped to the waist, weaving their dragon lanterns above their heads, they marched about, while crackers and fireworks exploded all round them. The soldiers, the revenue officers, the workers in the shops along River Road—they had all contributed to the occasion, hollowing out palm roots, filling them with nitre and sulphur and fine-grained sand, and then hammering all these things into the consistency of rock with innumerable hammer-blows. It was an extraordinarily beautiful sight—the half-naked soldiers marching in the lantern-light to the sound of drum-beats, while fire-crackers rained down on their backs and shoulders from long poles; and while the tempo of the drum-beats increased, the excitement of the people knew no bounds. When the fire-crackers were finished, an enormous cylinder of fireworks was roped to a bench in a corner of one of the large courtyards, the fuse was lit and slowly a ray of white light poured from the cylinder, but a moment later it would begin to explode with a terrifying sound of thundering tigers, shooting upwards three or four hundred feet into the sky, melting in a rain of flowers and fountains. Meanwhile, the boys bearing the lanterns would dance in circles under the rain of fire-petals, impervious to their heat. Green Jade and her Grandfather always enjoyed these processions, but for some mysterious reason they were never quite so enjoyable, or so memorable, as the processions of boats in the Dragon-boat festivals.

Green Jade had not forgotten the last occasion when she saw the dragon-boats. It had been a perfect day, but suddenly the rain began to fall and soon they were all soaked to the skin. To escape the rain, Grandfather, Green Jade and the yellow dog sought shelter under the eaves of Shun-shun's house. The place was crowded, and they were standing miserably enough in a corner when Green Jade noticed a labourer carrying a chair on his shoulders. It was the same man who had brought her home by torchlight; so she told Grandfather: "That's the man who brought me home. When he was carrying the torch, he looked exactly like a bandit."

Grandfather said nothing, but when the man passed again, he caught hold of his sleeve and said, smiling:

"Hey, you! You wouldn't come to have a drink in my house, you remember? You were afraid I might poison the wine, eh? And you're such an important old fellow—a future Emperor, most likely?"

At once the man recognised the old ferryman, and at the same moment he recognised Green Jade. So he laughed, and said:

"Green Jade is growing up all right! Second Master said the big fish would eat you up if you stayed by the river, but now you are getting too big for the fishes in our river!"

Green Jade said nothing, but smiled with her lips pursed together.

Though she heard Second Master's name spoken by the labourer who resembled a bandit, still she had not seen Second Master. From the conversation between her Grandfather and the labourer she understood that he was spending the day at Blue Wave Rapids, six hundred *li* downstream. But though she was introduced to T'ien Pao and even to the famous Shun-shun, she missed Nu-sung, even when her Grandfather praised the fat drake which Ti'en Pao had brought and Shun-shun begged his son to present it to the girl. And because he knew that the old ferryman was poor and could not afford the sweet rice dumplings wrapped in palm leaves which are eaten at all Dragon-boat festivals throughout China, Shun-shun gave them as many as they could hold.

While the most famous man on the river was talking with her Grandfather, Green Jade pretended to be looking over the river, but she was listening to every word. He was telling Grandfather that Green Jade had never been prettier, and he asked her age, and whether she had been betrothed. Grandfather praised Green Jade to the skies, but when it came to discussing her marriage, he became perfectly silent.

On the way home Grandfather carried the white drake and all the other things in his arms, while Green Jade led the way with the torch. They walked beside the city walls, the water on one side of them and the walls rising sheer on the other.

"Shun-shun could not be kinder, and T'ien Pao is also kind," Grandfather said. "They are all very good."

"Yes, yes, they are all very good!" Green Jade repeated. "But do you know them all, Grandfather?"

Grandfather did not understand what she was saying, and so he answered smiling:

"Green Jade, if T'ien Pao should want you to be his wife, if he sent a matchmaker, would you agree?"

"You're stupid, Grandfather. I do think you are stupid! I'll be as angry as anything if you ever say another word!"

The old ferryman kept silent, but it was clear that these ridiculous ideas still occupied his mind. Green Jade had never been so angry. She kept waving her torch from side to side, and walked on hurriedly, overwhelmed with anger.

"Green Jade, don't be silly. If I fall into the water, all the drakes will escape!"

"Who cares for the drakes?"

Grandfather thought he knew what made her so unhappy, so he began to sing the song of the rowers as they shoot the rapids. His voice was quavering and hoarse, but the words came clearly. Green Jade suddenly stopped.

"Grandfather, is it your boat which is shooting the rapids?"

Grandfather said nothing, but went on singing. It occurred to both of them that Nu-sung's boat was spending the festival at Blue Wave Rapids, but neither of them guessed what was in the other's mind. So they walked on silently. When they reached the ferry they found the man who had taken charge of the boat waiting for them on the bank; they all crossed the creek, went into the cottage and unwrapped the dumplings. When at last it was time for their old friend to return to the city, Green Jade promptly lit a torch for him so that he would not have to make his way home in the dark. And when he had crossed the stream and was making his way up the hill, Green Jade exclaimed:

"Look, there's an old bandit climbing our hill!"

Languidly Grandfather pulled at the boat, gazing at the thin mist which had descended over the stream, and as though he had caught sight of something extraordinary, he sighed gently. When they reached the bank, he told Green Jade to hurry home, for there were sure to be passengers returning from the festival; and he wanted to stay there alone to wait for them.

VI

That morning the old ferryman quarrelled with a paper merchant. He refused to take the money the merchant wanted to give him. It was as though the old man was hurt by the air of superiority which the merchant assumed, and therefore he forced it back into the merchant's hands, pretending the most scrupulous anger. But when the ferryboat came close to the shore, the merchant leaped on the bank, throwing the coins into the boat and smiling with triumph as he walked quickly away. Meanwhile the ferryman could not leave the boat, for he had to help the passengers to disembark. So he cried to his grand-daughter, who was standing on the top of the hill:

"Green Jade, don't let that paper-selling fellow go!"

Green Jade had no idea what had happened, but she barred the man's path with the aid of her dog.

"What's the matter? Why won't you let me pass?" the man laughed.

At that moment another merchant arrived and explained the situation. As soon as she understood, she took hold of the merchant's gown and kept saying: "You must stay here, you really mustn't go!" Meanwhile the yellow dog, in order to show his sympathy with his mistress, began to bark vociferously. All the other merchants crowded round, laughing. Then Grandfather ran up the hill, gasping for breath, thrusting the money into the man's hand and slipping some leaves of tobacco into his bundle. He kept on rubbing his hands as he said at last:

"Well, you can go now, we won't detain you any longer."
Then all the merchants went laughing on their way.

"Grandfather," Green Jade objected. "I thought he had stolen something from you; I even thought he had been fighting you——"

"Well, he gave me a lot of money. Who wants it? I told him I didn't want it, but he insisted on giving it to me—unreasonable!"

"Did you give it all back?"

Grandfather shook his head and once more his lips were pursed together in a grim smile, and at last he took a copper coin from his waistcoat and murmured:

"With the tobacco leaves I gave him he will have something to occupy his thoughts until he reaches Chen-kan!"

And then suddenly they heard the distant beating of the drums; the yellow dog listened with his ears pricked up. Greed Jade asked her Grandfather whether he could hear anything, and after a while Grandfather said he recognised the sound.

"I suppose that means there is another Dragon-boat festival soon," he murmured. "Do you remember T'ien Pao, who gave us that fat drake last year? He enquired about you when he crossed over the ferry this morning—he is going to East Szechuan. You haven't forgotten—it was the day when the rain came down in torrents. If we go there again, we'll come back by torchlight. Do you remember how we used a torch on our way home?"

Green Jade was musing over the two recent Dragon-boat festivals, but when the old man began questioning her she assumed the air of someone who is slightly offended, and she answered:

"No, I don't remember anything at all!" she said, shaking her head, but what she really meant to say was: "How could I possibly forget?"

Grandfather understood perfectly, and continued:

"Really it was more interesting the year before. There

you were, waiting all alone, and I thought you had been gobbled up by a big fish."

Green Jade made a little sound through her teeth as she burst out laughing:

"Grandfather, do you really mean that? You know, it was somebody else who said it, and then I told you about it. All you were thinking about was whether that friend of yours from the city would drink up the wine-gourd along with the wine. What a memory you have!"

"Yes, I am getting old and I can't remember things as well as I used to do. Now that you are growing up, I suppose you can go to the city alone and never fear the fishes in the river."

"I'm grown up now, and I can watch over the boat."

"No, that's a job for the old."

"I think the old ought to rest a litle bit."

"Good heavens, I'm still strong enough to hunt tigers. I'm not old in the least!" Saying this, he flexed his muscles, trying to make them appear as strong and supple as when he was a youth. "And if you won't believe me, try to bite it!"

Green Jade gazed tenderly at her Grandfather, whose shoulders were already stooping, but she said nothing. She could hear the sound of pipes coming from a long way away. She knew exactly what it meant, and in what direction the sounds were coming, so she made her Grandfather follow her into the boat and cross to the other side. She was so impatient to see the bridal chair that she climbed up until she stood beneath the shadow of the white pagoda behind her cottage. Soon a procession drew near: two flute-players, four strong peasant boys carrying the empty chair, a youth in a new suit of clothes who looked like the son of a captain, two sheep and a boy leading them, a jar of wine, a tray of cakes and someone to carry them. As soon as they got into the boat, Green Jade and Grandfather followed them. Grandfather pulled the boat across, while Green Jade settled up close to the bridal chair, gazing intently at the chair and the embroidered decorations. When they reached the bank, the young man who resembled the son of a captain took from his embroidered girdle a package of red paper and gave it to the old ferryman. This was the local custom, and Grandfather could hardly refuse it since wedding processions since time immemorial had paid toll at bridges and ferries. Taking the money in his hands he began to ask the youth where the bride came from, and what her name was, and how old she was. He had found out everything about the bride by the time when they reached the other side; and now the flutes were beginning to play again and the small procession was mounting the crest of the hill. Grandfather and Green Jade remained in the boat, but their thoughts followed the sounds of the flutes and did not return until they heard the flutes no longer.

Grandfather weighed the red paper package in his hand and said:

"The new bride at Sung is only fifteen years' old."

Green Jade knew exactly what he meant, but once again she remained silent. As she quietly pulled the boat along, she murmured to herself: "Well, what if she is fifteen!"

As soon as she reached the bank she ran home and found her own flute made of two small bamboo tubes, and begged Grandfather to play the tune "A Mother is Marrying her Daughter Away." While he played she lay down with the dog on the shadowy rock beside the house and gazed up at the clouds. Silently the day wore on. Grandfather dozed off, and soon they were all three sleeping in the sun.

VII

The Dragon-boat festival came round once again. Three days previously Grandfather had arranged with Green Jade that he would look after the boat while she went with the dog to Shun-shun's house overlooking the river. At first Green Jade refused; but later she decided to go, and then again the next day she refused for the second time, saying that either they ought to stay together or else they ought to see the festival together. Grandfather at once noticed what had happened: she was torn between her affection for him and her desire to see the boats. She was joined to her Grandfather by invisible bonds, and she could not unloosen them.

"Green Jade, what is the meaning of all this?" Grandfather smiled. "Everything was agreed, and you suddenly changed your mind. You know, that's not like the Ch'a-t'ung way of doing things. You ought to keep your words and not have 'three hearts and two minds.' My memory is not as bad as all that—I don't forget promises as soon as I have made them."

Though he spoke in this way, it was quite certain that he would agree to anything she proposed. He noticed that she was already too clever for him. He grew silent, and suddenly Green Jade asked:

"Who will keep you company if I go?"

"Well, there's always the boat——"

Green Jade knitted her brows and smiled ruefully.

"Huy! The boat keeping you company—that's a joke!"

Grandfather reflected in his heart: "Soon there will come a time when you will leave me," but he did not dare to say this aloud. Since there was nothing further to say, he went to the little garden behind the cottage to look at the spring leeks. Green Jade followed him.

"Grandfather . . ."

"Yes."

"I have decided not to go. We'll let the boat go, but I'll stay behind and keep you company."

"Then if you won't go, I'll go. Yes, and I'll put a red flower in my hair and disguise myself as an old grandmother."

They both burst out laughing.

Some time passed. Grandfather carefully examined the spring leeks. Green Jade plucked one of the stems and blew on it as though it was a flute. People were hailing them from the other bank. Green Jade refused to let Grandfather ferry the boat over, and instead she raced down to the creek, jumped into the boat and pulled the rope with all her strength. And all the while she shouted at Grandfather: "Sing, Grandfather, please sing——"

But Grandfather was silent. He stood on the cliff, gazing at Green Jade, waving his hands and saying nothing at all.

Something was weighing deep on his mind. Green Jade was growing up. Nowadays, when you mentioned certain things, she blushed crimson. Time was filling her out, urging her towards things of which she had cared little in the past. She liked to gaze at the brides whose faces were heavily powdered; she liked to hear stories about them; she liked to put wildflowers in her hair and listen to people singing. She began to appreciate the tenderness in the songs sung by the city people; and there were times when she felt lonely and liked only to gaze at a cloud or a star in the sky. If Grandfather said: "Well, Green Jade, what are you thinking about now—a penny for your thoughts?" she would answer in a low voice filled with unaccountable shame:

"Green Jade is not thinking about anything!"

But all the while, deep in her heart, she was asking herself: "What are you thinking about? I suppose I am thinking of many things, and they are all far away. I don't know what they are!"

She had no idea what she was thinking about. Her body had filled out, and the strangeness of some of the things that happened to her now that she was an adolescent filled her with unreasoning fears.

Grandfather understood perfectly what had happened; and his own feelings for her had undergone a change. For seventy years he had lived close to nature, but nature herself was now surprising him with all its curious complexities of change. And he began to remember, out of the stored wisdom of his age, incidents which happened in the long-dead past.

There had been a time when Green Jade's mother behaved exactly like this. Her long eyebrows, large wide-open eyes, rosy skin, he remembered all these as he remembered her pathetically artful and lovable ways, for she could make everyone happy. She, too, had seemed incapable of leaving her family. But tragedy came to her; she fell in love with a soldier. The old ferryman blamed no one: it was the dispensation of Heaven alone. And though he refused to speak out against Heaven, he knew it was wrong; and though he often declared he had put it out of his mind, it was still there, lurking continually in the background, and he knew he would carry the burden of the mystery to the end.

And then there was Green Jade. What would happen if she should behave as her mother had done, and once again he would be left with a baby to bring up alone. Even if he was willing to do this, Heaven would forbid it. He was too old. It was time for a long rest. He had suffered all the misfortunes and hardships which are the common lot of honest countrymen. And surely, if there was a God in the sky, with two powerful hands which managed the affairs of the world, yes, surely God would take him first, leaving the young life to grow up in its own splendour . . .

And yet Grandfather did not altogether agree with his own ideas. Now and then he would lie at full length on the rock beside the cottage, meditating under the stars. That Death would soon come to him he knew, if only because Green Jade was growing so tall. She had been given to him by her mother, and now she must settle down, following the course of her own life as it was decided by the stars. But first he must bequeath her to the care of some man, and thereby complete the cycle. But who should he give her to? And how could he be sure that she was not wronged?

A few days ago, while T'ien Pao was crossing the ferry, he had talked to the old man. His forthright words were all about Green Jade.

"Old uncle, you know—Green Jade is very attractive. As

soon as I am free to look after my own affairs at Ch'a-t'ung, instead of running about like a crow, be sure that I shall come to the stream every night and sing for her."

Grandfather encouraged him with a smile, fixing his small eyes on the boy as he pulled the boat along.

T'ien Pao continued: "Green Jade is so gentle. I am afraid she is better suited to serenades than to bother her head about household affairs. I wanted a girl who will listen to my songs, but I also need a wife to look after my house. 'I don't want my horse to eat grass, but she must run faster than anyone else.' It seems to me that these old proverbs were invented entirely for me."

The old man lazily let the boat drift round so that its stern touched the bank, and said: "Well, young man, all things are possible. Just wait and see!"

When the boy had disappeared, Grandfather mused over the truth of his words, and was alternately gladdened and made melancholy; for he wondered whether he was the best man for her, and whether Green Jade would accept him.

VIII

On the fifth day of the fifth moon, when the Dragon-boat festival is held, the rain poured down and the river was in flood, and had turned dark green. Grandfather decided to go to the city to do some marketing for the festival; he wore a hood of palm leaves, carried a basket and a gourd full of wine, and slung over his shoulders a black cloth bag in which he had put sixteen hundred copper coins, and proceeded on his way. It was a festival day; all the people from the surrounding hamlets, and even from the houses of the great lords, were congregating in the city, bringing money or merchandise to the fair; and they had all risen early. As soon as Grandfather had gone, Green Jade went down to the stream to look after the boat, accompanied by the yellow dog. She, too, wore a new palm-leaf hood. When the boat came near to the shore, the yellow dog would leap to the bank, holding the rope in its teeth, and always attracting the attention of the passengers. Sometimes people came to the ferry bringing dogs of their own; and according to the old proverb that dogs should be kept at home, otherwise it betrays an invincible weakness, so now whenever the yellow dog espied another, he would walk up, tail wagging, to sniff at the newcomer, and always with a glance at Green Jade to show that he understood her; and seeming to understand her perfectly, he never behaved in anything except the most proper manner. But once ashore, letting go the rope from between his teeth, he would bark at the strange dog disappearing slowly along the crest of the hill, or perhaps he would bark at the dog's master and run after him, until Green Jade called out angrily:

"Dog, dog, have you gone mad? There's so much work for you to do, and all you can think about is running away!"

Then the yellow dog would hurry back and begin to sniff all over the boat.

"What's all this nonsense?" Green Jade would exclaim. "Who taught you to behave like this? Lie down there, and behave yourself!"

And as though he really understood her, he would lie down quietly in his proper place, but sometimes the memory of a past event would fill his mind, and you would hear a few inexplicable, short barks.

The rain continued, and soon there was a great cloud of smoky rain lying over the river. Because there was nothing to do on the boat, Green Jade began to think of her Grandfather's journey to the city. She knew exactly where he would go, who he would meet and what they would talk about. As though she was actually seeing it with her eyes, she imagined the appearance of the great gateway and of River Road. She knew all her Grandfather's characteristic ways. She could conjure up out of her imagination the way in which Grandfather greeted his friends in the army, whether they were stable-boys or cooks. It was something like this:

"Greetings, old fellow, may you eat and drink your fill throughout the festival!"

"Hey you old ferryman, the same to yourself!" the stable-boy would reply, or else perhaps he would say: "It's a poor time we are having now, old ferryman. How can I fill my belly with four ounces of pork and two bowls of wine!" And then Grandfather in all sincerity would invite the man to have as much wine as he could drink at the Blue Stream Valley. Perhaps, too, Grandfather's friend might like to take a swig at the gourd hanging from his belt: in that case Grandfather was only too pleased to assist him, and while the army man drank the wine and licked his lips with a lolling tongue and even went so far as to praise the wine, Grandfather would be delighted beyond words and invite him to take another swig. So the wine disappeared, and Grandfather would find himself going to the wine-seller to have the gourd refilled. After that—and Green Jade summoned all these pictures into her imagination—after that Grandfather would wander along the dockside, talking to the sailors whose junks had only just arrived, asking about prices down-river, and sometimes he clambered into the holds redolent of seaweed, oil, vinegar, squid and innumerable other smells. The sailor would claw up a handful of red dates from a small jar and give them to him; and if it should happen that Green Jade should complain when he reached the cottage, the plump red dates offered a means of making peace with her. When he reached River Road—Green Jade was still following him in her mind's eye—the shopkeepers strove to press all kinds of presents on him in order to show their respect for an old man who so faithfully accomplished his duty, and Grandfather would cry out in a loud voice:

"So many things—they will only break my poor old back!"

But he would have to accept them, if only to acknowledge their great kindness. He would go along to the pork-shop and try to buy some meat, but they always refused to accept his money, and he would go off in search of the one particular meat-shop where he thought they might accept his copper coins, but he was always thwarted.

"What's the matter with the old 'un?" they would say. "He's becoming real rude nowadays. Does he think he is a ploughshare ploughing the fields?"

Very well! They refused to take payment, did they! He would count out the money beforehand, throw it into the bamboo cash-box, on which someone had inscribed the inscription: "Yellow Gold and a Myriad Cash," and having done this, he would snatch the pork and hurry on his way. Some of the butchers recognised this habit of his, and so they prepared the most tender portions of the meat and reserved it for him, and always weighing out much more than he demanded. And then, if he noticed them, he exclaimed:

"Hey, you old butcher! I'm not begging for any favours! Tenderloin is only for the city people who like cooking them with squids and little slivers of pork. I want a cut off the neck—something fat and rich. I'm just an old boat-hand, so I want to boil it with carrots and serve it with a little wine!"

At last he would take the pork and hand over the money, first counting it carefully and begging the butcher to count it again. If it so happened that the butcher accepted the money, he would simply throw it into the bamboo cash-box without ever dreaming of counting it; and then Grandfather went on his way, smiling with indescribable charm, while the butchers and all the other merchants gazed after him, laughing happily until they were sore, but only because they had seen that charming smile of his.

Green Jade saw all this, and she saw him going down to Shun-shun's house along River Road.

She recalled everything she had seen and heard during the previous two festivals, and seeing these things her heart was filled with happiness exactly as when, in the morning when her eyes were closed, she saw yellow butterflies and sunflowers, which were perfectly vivid and clear, yet no hands had ever plucked them.

"Are there really tigers at White Cock Pass?" she asked herself, but she had no idea why White Cock Pass should have suddenly entered her mind.

Then the thought occurred to her: "There are thirty-two men pulling at six oars, and there is a great white sail made of a hundred pieces of cloth rising against the wind and tide. Crossing the T'ung-ting Lake on a ship like this . . . ridiculous!" She had no idea how large the T'ung-ting Lake is, and she had never seen such large ships, and what was still more curious was that she had no idea why she was thinking of these things.

Some passengers were approaching, men carrying loads on poles stretched over their shoulders, some people who looked like errand-boys, a mother and her daughter, the mother in stiff starched blue cloth, her daughter wearing bright new clothes and with two thick circles of rouge on her cheeks which resembled two cakes. It was obvious that they were going to the city to pay visits and see the dragon-boats. All the time they were crossing the stream, Green Jade could not take her eyes away from the girl. The girl was about ten years old, and quite spoilt, so that it seemed impossible to believe that she would ever leave her mother. She wore a pair of nailed boots, newly oiled, and slightly stained with yellow mud. Her trousers were onion-green, but sometimes you could see purple lights in them. Seeing Green Jade incessantly gazing at her, she turned to Green Jade a pair of eyes as transparent and as bright as little crystal marbles. The woman who appeared to be the girl's mother began to ask Green Jade how old she was. Green Jade smiled, making no reply, and instead she asked the age of the little girl. Hearing that she was twelve, she burst out laughing for no reason at all. It was clear that the girl was the daughter of a very rich man indeed. Green Jade began to examine her closely, noticing the twisted silver bracelets which sparkled with a shimmering white light on her wrists; and she wished they were hers. When the boat reached the bank, and the people climbed ashore, the woman took a copper coin from her pocket and thrust it into Green Jade's hand, and so went on her way. This time Green Jade forgot her Grandfather's rule, and even forgot to give her thanks, but instead she gazed after the girl like someone possessed. It was only when they were already half way up the hill that she began to run after them, intent on returning the copper coin. The woman exclaimed: "How strange! I've just given it to you!" Green Jade made no reply. She shook her head dumbly and raced back towards the boat before the woman could say another word.

There were more people waiting to cross, and she hurried over the ferry. This time there were seven of them, including two small girls who had changed into new clothes for the festival. But they were not very pretty, and it was still more difficult for Green Jade to forget the first girl.

There was an extraordinary number of people crossing the ferry, and far more girls than ever before. Because she was pulling at the boat, Green Jade was able to accumulate a variety of strange impressions: the pretty girls, the queer girls, the obviously clever girls, the girls with bloodshot eyes. And when there were no passengers, and Grandfather was still in the city, she would amuse herself by passing all these girls in review. And she would sing quietly to herself:

"*There comes the Tiger from the White Cock Pass,
And he will only bite the Chieftain's daughter.
My eldest sister has a gold-pin in her hair,
My second sister has silver bracelets on her wrists,
But I, the third maiden, have nothing to wear
But a bean-sprout behind my ears all the year round . . .*"

There came a man from the city who had seen the old

ferryman in front of a wine-shop, offering his gourd to a young sailor and begging him to taste this new white wine. Green Jade asked him to tell her everything he had seen, and as he spoke of her Grandfather, always so generous, but always generous at the wrong time, she burst out laughing. When the passenger had gone, she hummed to herself the song of the witches welcoming the gods; and the low tone of her song suggested that her joy was mingled with melancholy. The song ended in this fashion:

"Joy without end and endless riches are gifts of God,
The gentle rain and the timely wind are of his favour,
Fine wine and fine rice are set before you,
The fat pork and the fat lamb are cooked on the fire . . .

Hung Hsiu Chuan, Li Hung Chang,
In your time you were heroes,
You had your own reasons for massacring and burning,
You had your own reasons for proving your loyalty to a master,
But surely there is no harm in coming to share our feast . . .

Eat slowly, drink slowly,
You can cross the rivers under a bright moon and with a fresh wind,
Holding each other's hands if you happen to be drunk,
And then I will sing another song for you . . ."

As soon as she had finished singing, Green Jade felt a sweet sadness creeping into her heart. She thought of the bonfires and bugles in the fields when people performed thanksgiving in autumn.

She heard drumbeats in the distance. She knew that the vermilion dragon-boats were now being launched, at this very moment. A fine rain was falling over the river, and thick clouds of vapour were rolling down the hills.

IX

When Grandfather came home, it was nearly time for early lunch. He hailed her from the other side of the river, his shoulders and his hands loaded with all the things he had brought back from the city. So many people had been making their way to the city that Green Jade felt nervous in the small boat, but as soon as she heard her Grandfather's voice her spirits rose, and she answered shrilly: "I'm coming, Grandfather—I'll be there in a moment!" The old ferryman laid all his things on the prow of the boat and helped to pull it across, smiling at Green Jade like a child and saying modestly and shyly: "You were worried to death, weren't you?"

Ordinarily she would have scolded him for such a remark, but now she said:

"I know exactly what you were up to. You were trying to make them drink your wine. It was so funny!"

She knew that Grandfather liked to wander down River Road, looking over the shoulders of the sailors as they played mahjong, but she said nothing about this, knowing that he would feel ashamed, and perhaps he might even explode in anger. She counted all the things he had laid in the prow of the boat, and noticing that the wine-gourd was missing, she laughed through her teeth—the little impish laugh which always amused him.

"Grandfather, you are really generous—I never thought you were so generous. You give all the soldiers and sailors your wine, and then you allow them to swallow the wine-gourd as well!"

Grandfather laughed silently.

"Do you know what happened. Old Shun-shun took my wine-gourd away, because he found me giving my wine away to the sailors in River Road. He said: 'Hey, you old ferryman, what are you up to—giving wine away like that? You don't own a wine-press, do you? You can't go on behaving like that! Put down that wine-gourd of yours, and let *me* drink it for you!' That's what he said. 'Let me drink it for you!' So I left it with him. I suppose he was only joking with me. He has got enough wine in his house! Green Jade, my dear, do you think——"

"You think he was only joking with you——he didn't really want your wine?"

"That's right."

"Don't worry, Grandfather. He wanted to keep your wine-gourd because you were giving so much away. He'll send it back to you! Now do you understand?"

"Yes, well, perhaps there's something in that! I'm getting too old now, but there's something in what you were saying."

They were still talking when they came to the bank. Green Jade wanted to take everything up to the cottage, but she was only allowed to take the fish and the sackcloth which once held the cash, though it was all spent now, and in its place there was only some white sugar and some sesame cakes.

They had just reached the cottage when someone hailed them from the bank. Grandfather warned Green Jade to keep an eye on the meat and vegetables lest some wildcat ran away with them, and then ran back to the stream. A few minutes later he returned with a strange man—a man who was carrying a wine-gourd. From a long way away she could hear Grandfather shouting at her:

"You were quite right, Green Jade—quite right! They've sent the wine-gourd back to me already!"

Green Jade scarcely had time to run to the oven when Grandfather entered the cottage, followed by a dark, broad-shouldered young man.

Grandfather kept on talking about it, and all the time Green Jade and the strange young man were laughing. The new visitor smiled at her. She seemed to understand why he was gazing at her, and suddenly she grew shy, and retired behind the oven to kindle the flames. It happened that at that moment someone else began hailing from the other bank. It was still raining, but for some reason there was a continual stream of passengers and Green Jade found herself continually going backwards and forwards between the banks, and all the while she was musing about her grandfather. Then there was the strange man who brought the wine-gourd—it occurred to her that she had seen him before, but she could not remember where. And because there were things she refused to think about, because they were too familiar and dear to her, so for the same reason it was impossible for her to discover why his image remained in her mind.

"Green Jade, come here!" Grandfather called from the rock. "Come up and rest, and keep our guest company!"

There were no passengers now, and she had been thinking of returning in order to fill the stove with firewood; but now she preferred to remain in the boat.

The strange guest was saying to Grandfather: "Tell me, don't you want to see the festival?" and Grandfather replied: "There's the boat to look after—I can't leave it." Then they went on to talk about other things until at last the guest decided to speak out what was really on his mind.

"Old Uncle, let's talk of Green Jade. She's growing up now, and she is very pretty indeed."

"Just like his brother," Grandfather thought. "Straightforward and forthright. I like that." But instead of saying this aloud, he said: "Second Master, you are the only person in the city who deserves such praises. Everyone says you are handsome. What do they call you? The Leopard of Eight-Face Mountain, eh? Or the Pheasant of Thousand-Field Stream? That's what they call you!"

"You're only joking!"

"Not at all! I've heard the sailors saying that the last time you took a junk down-river, you had an accident at

White Cock Pass, and you saved three men from drowning, and all the women came down to your camp and sang for you all night. Isn't that so?"

"No—not the women singing—only the wolves roaring. It's famous for its wolves, and they tried to eat us up."

The old man burst out laughing. "Well, that's even more wonderful! What they say is still true. The wolves only like young girls and children and handsome young men—they don't like old bones wrapped in skin!"

"Well, you've seen twenty thousand suns pass down the sky, and people say that the 'wind and water' signs are favourable here to the birth of a great man, but why is it that not a single great man has appeared?"[1]

"You think there ought to be some really great man because the 'wind and water'[1] signs are favourable, but—do you know—I don't think it does any harm if we don't have great men born in a little place like this. We have some honest, brave and long-suffering young men, isn't that enough? Men like you, your father and your brother. That's glory enough for us."

"So it is," the youth laughed, "and I agree with you, and it's true there are no really bad men here, they're all good. There can't be many men like you, though, old and as strong as an oak-tree, firm as a rock, generous——"

"Enough of that! I'm a tin can filled with old bones! I'm nothing to talk about! The sun, the rain, long journeys, heavy loads, good food, good wine, cold and hunger—I've had my fair share of them, and soon I'll be lying in the icy earth and feeding the worms. In this world everything is for the young. Work well, the sun won't wrong you as long as you don't wrong the sun!"

"Perhaps you are right. You are a remarkable old man, and you've set the pace for the young."

They talked for some time, and soon Nu-sung made

[1] Referring to geomancy.

preparations to go. The old ferryman stood at the gate calling to Green Jade to come up and boil the water for the rice, while he looked after the boat. But Green Jade refused to move from the boat; and when both Grandfather and the stranger were being pulled across by her, Grandfather said in a tone of complaint:

"Why didn't you come up when I called you? Did you want me to stay at home and look after the rice like any housewife?"

Green Jade stole a glance at the young man, noticing that he was gazing at her. She turned her face away, pursed her lips together and went on pulling at the rope in a terrible fit of self-consciousness. Slowly the boat approached the other bank. While still standing at the bows, the stranger said:

"You are coming to the boat-race with your Grandfather after lunch, aren't you, Green Jade?"

She was afraid of being rude, and though she had no desire to answer him, she said:

"Grandfather is not going, because there will be no one to look after the boat."

"And what about you?"

"I'm not going either, because Grandfather——"

"You want to take care of the boat too?"

"I want to be with Grandfather."

"Well, if I get somebody to look after the boat, will you come?"

At that moment the prow swung against the beach; they had reached the bank. Nu-sung stepped ashore.

"Thank you, Green Jade," he smiled, "I'll send a man to look after the boat as soon as I reach home. So have lunch quickly, and come along with your Grandfather to watch the race. There will be thousands of people there!"

At first, Green Jade did not understand the stranger's kindness, nor why he insisted they should come and watch the races from his house. She smiled, but still with her lips closed, and pulled the boat back to the cottage. But when she reached the house, he was still there, standing on the hill above the stream and gazing at her. She went into the cottage and while she was thrusting the damp hay into the oven, she said to Grandfather as he sipped the new wine which had been poured into the gourd.

"He said he would send a servant to look after the ferry, so that we can see the races. Are you going?"

"Do you want to go?"

"Yes, if we could both go. He is very nice. I've seen him somewhere before. Who is he?"

Grandfather mused to himself: "What could be better? They both think so much of each other." Aloud, he said: "Don't you remember the man who said the big fish in the water would come out and bite you?"

It was all perfectly clear to her now, but still she pretended that it was incomprehensible to her.

"Who is he?"

"Why, it's the Second Master—Nu-sung! Didn't you recognise him?" Saying this, he sipped a little of the wine, and as though praising the wine, or perhaps because he was praising the man, he said: "Fine! Excellent! Never seen better!"

There were some more passengers at the ferry, hailing him from below. As he hurried down to the boat, he kept on murmuring, "Fine! Excellent! Never seen better in my life!"

X

While they were still eating, someone called to them from the other side of the stream. Green Jade scampered down the bank, and found that the man had been sent from Shun-shun's house to look after the ferry. As soon as he saw Green Jade, he exclaimed:

"Hurry up! Second Master wants you to go to the house as soon as possible."

When he saw the old ferryman, he repeated what he had said to Green Jade.

If you listened with your ears wide open, you heard the drumbeats coming faster and faster, and hearing these tenuous quick notes, it was not difficult to imagine the slender lines of the dragon-boats in the pool.

The newcomer refused the tea that was offered him, and at once took up his station in the boat. Grandfather tried to press on him a glass of wine. Again he refused.

"I think I ought to stay behind," Grandfather said at last. "What do you say? He will be so lonely—"

"If you don't go, I won't go."

"And if I go alone?"

"I don't want to go, but if you go I'll keep you company."

Grandfather smiled.

"Then it's all settled. We both go——"

There were thousands of people milling along the banks when they reached the city. The rain was no longer falling, but the earth was still wet. The old ferryman begged Green Jade to take shelter in Shun-shun's house on River Road, but Green Jade preferred to remain on the bank. But they had hardly taken up their places along the bank when a servant came down from the house—Shun-shun had sent for them. The house was crowded. Green Jade recognised the woman with the beautiful daughter who had crossed the ferry earlier in the morning; they were standing at the window which offered the best view. As soon as she saw Green Jade, the girl shouted: "Please come here," and Green Jade shyly went along to share the view. Grandfather thereupon disappeared.

He never saw the boat-race. He met a friend of his, and together they wandered half a *li* up the river to inspect a new water-mill. He had some knowledge of mills. Hard by a mountain, at the water's edge, a thatched roof sheltered a stone cylinder which moved on a horizontal shaft and lay slantwise over a stone trough. When the sluice-gates were opened, the stream of water flew over a small wheel lying below the surface of the water, and this in turn moved the stone cylinder. The owner would pour the whole grain into the stone trough, and then remove the ground rice and sift it through a sieve, which lay in the corner; and so the chaff and the dust were sifted away. There were husks scattered all over the floor: there was dust all over the white kerchief he wound round his head, and there was dust all over his face and shoulders. When the weather was fine, he would plant turnips and cabbages, garlic and onions in the little patches of land round his cottage. When anything happened to the dam, he would take off his trousers and wade out into the stream, to fill up the wall with stones or repair the channels. It was quite obvious that managing a mill was more interesting than managing a ferry. But no ferryman could ever afford to own a mill: mills belonged only to the rich. The old ferryman discovered the name of the mill-owner as they walked along on their tour of inspection.

Kicking the new mill-stone, the man said: "The man who owns the mill lives up in the mountains. That's why he wants to have the mill near the stream. Old Captain Wang—that's who it belongs to, and it cost him a pretty sum of seven hundred thousand large cash, I can tell you!"

The old ferryman rolled his little eyes, and gazed jealously and earnestly at everything he saw, continually nodding his head and making the appropriate gestures. A little while later they sat down on a white unpainted bench which was not yet completed. They began to talk about the future of the mill, and the man said it was going to be the old captain's dowry for his daughter. And then he went on to question Grandfather about Green Jade, exactly as he had been ordered to do by T'ien Pao.

"Let's see, how old is she?"

"Fifteen now," the old ferryman answered, and at once his mind began to travel back in the dim past.

"She's a bright girl for fifteen! He will be a lucky man who gets her!"

"Why happy? She won't be getting a mill for a dowry—just her bare hands!"

"Now don't say that, old fellow. Her two hands may be worth five mills. Remember that the bridge at Loyang was built by Lu Pan with his bare hands."

The man laughed as he said this, and the old ferryman joined in the laughter, saying: "I can't see Green Jade building a bridge with her bare hands, can you?"

There was a short pause.

"Have you noticed what sharp eyes the youngsters have nowadays," the man continued. "They're very expert at choosing their wives. I'll tell you a story if you have got time."

"Go on."

"Don't take it too seriously—just a midsummer night's dream," the man said, and he went on to tell the story of how T'ien Pao was continually praising Green Jade's beauty, and how he had asked him to find out what the old ferryman's views were in the matter, and he went on to describe a conversation he had had with the First Master:

"'First master,' I said, 'what's the game—is it serious or are you only joking?' and then he said: 'I want you to find out what the old fellow thinks of me. I'm in love with Green Jade, I want her to be my wife and I'm desperately serious.' That's what he said. Then said I: 'I'm no good at this kind of thing. The old man will just slap my face if I am not careful.' And then said he: 'If it's like that, just pretend you're telling him a tale—a midsummer night's dream—and then perhaps he won't slap that fat face of yours.' That's how it is, old fellow—just an idle tale, or something serious, take it how you will ... And now what shall I tell him when he comes back from East Szechuan on the ninth?"

The old ferryman recalled what T'ien Pao had told him,

and he knew T'ien Pao was serious. He knew, too, that Shun-shun possessed a deep affection for the girl, and so he was glad at heart. But according to the traditional custom, the man himself ought to come with a gift of cakes to the cottage, and so he said:

"When you see him, I want you to tell him something. I've heard your midsummer night's dream, and here's another one for you. It's like this—you know the old proverb: "There's a road for carriages and a road for horses." If T'ien Pao prefers the carriage road, he must first ask permission, and send a go-between to come and talk with me in the proper manner, but if he prefers the road for horses, then that's clear too—all he has to do is to stand on the cliff over the stream and sing to Green Jade for three years and six months."

"Well, yes. But if it comes to singing for her for three years and six months, I would gladly do it myself."

"Surely you don't think I would refuse to let her go—it's her own affair."

"People say that if you gave a promise, she would follow whatever you said."

"No, no, it's her own affair."

"That may be, but people do say that a word from you is worth more than three years and six months' singing, in sunshine or moonlight. That's what they say!"

"Well, this is what I say to you. Wait till he gets back from East Szechuan, and then let him talk it over with his father. And I'll go and ask Green Jade what she thinks about it. If she prefers to listen to him singing for three years and six months, I'll ask you to advise him to take that road."

"That's excellent. When I see him, I'll say: 'I've told him your midsummer night's dream. The rest depends on your destiny—nothing else. But I still think his destiny lies in your hands, old man."

"No, you can't say that. It's not my affair, it's hers. If

I was the only person concerned, I would decide right away."

Soon afterwards they went to look over the three-cabined junks which Shun-shun had recently purchased. Meanwhile all kinds of strange things were happening in the house overlooking the river.

Green Jade was sitting beside the girl near the window, enjoying a splendid view of the river, but she was continually restless. It seemed to her that people at the other windows were rolling their eyes in her direction, and sometimes they would pretend to have some important mission and deliberately cross the room in order to be near the girls who were sitting at the best window. She had no idea what to do. She wanted to run away. Soon there was the sound of a gunshot from somewhere on the river, and immediately afterwards the boats which had been lined up in the distance came swiftly towards her. There were four boats very close to one another, and they shot like arrows over the river. Two boats took the lead in the middle of the course, and soon one of them began to forge ahead to arrive in front of the Revenue Office at the exact moment when another gunshot sounded. Victory had gone to the boat belonging to people living in River Road. Fire-crackers began to explode everywhere. The boat began to glide close to the houses which overhung the water, drums playing, while yells of joy and congratulations resounded from the banks and from all the houses. There was a young man standing in the prow of the boat with a red cloth wrapped round his head, and he was controlling the boat by means of little flags which he carried in his hands; and suddenly it occurred to her that she had seen him before—he was Nu-sung, who had brought the winegourd to the cottage. And now things that happened two years ago rose up in her mind.

"Don't be surprised if a fish comes out of the water and bites you!"

"Even if a fish does bite me, I'll never have anything to do with you."

"It's all the same to me—"

"Dog, dog, take care what people you bite!"

Not till then did Green Jade discover that the yellow dog had disappeared: she left her seat and searched everywhere in the room, forgetting the man who stood on the prow of the boat. While she was still searching she overheard a woman with a large face saying:

"Who is she—the girl sitting in the best position of all near the window?"

"She is the daughter of old Captain Wang," someone else answered. Just come to stare and be stared at! She has the right to the best place in the room."

"To stare at—what on earth do you mean? Who's staring at her?"

"The Wang family is very keen on Shun-shun."

"Which is it?"

"Nu-sung, I do believe. Wait and see our handsome youth coming up to meet his future mother-in-law."

"He'll be the luckiest man in the place if he marries her," someone interrupted. "They're going to give that new mill of theirs as a dowry. Better than labourers, eh?"

"What does he say about it?"

"He said there wasn't a dog's chance. The last thing he wants is to own a mill."

"You really heard him say that?"

"I heard someone else saying it, and what's more, they say he is in love with the girl down at the ferry."

"Does he prefer the ferry to the mill?"

"Who knows? Sometimes people cook beef with garlic—it's all a matter of taste. The ferry may be just as good as the mill."

While they were talking, they were gazing down at the river, and neither turned to Green Jade, who was standing just behind them. Green Jade went away, her face burning. Two more people were discussing the forthcoming marriage, saying: "Everything is arranged, they're only waiting for

Nu-sung's word now," and then she heard the other speaking in excited tones: "It is quite certain he is in love. There must be a yellow-flower maiden on shore who has given him all that courage."

Green Jade was too small to see what was going on in the river. She heard the drumbeats drawing nearer and louder, while the shouts from the shore became more vociferous. And she knew Nu-sung's boat was passing beneath the house, for she heard his name shouted by the people in the house. Fire-crackers were being set off near the captain's wife. Suddenly there came to her ears other sounds, of terror and suspense, and people were running down towards the river, struggling past the little gate which led to the river. Green Jade had no idea what was happening. She wondered whether she ought to go back to her seat, or whether she should continue to stand behind the other people; and at that moment she noticed a servant bearing a tray containing sweet cakes and dumplings specially prepared for the festival, and handing it to the people sitting near the great window. This decided her. She no longer had the courage to go over to the window, and decided to go downstairs, through the crowded gate, and so out along the river. She made her way down a little lane, past a salt-shop, under the pillars supporting the house, and suddenly she noticed a crowd of people coming in the opposite direction: among them was Nu-sung, with his head still swathed in the red turban. As soon as he saw Green Jade, he exclaimed:

"I'm so glad you have come. Where is Grandfather?"

Her face was burning. She said nothing, for she was wondering where the yellow dog had got to.

"Why don't you stay up in the house? I've told them to give you the best seat."

Green Jade was thinking: "It must be wonderful to have a mill for a dowry."

He could not persuade her to return, and at last they parted. When Green Jade reached the river, she was filled with indescribable emotions. She did not know whether it was annoyance or melancholy or happiness. What was it that made her so happy? Was it anger?—yes, she was really angry, and it was this which had made her so delightfully happy. The banks were crowded with people. In the shallows beside the docks, on masts, on cabin-awnings, hanging on the columns supporting the houses—there were people everywhere. "So many people," she murmured. "What is the fun of seeing so many people?" She thought she might find her Grandfather somewhere on one of the boats, but though she searched for him for a long time she did not find him. She thrust her way through the crowd towards the water's edge, and suddenly she saw the yellow dog wagging its tail and enjoying the scene from a little boat moored some distance from the shore, and in the boat there was one of Shun-shun's servants. Green Jade cried out in a sharp voice, and the yellow dog pricked up its ears, raised its head, looked around and then, and only then, jumped into the water and swam towards her. When he reached her, he was wet all over. He began to shake off the water and run about.

"Enough of that!" Green Jade said reproachfully. "The boat didn't turn over. Who wanted you to get into the water?"

They went in search of Grandfather, finding him at last in a nearby timber-yard.

"I've just seen the most wonderful mill!" he exclaimed. "The mill-stone is new, the water-wheel is new, the thatched roof—all new! The stream is dammed up beautifully, and when the sluice-gates are opened, the water-wheel turns like a top!"

"Who's is it?" Green Jade asked affectedly.

"Who's is it? Why, it belongs to Captain Wang, who lives up in the mountains. It's going to be given as a dowry to his daughter. How rich they are! The building alone cost seven hundred thousand large cash, and that's not including the wind-mill and the furniture."

"Who is going to marry her?"

Grandfather looked at her and laughed roguishly: "The big fish will bite you, the big fish will bite—"

Green Jade already knew about the forthcoming marriage, but she pretended not to understand, and once again she asked her Grandfather: "Who is going to have the mill?"

"Well, it's Nu-sung," he answered and went on, as though talking to himself: "Some are jealous because Nu-sung is going to get the mill, and some are jealous because the mill is going to get Nu-sung."

"Are you jealous, Grandfather?"

"I? . . ." he asked, and he burst out laughing.

"You are drunk, Grandfather," Green Jade said. "Really you are drunk."

"Yes, yes, I'm drunk. He was always praising your beauty to the skies."

"You must be mad."

"No, I am not drunk and I am not mad. Come on, let's go and see them letting loose the drakes." He was about to say: "When Nu-sung gets the drakes, be sure he is going to present them to us," but Nu-sung was already standing before them, and smiling down at Green Jade.

And they went into the house.

XI

A man had come to Blue Stream Valley with presents. Shun-shun had engaged a matchmaker for his son. The old ferryman ferried the man over the stream, feeling nervous and excited, and he had led the man up to the cottage. Green Jade was shelling peas in the garden, and paid very little attention to them. But when the man began to congratulate her as he passed through the gate, she became self-conscious and dared not pass the time there any longer. Pretending to chase the chickens out of the kitchen garden, waving the bamboo flute and calling out to them in a soft voice, she ran towards the white pagoda.

They went on talking about the most irrelevant things, but at last the matchmaker returned to the original proposition. The old ferryman had no idea how to reply, but kept on rubbing his old gnarled hands together. He seemed to be saying: "That's fine, that's splendid!" but actually he never uttered a word. At last the matchmaker finished what he had to say, and turned to Grandfather for his opinion. The old ferryman nodded and said:

"So T'ien Pao wants to take the carriage road? I'm glad, but you know I must ask what Green Jade thinks about it."

Soon the matchmaker departed, and Grandfather hailed Green Jade from the boat.

Green Jade returned with the basket of peas in her hands. She was very self-conscious as she settled herself in the boat. "What is it, Grandfather?" Grandfather smiled and said nothing, but kept gazing at Green Jade for a long while; and Green Jade sat in the prow with lowered head, still shelling the peas, still listening to the golden orioles in the bamboo grove. She thought: "The days are getting longer now, and Grandfather's silences are getting longer too." Her heart was beating fast.

It was some time before Grandfather asked her whether she understood why the man had come.

"I really don't know," Green Jade answered, but her face and neck turned crimson.

As soon as he saw this, he knew what she was thinking about, and so he looked away into the far distance. In the empty mists of the past, he saw her mother as she was sixteen years ago, and his heart grew heavy, and he began to speak in a soft, slow voice: "Every junk must come to harbour, and every bird must have a nest," and saying this, he felt a sharp pain over his heart. But he forced himself to smile.

Meanwhile Green Jade's imagination was filled to overflowing with visions of singing orioles and cuckoos in the hills, and the woodcutter chopping down the bamboos, and then too she thought of the tigers who bite men, and of those four-line folk-songs which are always sung in anger, the square troughs in the paper mill and the molten iron pouring out of the furnaces—she reviewed all the things she had seen and heard, and she did this in order to forget the present. But what she was doing was quite incomprehensible to her.

"Let me tell you what happened," her Grandfather began. "Shun-shun sent a messenger—a matchmaker—wants you to be the wife of T'ien Pao—asked me whether I was willing— well, I'm old, and I won't last more than two or three years. It's nothing to do with me, but I'm quite willing, but you must think it over and decide for yourself. If you are willing, then that's very good, and if you are not willing— why, that's good too!"

Now at last it was clear. It was T'ien Pao they were trying to marry her to. She did not raise her head, because her heart was beating wildly and her face was still burning, and she was still shelling the peas and throwing the empty pods into the water, watching them as they drifted quietly away. And somehow, as she watched them, her heart felt quieter.

Because she was silent Grandfather laughed and said: "Green Jade, it doesn't matter if you want to think it over for a few days. Loyang Bridge was not built in a night— these things take days. The matchmaker told me this, and I told him that for carriages there are carriage roads, and for horses there are horse-roads. Yes, let them choose between the two ways, and if he chooses the carriage road, this is his own affair, but if he chooses the other way, let him sing for three years and six months, and do you know, I believe he will sing to you under the moon until he vomits blood and he wears out his throat under the strain!"

Green Jade remained silent. She would have liked to have wept, but she could find no reason for tears. Grandfather went on to speak of her dead mother, and suddenly fell silent. Green Jade saw that his eyes were filled with glittering tears. She was astonished and frightened, and she asked timidly: "Grandfather, is anything the matter?" Again Grandfather was silent. She saw him rubbing his eyes awkwardly with his large, hairy hands, then he laughed like a child, leapt ashore and made his way to the cottage. Green Jade thought of following him, but after a while she decided to remain in the boat.

It was fine now after the rain. The sun fell hot and strong on shoulders and backs. The reeds and the willows by the stream, and the vegetables in the garden grew powerfully with a kind of wild health. Green grasshoppers flew among the grass-blades, their tremulous wings making a sound of continual whispering, and the voices of the young cicadas in the branches grew louder, and still there came the cries of the yellow orioles, the pheasants and the cuckoos from the deep-woven bamboo groves on the hills. Green Jade saw them; she could understand them; and all the while she listened and thought: "Yes, he is nearly seventy now . . . three years and six months . . . who gave me the white drake? . . . yes, and the mill, how proud they must be! . . . or perhaps the mill is proud? . . ."

She was still meditating, but suddenly she stood up, and at that moment she let go of the basket of peas and watched them streaming into the river. As she pulled the basket out of the water, she heard someone calling across the stream.

XII

On the next day, when she was again asked the same question by her Grandfather, her heart began to beat wildly, she lowered her head and looked away from him, and all the while she was plucking the spring leeks. Grandfather laughed silently and murmured: "Better wait till some other time, or all the leeks will be plucked." But at the same time he felt something strange in the atmosphere, and in the girl's silence, and he decided to wait before pursuing the matter. And so, instead of speaking of her marriage, he told her a story.

It was nearly the sixth moon of the year, and the heat was increasing daily. The old ferryman found an old jar, dust-covered, which had been lying unused in some old corner of the house, and now he amused himself by making a round lid for it from some spare pieces of wood, and he sawed up some logs to make a stand for it; and then he cut and smoothed some bamboo in the shape of a dipper with a rattan handle, and this was to be placed beside the jar. Then the jar was taken down to the stream near the house, and every morning Green Jade boiled a cauldon of water and poured it into the jar. Sometimes tea-leaves were thrown into the fire, and sometimes scorched rice burnt in the fire would be thrown in while it was still hot. And he still prepared herbs and the bark of trees against sunstroke, stomach-ache, boils and wounds, and these were placed in some convenient spot in the house, and whenever he saw a passenger who seemed to be unwell, he would hurry to the cottage and oblige him to take the medicines, explaining how they should be used and that he had obtained them from the army surgeons and the witch-doctors in the city. All day he stood on the square-ended boat in the stream, his arms bare, his head uncovered, the short white hair glistening in the sunlight like silver. Green Jade was as happy as ever. She ran and sang about the house. When she was not moving about, she would sit in the shade of a tree out on the rocks, and amuse herself by playing on her bamboo flute. It seemed that Grandfather had entirely forgotten T'ien Pao's proposal of marriage, and Green Jade no longer thought about it.

But before long the matchmaker came again, and once again Grandfather shifted the responsibility onto Green Jade's shoulders and sent the matchmaker away. Then he talked about the matter with Green Jade, but they came to no conclusion.

The old ferryman could not understand why she delayed. At night, as he lay in bed, he would meditate, and he dimly perceived that something . . . but whenever his mind came to this point, he would smile reluctantly and as though afraid. But really he was alarmed, for it had occurred to him that she was exactly like her mother, and he wondered whether they were destined to share the same fate. As he tried to sleep, he would find that his mind was thronged with memories, and no longer able to keep silent, he fled from the house alone and made his way to the cliff overlooking the stream, and there, gazing at the stars and listening to the murmur of the grasshoppers, which was like rain, he remained for hours. It was early the next morning before he returned to bed.

Green Jade was entirely unaware of all this. All day she played and worked, conscious of some stirrings in her heart, mysterious and invincible, but at night she slept soundly and never thought of them again. But even then time was changing her; and the succession of days marching forward like an army were more powerful than the quiet and uneventful incidents of daily life.

Meanwhile, in the house overlooking the river, T'ien Pao had told Nu-sung that he was in love with Green Jade, and he was surprised to discover that his brother was also in love with the same girl. This did not altogether surprise the people of Ch'a-T'ung, for there was a well-known proverb:

> "The fire burns everywhere,
> Water flows everywhere,
> The sun and the moon shine everywhere,
> And love reaches everywhere."

It was not, therefore, unheard of that the son of a rich river-judge should fall in love with the daughter of a poor ferryman. The difficulty lay in deciding which of the brothers should have her, and according to the conventions of Ch'a-t'ung the decision could only be reached by bloodshed. And though it was inconceivable that the brothers would fight over her, it was equally inconceivable that they would "surrender the beloved" according to the traditions of the cowardly dwellers in cities, who are only too often deserving of a better fate.

One day the two brothers went to a shipbuilding yard upstream, where their new junk was berthed, and there T'ien Pao explained that he had loved the girl for two years and had decided to marry her. Nu-sung listened quietly, smiling to himself, and a little later, when they went to visit the mill, T'ien Pao resumed the conversation, saying:

"You are the lucky one, for you will have the mill, and as for me I shall have the ferry. I shall buy up the hills all around and build a stockade and cover the hills with red bamboos."

Nu-sung listened patiently, scything the grass and the small trees by the roadside with the crescent-shaped scythe he held in his hand. But when they reached the mill, he stopped scything the grass and turned to his brother:

"Perhaps she is already in love with someone else?" he said mysteriously.

"I don't believe it."

"Does it occur to you that perhaps the mill will never belong to me?"

"No."

They went into the mill.

"Perhaps there is no reason why you should believe it, but if I tell you that I, too, fell in love with her two years ago, and I have never wanted the mill, what then?"

T'ien Pao was frightened. He gazed at his brother who was sitting astride the axle of the mill-stone, and he knew that Nu-sung was not lying. He came closer to his brother, caressed his brother's shoulder and even considered pulling him down. And then it suddenly occurred to him that all his brother had said was true, and he burst out laughing.

"Yes, I believe you are telling the truth," he said.

Nu-sung gazed at his brother and said earnestly:

"Please believe me! I've thought it all out long ago, and even if our family objects, I am prepared to look after the ferryboat. Now tell me what you propose to do?"

"Father has already consented. He told Yang, the stableman, to be the matchmaker, and Yang has already seen the ferryman." And afraid that Nu-sung might be laughing at him, he added quickly: "The old ferryman said there was a road for carriages and another for horses, and I am taking the carriage-road."

"And what happened?"

"Nothing."

"What about the horse-road?"

"The horse-road? The old ferryman said that if I take the horse-road, I must sing for three years and six months beside the stream."

"Good idea!"

"Oh yes! So you think a stammerer can sing songs even when he can't talk. I'll have no say in the matter. I am not a nightingale, and I don't know how to sing. The Ghost knows what's in the old fellow's mind, whether he wants to marry his grand-daughter to a singing water-wheel, or find a real man!"

"Then what are you going to do?"

"I'm going to ask him for one word—just one word. If he refuses, I'll go downstream to Taoyuan, and if he accepts, even if I have to look after the ferryboat, I'll obey!"

"What about singing?"

"That's for you. You can go and sing like a nightingale as long as you like."

Listening to his brother speaking in this way, Nu-sung understood the sorrows of his heart as he understood the rough, straightforward simplicity which his brother shared with the people of Ch'a-t'ung, who were so generous that they would claw out their own hearts for a friend, though they would fight their own uncles to the death if they felt insulted.

T'ien Pao had imagined that it might be necessary to take the horse-road if he failed along the carriage-road, but as soon as he heard Nu-sung's confession, he knew that that way was marked out for him, and that his own hopes were already disappearing. And he found it difficult to conceal his annoyance and resentment.

Then Nu-sung suggested that they both go to Blue Stream Hills and sing on moonlight nights. They would sing in turns, revealing to no one that there were two of them, and the one who received an answer would continue to sing for her. T'ien Pao was not good at singing, and Nu-sung would therefore have to sing for him when it came to his turn. So the question would be settled by luck, and this would be perfectly fair. T'ien Pao said that it was impossible that he should sing, neither did he wish his brother to be his nightingale. But Nu-sung, invoking the poetic justice of the contest, insisted, for it seemed to him the only way in which they could reach a fair decision.

T'ien Pao thought for a while, and then laughed sadly: "Mother's, I'm not a nightingale, and why should I ask my brother to be my nightingale? Let us sing by turns, but I shall not need your help. The owl in the woods has an ugly voice, but it sings itself when it wants a wife."

So the matter was settled, and they counted the days. "To-day's the fourteenth, to-morrow's the fifteenth, the day after's the sixteenth..." On the three following nights there would be a full moon, and since it was midsummer and neither too hot nor too cold at midnight, they would wear their homespun clothes and wander along the moonlit cliffs, singing from their full hearts according to the customs of the people for the sake of the "new-born calf," the yellow flower girl. Not before the dew had fallen and their singing had grown hoarse would they return home by the light of the fading moon. Or perhaps they would stay in a mill, for the mill-workers did not stop working at night, and there they would sleep until daybreak. So everything was arranged, and neither of them knew what the outcome might be. They decided that the contest should begin that night, for they were determined not to avoid the issue.

XIII

When dusk came Green Jade was sitting beneath the white pagoda behind the house, gazing up at the transparent clouds now molten-red in the setting sun. On the fourteenth of the moon there was a fair in the hills, and many merchants left the city and climbed the mountains in search of the natives' wares. So there were more people than ever crossing the ferry, and Grandfather was kept busy all day. Night was approaching. All the birds except the cuckoo, which clamoured incessantly, had gone to their rest. The earth and the rocks, the grass and the trees had basked all day in the heavy sun, and now they gave off their thick vapours. The air was full of the smell of the soil, of the leaves and of beetles. Gazing at the molten-red clouds in the sky and listening to the confused voices of the wandering peddlars crossing the stream, Green Jade felt a silent melancholy creeping over her heart.

The twilight was as beautiful and peaceful as always; and all those who watched this evanescent tranquillity must have suffered the same sorrow in their hearts. For them there is sorrow in every day that passes. Green Jade felt that something had been lost in the world. She was helplessly watching the days pass by, and she was never able to detain them with a bright passion of excitement. It seemed to her that all life was commonplace, and there was no end to it.

"I would like to sit in a junk and float down quietly towards Taoyuan, and disappear in the direction of the T'ung-ting Lake. Grandfather will call my name, and beat gongs for me all over the city, he will send out messengers with lanterns and torches and he will never find me!"

For some reason she pretended to be passionately angry with her Grandfather, and she imagined him searching for her and never finding her, and then he would lie at full length in the boat, prostrate with grief.

"Yes, people will call out: 'Where's the ferry? I want to cross the river. Old uncle, what's the matter with you?' And then Grandfather will answer: 'What's the matter with me? Why, Green Jade has gone away! She has gone down to Taoyuan all alone!' Then the people will say: 'What are you going to do about it?' And he will answer: 'What am I going to do? I'm going to take a knife and hide it in my things and go downstream and kill her with it' . . . "

Green Jade really thought she could hear these words, and she grew frightened. She called shrilly to her Grandfather and ran swiftly down the hillside towards the ferry, and when she saw Grandfather pulling in midstream, the passengers talking quietly together, she felt as though her heart would burst.

"Grandfather, Grandfather, bring the boat back at once! You must——"

He did not understand her, and thinking that she wanted to take his place, he called out:

"Wait a moment! I'll soon be coming back——"

"Are you sure?"

"Yes, yes! I'll soon be coming back——"

She sat near the stream, gazing at the people in the boat bathed in the falling twilight. Someone was striking a flint to light his long pipe, and then he tapped the pipe against the rail to empty the ashes. Suddenly she burst into tears.

When Grandfather pulled the boat to the other side he found Green Jade sitting on the bank and gazing in front of her with glazed eyes. She made no reply to his questions. He wanted her to build a fire and cook the rice. She thought meditatively for a while, and then deciding that it was ridiculous to fall into tears, she went back to the cottage alone. She made the fire and then hid in the dark corner of the kitchen behind the oven. A little while later she went out on the cliffs and once again she called to her grandfather to come home. The old ferryman took his duties seriously, and knowing that the passengers were hurrying home to dinner, he worked on the ferry even if there was only one man to be taken across, for he detested to see people waiting there helplessly. It was impossible for him to come ashore; and when she called, he only stood up in the prow and begged her to wait until the last passenger was taken ashore. And when Green Jade called to him yet again, he said nothing, and she was left to brood alone on the cliffs overlooking the river.

It was dark now. An enormous firefly, flashing a blue light on its tail, flew past her, and she thought: "Let me see how far you can fly!" And she followed the blue light with her eyes. Cuckoos began to sing again.

"Grandfather, why don't you come up? I want you!"

Hearing her coaxing, reproachful voice, he answered gruffly: "I'm coming, do you hear? I'm coming!" And then he murmured under his breath: "Oh, Green Jade, what will you do with yourself when I am gone?"

When he reached the cottage at last, he found the house in complete darkness except for the small fire gleaming in the oven. Green Jade was sitting on a bench near the stove with her hands over her eyes. It was not till then that he realised that she had been weeping for a long while. All afternoon he had been pulling the boat backwards and forwards across the stream, his back bent, and now his arms and his waist were aching. Usually, when he reached home, he would smell the vegetables warming in the pan, and there was Green Jade flitting about the room as she prepared their dinner.

"Green Jade," he complained, "I'm only a little late, and there you are crying! What if I were dead?"

Green Jade said nothing.

"Don't cry! Be a good girl! You ought not to cry, whatever happens. You must be stronger—stronger—if you want to live on this earth!"

She took her hands from her eyes and drew closer to Grandfather.

"I won't cry any more," she said.

While they were cooking the rice, Grandfather told her some stories and even mentioned her dead mother. When they had taken dinner beneath the bean-oil lantern, he treated himself to half a bowl of spirits, for he was tired after the long work in the afternoon, and he went out on the cliffs to tell her more stories under the moonlight. He talked about her poor mother's bright intelligence, and her strength of character. And, listening to all this, Green Jade was lost in admiration.

She sat beside him in the moonlight with her hands clasped round her knees, and all the while she kept questioning him about her mother. Now and then she would sigh as though a heavy weight lay over her heart; and she thought that if she sighed, the weight might be made to disappear. But it always remained.

The moonlight was pure silver, pouring over the whole countryside. Only the bamboo groves in the hills shone black in the silver moon. The songs of the insects were like rain. Once in a while a grass-owl could be heard uttering its lament, but a moment later the grass-owl would discover that it was past midnight, close its eyes and go to sleep again.

Grandfather was unusually high-spirited that night. There was no end to his stories. He told her how the people of Ch'a-t'ung were famous twenty years ago all over Szechuan and Kweichow for their singing. He told her that her father had been a famous singer, and knew all the verses by which love and hatred are made known. Grandfather even talked about this! And he told her how her mother loved singing, and how her mother and her father sung together in the days before they knew one another, her father cutting the bamboos on the hillside while her mother carried the ferry across the stream.

"And what happened afterwards?" Green Jade asked.

"It's a very long story," he answered. "The most important thing is that they sang and sang and in the end you were born!"

XIV

He was tired from his long day's labour and soon he went to bed; and Green Jade was also tired from weeping, and she too went to bed and slept. But as she slept she could not forget the things her Grandfather had told her, and her soul was lifted up by the sound of such singing as she had never heard before. It seemed to come floating along the white pagoda, from the garden, from the boat, from the walls of the high cliffs overlooking the river. What was she doing there? Gathering tiger-lilies? She had seen these round lilies high up on the cliff-walls when she was ferrying the boat across the stream.

Everything was happening just as Grandfather had foretold. Green Jade lay sleeping on her straw mattress under the coarse linen curtains, and it seemed to her that the dream was more charming than anything she had experienced before. But Grandfather lay wide awake, listening in the half-light to the voice of the singer coming across the stream. He knew who was singing. He knew it was T'ien Pao making his first halting steps along the horse-road. He listened with sorrow and gladness. He did not attempt to waken Green Jade, for he knew that she was tired from her long weeping during the day.

In the morning they both awoke at daybreak. She washed her face in the stream, and then forgetting that one should never tell one's dreams, she ran up to Grandfather and told him what had happened during the night.

"Grandfather, you were talking about singing, and last night in my dreams I heard songs, so soft and so gentle! I was led by the voices along the cliffs of the stream, and there I found the tiger-lilies, but I have no idea whom I gave them to. The dream was so beautiful, and I slept so soundly."

Grandfather smiled gently, but he told her nothing of what had happened the previous night.

"It would be still better if you dreamed dreams all your life," he thought; "there are even people who dream of being prime ministers!"

The old ferryman still thought it was T'ien Pao who had been singing the previous night, and during the day he asked Green Jade to look after the boat while he went to the city on the excuse that he must be sending some medicines. On the way he met T'ien Pao. He caught hold of the boy's sleeve and said happily: "So you're taking the horse-road as well as the carriage-road, eh? What a sly old fellow you are!"

But he had made a mistake, "putting Chang's hat on Li's head," for it happened that the two brothers had gone to Blue Stream Valley together, and because he had already taken the carriage-road, T'ien Pao had insisted that his younger brother should sing first, and as soon as his brother opened his mouth he knew that he was lost, and refused to sing at all. So it was Nu-sung's voice that they heard. And later, when they were returning home T'ien Pao had decided to take the newly-varnished junk downstream, so that he could forget the girl. He was on his way now to load up the new junk. The old ferryman found him cold, and not understanding in the least what had happened, and thinking that T'ien Pao was merely behaving shyly, he patted him on the back and said quietly:

"You sang splendidly. She heard your songs in her dreams, and she was carried away by them!"

T'ien Pao gazed at the ferryman's mischievous old face and said sadly:

"Do not let us discuss it. The precious child belongs to the nightingale."

The old man was completely bewildered. The boy left

him and went down towards the river through a narrow lane between the overhanging houses, the old ferryman following him. Arriving at the riverside he saw a new junk being loaded; there were hundreds of bamboo oil-casks lying about the bank, a sailor was weaving hay into fenders, and another was rubbing bacon-grease on the oars. The old ferryman asked the sailor who was making the fenders in the strong sunlight, when the junk would depart, and who was in charge of it. The sailor only pointed to T'ien Pao. Rubbing his hands together and approaching T'ien Pao, the old ferryman said:

"Young man, please listen to me for a moment—I have some serious things to say to you. It was wrong for you to take the carriage-road, but you were splendid when you were driving down the horse-road!"

"Look, uncle," T'ien Pao pointed to a nearby window. "You want a nightingale for a son-in-law, and there he is!"

Grandfather lifted his face and saw Nu-sung mending a fishing-net on the windowsill.

When he returned to Blue Stream Valley, Green Jade exclaimed: "Have you been quarrelling with anybody—you look so ill!"

He only smiled. He did not tell her what had happened in the city.

XV

T'ien Pao sailed downstream in the new oil-junk, leaving Nu-sung behind. The old ferryman imagined that the singing would be resumed, since it was Nu-sung who had sung on the previous occasion. And as night came on he tried to distract Green Jade's attention from the things that occupied her in order that she might think only of the singing. After supper, as they sat in the house, the mosquitoes came up from the stream and hummed in their ears, and Green Jade lit a bundle of mugwort and waved the smoking light in all the corners of the house. And when she thought that the fumes from the burning brand had entered every cranny and hole in the house, she laid it beside her bed. Then she sat down on a small stool and listened to Grandfather telling stories.

"Green Jade, listen to me. When you hear songs in dreams and go gathering tiger-lilies, this is one thing; but if someone should really sing for you from the cliffs, what would you do?"

Thinking that he was joking she replied:

"I would listen to him as long as he kept on singing."

"And what if he should sing for three years and six months?"

"Yes, I would listen to him for three years and six months if he sang well."

"Isn't that being unfair?"

"Why? If he wants me to listen to him——"

"Cooking for someone else to eat and singing for someone else to listen to—that's perfectly proper, but what if he should want you to understand the thoughts behind the words he is singing?"

"What kind of thoughts?"

"The thoughts are burning in his heart — it's just like listening to the nightingale if you cannot hear the words of his heart."

"Yes, and what happens if I hear the words of his heart?"

Grandfather clapped his hands over his leg and burst out laughing.

"Green Jade, you are clever, and your old Grandfather is quite stupid. Don't be angry if I can't speak more plainly. Let me tell you a story. It's no more than a midsummer night's dream, and you mustn't take it as anything more than that. T'ien Pao preferred the carriage-road, sent a match-maker to ask for your hand, and all the time you seemed to be unwilling. But what if he has a brother who is prepared to sing for you?"

Green Jade was amazed, lowered her head and did not

know how to reply, for she had no idea how much truth remained in the midsummer night's dream, and she did not know whether her Grandfather or somebody else had made it up. She smiled suddenly and said in a low voice:

"Grandfather, please don't tell me such stories!"

She rose to her feet.

"And what if this story is the truth?"

"You are really so silly, Grandfather," she answered as she went out.

"Yes, it's only a story I have made up," he called after her. "Please don't be angry."

She came back, for it was impossible to be angry with the old man.

"Look at the moon!" she exclaimed. "It's so big!" She was standing on the threshold, gazing at the cool light which flooded the whole countryside, and soon Grandfather came and stood beside her while she kneeled down on the white rock which had been burned all day by the fierce sun, and now the rock was exhaling the heat which it had consumed during the day.

"It's dangerous to sit on the rocks," he murmured, but after he had felt it with his hands, he too decided to sit down there.

The moonlight was very soft. A thin layer of white mist lay over the stream. To the old man nothing could be more beautiful than that someone should sing across the stream, and the girl answering him. Green Jade remembered the idle tale she had been told. Her ears were not deaf, nor were Grandfather's words spoken in a thick voice, and she remembered the story of the brother who sang for her through three years and six months. She seemed to be waiting for the voice of the singer, and for a long while she was silent.

They were still waiting. She was perfectly willing to listen to someone singing, but she heard only the murmuration of the grasshoppers, sweet and clear. She returned to the cottage, searched for her bamboo flute, and, finding it, she returned again under the moonlight. She was not playing well, and so she handed it to Grandfather, begging him to play. He put the flute to his lips, and as the music flowed from the pipe, her heart softened. She leaned against her Grandfather, and suddenly smiled at him:

"Grandfather, who was the first person to make a bamboo flute?"

"He must have been one of the happiest men in the world, for he has given such happiness to people, but perhaps he was one of the most melancholy, for he has given them sadness, too."

"Grandfather, are you sad? Are you angry with me?"

"No, why should I be angry with you? I am very happy with you."

"And what if I should run away?"

"You wouldn't——"

"No, but if I should—what would you do?"

"I would take the ferryboat out and go in search of you."

She burst out singing:

> "*Green Thatch Rapids and Phoenix Rapids are not really strong,*
> *Nor are the Red-rooster Rapids, which are found downstream,*
> *For they are still easy to cross,*
> *But the waves of Blue Wave Rapids are as high as houses!*"

"Yes," she smiled. "So you are really going to take the boat down the Phoenix Rapids, the Green Thatch Rapids and the Blue Wave Rapids? But you said yourself that the water there behaves like a mad person?"

"If you go away," he said slowly, "I myself shall be like a mad person, and I shall have no fear of the great waves."

Green Jade meditated quietly. At last she said, as though she had come to a decision:

"I am not going away. But what if you go away? What if someone takes you?"

Once again he was silent, thinking of death. He had long meditated the subject of his own death, and now gazing at a star in the southern corner of the sky, he thought:

"In the seventh and the eighth moon there are always shooting stars, and perhaps I, too, shall die in the seventh or the eighth moon." And he thought of the conversation he had had with T'ien Pao, of the mill, and of Nu-sung. Thinking of so many things, his heart was confused.

Suddenly Green Jade exclaimed:

"Grandfather, please sing for me!"

He sang ten songs while Green Jade leaned against him and listened with her eyes closed. When he had finished, she whispered to herself:

"While you were singing, I was gathering more tiger-lilies."

He did not tell her that he had been singing the songs he had heard the previous night.

XVI

Nu-sung never sang again at Blue Stream Valley. The fifteenth and the sixteenth day passed, and on the seventeenth the old man could no longer control himself and he went down to the city in search of Nu-sung. At the city gate he met Yang, the stableman, leading a horse, and as soon as Yang caught sight of the old ferryman, he said:

"Old uncle, I was just coming to see you, and here you are!"

"Has anything happened?"

"That's just it. T'ien Pao was taking a junk downstream, and they have met with an accident at Green Thatch Rapids. He fell into a whirlpool and was drowned. We only heard of it this morning, and Nu-sung has gone immediately to the rapids."

The news struck Grandfather like a terrible slap across the

face. He could not believe it. Scratching his cheeks, he said shamefacedly: "T'ien Pao drowned? Nonsense! I've never heard of a drake who could be drowned in water."

"But he was drowned all right! And do you know, I approve of your wisdom in not letting a young fellow like that have a smooth progress along the carriage-road."

Hearing this, Grandfather still doubted the stableman's words, but when he looked at the stableman's face, he knew it was true. He said dejectedly:

"What do you mean by wisdom? This is Heaven's will..."

His heart was filled to overflowing with sadness.

To discover whether the stableman was really speaking the truth, for even then a doubt remained in his heart, he hurried towards Shun-shun's house where people were talking quietly together and someone was burning paper money for the departed ghost. He joined them and heard them speaking about the same thing which the stableman had told him. But as soon as these people noticed that the ferryman was present they began to discuss the rise in the price of oil. He was utterly disturbed, and thought of asking one of the sailors, but at that moment Shun-shun himself appeared, downcast and ill-at-ease, preoccupied with the thought of his loss, like a man trying to stand up against the blows of fate. As soon as he saw the old ferryman he said:

"Uncle, we'll have to put aside the matter we were discussing some time ago. You've heard the news?"

The old ferryman's eyes were red with blood. He rubbed his hands together and said: "What happened? Is it true? When did it happen? Yesterday? The day before?"

At that moment someone came running along with the news: "It was on the forenoon of the sixteenth; the junk crashed against some rocks and the water came in through the prow. T'ien Pao tried to edge the boat off the rocks with a pole, but he failed and fell into the river."

"Did you see him fall with your own eyes?"

"Yes, and I followed him into the river."

"Did he say anything?"

"No, he had no time to say anything. All the time he had been angry, and refused to speak."

The old ferryman shook his head and glanced at Shun-shun's eyes. Shun-shun seemed to understand what was going on in his soul, and said gently:

"Uncle, this is Heaven's will! Let's forget about it! I've got some fine wine here, sent up from Tahsing village." A servant filled a bamboo cup with wine, covered the top of the cup with a fresh tung-oil leaf and gave it to the old ferryman, who took the wine and went on his way. At first he went along to the dock where he had seen T'ien Pao. The stableman Yang was still there, for he had brought the horse to gallop along the sand, while he himself enjoyed the cool shade of the willows. The old ferryman invited him to taste the wine, and soon they were more cheerful, and Grandfather even went on to talk of how the two brothers had been singing over at Blue Stream Valley. The stableman listened quietly, and at last he said:

"Grandfather, tell me, is Green Jade in love with Nu-sung?"

He had no sooner said this when Nu-sung himself appeared along the road. He looked as though he was about to undertake a journey, and he turned back as soon as he saw the old ferryman. So it was Stableman Yang who called out to him: "Nu-sung! Nu-sung! Come here! There is something I want to talk to you about!"

"What is it?"

"I heard people saying that you had gone away—now come over here, and let me talk to you. I'm not a tiger, I won't eat you up!"

Nu-sung was broad-shouldered, strong and more robust than most of the other people in the city. He came forward, a forced smile of greeting on his long face; and when he came into the shade of the willows, Grandfather said plaintively:

THE FRONTIER CITY

"Nu-sung, they tell me that soon the mill will be yours. Will you let me be the caretaker?"

Nu-sung appeared to have no love for disguised questions, and noticing that there was an ill-wind between them, the stableman interrupted and said: "Nu-sung, are you really going downstream?" The boy nodded, saying nothing, and went away.

The old ferryman felt that he had only brought disgrace upon himself, and he returned silently to the hills. On the ferryboat he told Green Jade with assumed nonchalance what had happened in the city.

"Green Jade, listen to me. T'ien Pao was taking a junk laden with oil downstream to Chenshow, and he was drowned at Green Patch Rapids. That man—strong as a tiger and as full of vitality as a dragon. They say a man may look down on the mountains but not on the water."

Green Jade did not understand what he was saying, and at first she paid no attention to his words. Then he said:

"It's quite true. Stableman Yang, who came here the other day as a matchmaker, said I was very wise not to consent so early."

Green Jade threw a glance at Grandfather, and noticing that his eyes were bloodshot and that he had been drinking, she said:

"Are you angry with something?"

He said nothing. When they reached the bank, he walked up to the cottage with a vague smile on his face. Green Jade remained to look after the boat, but not hearing him, she decided to go up to the house and see what had happened. She found him sitting on the threshold and weaving a new pair of sandals. Because he looked ill and grief-stricken she knelt down beside him.

"Grandfather, is anything the matter?"

"Darling, he is really dead," Grandfather said. "Nu-sung is angry with us. He believes it was all due to us."

Someone was calling to them from the other bank. Grandfather hurried away. Green Jade knelt on the heap of straw, and it seemed to her that she had never felt so unhappy in all her life. She waited for a long while but Grandfather did not return, and soon she noticed that she was weeping.

XVII

For some reason Grandfather seemed more than ever preoccupied and angry, there was rarely a smile on his face and he paid less attention to Green Jade than before. Green Jade sensed rather than felt that he loved her less than he had loved her at other times, but she could find no reason for the change in him. Yet this was only an interlude. After a few days everything was the same again, they still tended the boat in the same way and nothing had changed in the daily uneventful life of the ferry. But Green Jade was conscious of a gap in their lives which could never be bridged. Whenever Grandfather went to the city, he was entertained by Shun-shun, but it was only too evident that the father had not forgotten the cause of his son's death. Nu-sung had travelled six hundred *li* downstream to Chenshow through the North River, and in vain he had looked for the body of his brother. He put up posters announcing a reward for the recovery of the corpse, and these were set up at all the revenue offices along the river, and having done this he returned to Ch'a-t'ung. Soon afterwards he set out for East Szechuan on a trading mission, and on his way he crossed over the ferry at Blue Stream Valley. The old ferryman imagined that the boy had forgotten all about what had happened in the past, and so he said:

"What do you mean by going to Szechuan again when there's such a fiery sun overhead."

"We must get rice to eat," the boy answered. "Even when there's a fiery sun, we must eat!"

"Nonsense! There's no lack of rice in your house!"

"That's true, but our father always says that it is bad for us to idle at home."

"Is your father well?"

"He can still eat and work. Why should he be unwell?"

"Because your brother was drowned. He looks much older now."

Nu-sung was silently gazing at the white pagoda. He remembered that other night, and therefore he was filled with melancholy. The old ferryman glanced up at him timidly, a smile spreading over his face.

"Nu-sung, listen to me. Green Jade tells me that she had a queer dream that night." He looked craftily at Nu-sung, and noticing that the boy appeared to be neither surprised nor bored, he continued: "A very queer dream. She says she was lifted up on the wings of song, and she went high above the cliffs and gathered tiger-lilies."

Nu-sung smiled sadly as he thought: "He is a crafty old fellow!" Seeing the boy's smile, the old man was able to read his thoughts.

"Don't you believe me?" he asked.

"How can I not believe you? I was a fool to sing on those cliffs all night!"

The old man was surprised by this unexpected and honest confession, and he kept saying in a weak voice: "It was true . . . yes, true perhaps . . . I am sure it was true . . ."

All he had wanted to do was to make the situation clearer. But from the very beginning his thoughts had been confused, and he knew he was faltering. When the boat reached the bank, the boy leapt ashore and the old man called to him:

"Nu-sung, Nu-sung, wait a moment. There's something I want to tell you. Didn't you say you had once made a fool of yourself? Oh, but it's not true. Someone else was made foolish by your songs."

The young man paused and whispered:

"That's enough. Please don't say any more."

"Nu-sung," the old man continued. "I've heard people saying you want a ferryboat more than you want a mill. Stableman Yang told me. I don't suppose it is true, though."

"What if I should want a ferryboat?"

Looking at the boy's face, the old ferryman felt suddenly at rest, and he called to Green Jade to come down. Perhaps she was hiding in the house, perhaps she had disappeared among the woods, but she did not appear, and neither did he hear her voice till long afterwards. After waiting for some time and gazing at the old man's face, Nu-sung strode away, still smiling, with the porter who was carrying rice noodles and white sugar on his back.

After a while, when they were passing through the woods, the porter turned to Nu-sung and said:

"Judging from the fellow's face, it looks as though he likes you more than most."

Nu-sung was silent. The porter continued:

"He asked you which you wanted most—the mill or the ferryboat. Do you really want to be his grandson and the heir to a boat?"

Nu-sung laughed, listening quietly when the porter went on to say that anyone in his senses would prefer the mill, which brought in seven *shen* of rice and three pecks of husk a day."

"When I come back," Nu-sung answered, "I'll ask my father to approach old Captain Wang, and we'll marry his daughter to you and see that you get the mill. I prefer looking after a ferryboat. It's only the old fellow who is bad—he killed my brother!"

The old ferryman was downcast at the thought that he had taken leave of Nu-sung in such a manner. There was no sign of Green Jade when he went back to the cottage. It was some time later before she returned from the bamboo grove with a basket in her hand; she had been cutting bamboo shoots.

"I was trying to find you," he complained. "Didn't you hear me shouting?"

"No. Why were you shouting?"

"There was a passenger—someone you know. I called to you, but you did not reply."

"Who was it?"

"Guess . . . Surely you know who it was!"

Green Jade remembered all that she had overheard in the bamboo grove, and she blushed crimson. For a long while she was silent.

"How many bamboo shoots have you found?" he asked after a while.

She emptied the basket at his feet: there were only ten bamboo shoots, but there were innumerable tiger-lilies. He looked into her face. Her cheeks were burning. As soon as she saw him smiling at her, she ran away.

XVIII

The days passed. In these long days nothing happened except that the wounds of their hearts were gradually healed. The weather had never been hotter. Everybody was out in the fields making fermented rice-wine, washing the rice in cool water and basking in the sun, thinking of nothing except the heat. Every afternoon Green Jade walked to the white pagoda and slept in its shade. It was cool in the high places among the bamboo groves and there were always nightingales and other birds singing amid the glades; and listening to their songs she would lose herself in dreams, and sometimes they were the wildest imaginable dreams, dreams which filled her with joy and at the same time with fear. An unknown future was beginning to shake her with unconcealed violence, and she could no longer hide her most secret thoughts from her grandfather.

Grandfather knew nothing, and at the same time he knew everything. He knew that she liked Nu-sung, but he could not discover what lay in the boy's mind. He felt discouraged both by Nu-sung and by Shun-shun, but he never lost hope.

"It was my fault. The next time I must arrange it better."

With wide-open eyes he experienced dreams which were wilder and more boundless than any of Green Jade's.

Whenever someone from the city crossed over the ferry, he would ask after Nu-sung and Shun-shun as though they were members of his family. What was strange was that he began to grow afraid of meeting them, and whenever he saw them, no words came to his lips and he only rubbed his hands together in the old way and gazed round with a stare. The father and the son understood him perfectly, but the dead boy remained like a heavy memory over their hearts and they pretended to ignore the old ferryman's pleas. So the days passed in continual waiting.

Though he had not dreamed at all the previous night, Grandfather would murmur into Green Jade's ears: "I had a terrible dream last night, Green Jade."

"Was it very terrible?"

As though reflecting upon the dream he gazed seriously at her small face and long brows, and began to relate to her one of those dreams he had experienced with wide-open eyes. It was not a particularly terrible dream. All rivers run into the sea, and although he might begin to talk about some wholly unfamiliar subject, sooner or later he would always return to the subject which made Green Jade uncomfortable. Sometimes Green Jade would show that she was not entirely pleased with the story, and at such moments he would feel afraid, introduce gratuitous explanations and irrelevancies to conceal his real intentions. "I shouldn't have said that, should I? But you know, I'm getting old and muddle-headed and I make so many mistakes." But more often, even when he was continually losing himself in his wild dreams, she would remain silent with her lips pursed together, or else she would interrupt him quickly, saying: "Grandfather, you really are muddle-headed!" He would be on the point of saying: "Yes, I am terribly muddle-headed!" but always at that moment someone would call to him from the shore.

The hot days continued, and the passengers who came to the ferry with their heavy loads would crouch down beside the tea-jar in the shade of the rocks, enjoying the coolness, drinking the cool tea, offering one another their pipes and chatting with the old ferryman. Sometimes he would see them going down to the stream to bathe, and when they returned he would hear all the rumours of the town. Some of these rumours he would tell later to Green Jade. They would talk of the rise and the fall of prices, of the sedan-chair fares and the cost of hauling a junk upstream, of the big-footed women who made up the opium-pipes as they lay beside you. Everything, everything without exception, could be learnt at such meetings.

Then Nu-sung returned from East Szechuan, bringing a consignment of goods to Ch'a-t'ung. It was growing dark. It was very quiet on the stream. Grandfather and Green Jade were examining turnips in the garden. She was feeling terribly lonely, but while she had been sleeping in the afternoon she heard someone hailing the ferryboat in a deep-throated voice, and she had hurried down towards the creek only to find that it was Nu-sung and his porter. She was so confused that she turned back and hid in the bamboo grove like a young animal escaping from the hunter. They heard her footsteps, turned and understood exactly what had happened. Waiting for a while without seeing anyone, they called again in the same deep-throated voice. The ferryman heard, but he was still counting the turnips, and it seemed strange to him that, having seen Green Jade on her way down, they should still be calling, and then he realised that she must have hidden herself away because there was someone she did not want to see. So they kept on calling, and at last Nu-sung turned to the porter, who asked:

"It's very curious. The old fellow must be lying on his death-bed, and Green Jade is in hiding."

"Let's wait a little—we have enough time on our hands."

Meanwhile the old ferryman was thinking: "Is it possible that it is Nu-sung?" but he still remained where he was.

Once again a voice came from the creek, and this time he

recognised without any doubt that it was Nu-sung's. Was he angry because he had waited so long? As he ran down to the boat, the old ferryman still wondered what had happened, and then he noticed that they had entered the boat, and now he was quite sure he could see Nu-sung. He shouted out:

"Is it you, Nu-sung, really you? Have you come back?"

The boy seemed to be annoyed.

"Yes, I'm back," he answered. "What's happened to the boat? I've been waiting half a day, and no one has come!"

"I thought—" He looked round, but there was no sign of Green Jade. He noticed the yellow dog running out of the bamboo grove, and he knew that she was hiding there. And instead of saying what he had intended to say, he answered: "I thought you had already crossed over."

"How could we have crossed?" the porter asked. "No one dares to touch the ferry without you in it." A pair of white-winged water-fowl skimmed over the surface of the stream, and he said: "The white-winged bird is returning to its nest, and we have to wait for our dinner."

"It's still very early," the old ferryman answered, leaping into the boat, and to himself he said: "I thought you once said you wanted to inherit this boat?"

"Ah, the dust and the heat, Nu-sung . . ."

They both listened to the old ferryman's words, but neither said anything. The boat reached the bank, the young man and the porter climbed the hill and disappeared. They had been so indifferent to him that the old man immediately grew sullen, he clenched his fists, waved them threateningly in the air, and returned slowly to the other side.

XIX

Green Jade had escaped into the bamboo grove, the old ferryman had refused to come down—Nu-sung interpreted both these events in a manner which was curiously wrong-headed. The old man had tried to excuse himself and he had completely failed in his purpose. Nu-sung remembered his brother. He was a little indignant and a little irritated.

Three days after he returned home, a man came to stay at Shun-shun's as an intermediary from Captain Wang, who wanted to know whether the boy still wanted to possess the new mill. Shun-shun asked Nu-sung what he thought about it.

"Father," Nu-sung answered, "if you wish to marry me for your own sake, and if it makes you happy to possess a mill, then you may promise them that I will marry her. But if you are thinking of my happiness, let me think about it for a while, for even now I do not know whether I prefer a mill or a ferryboat, and perhaps it is my fate to guard over a small boat!"

The messenger committed these words to his memory and returned to the hills, but on his way he crossed the ferry and he smiled to himself when he noticed the old ferryman. The old ferryman discovered who he was, and then asked him about his business in Ch'a-t'ung.

"There was not much business," the man answered. "I was staying at Shun-shun's house in River Road."

"Then surely you had some business?"

"We talked for a while."

"Tell me, did you talk about—?" The old ferryman did not know how to begin, but at last he went on. "They say that Captain Wang is going to give his daughter to their family, and perhaps he will also give them the mill. Is the affair progressing?"

The man laughed aloud. "Well, we'll soon see how things are. I've been to ask Shun-shun and he's willing," and I've asked the boy—"

"What did the boy say?"

"Well, he said it was a choice between a mill and a ferryboat, and he had decided on the mill. A mill has roots, it stands before all the winds that blow, it's not a transitory thing like a ferryboat."

He was a clever man, a rice-broker and careful in his

speech. He knew exactly what was meant by the ferry-boat, but he did not put it into words. He noticed that the old ferryman was deeply disturbed, his lips were trembling and he was about to speak, and so he said gently:

"It's Heaven's will—men can do nothing without the help of Heaven. There was T'ien Pao—you couldn't have asked for a finer man, but he was drowned!"

The old man felt that he had been stabbed over the heart, and therefore he did not say what he had intended to say; and for a long while after the man had gone ashore, he stood on the prow of the boat, sunk in thought, stupefied by the words he had just heard, remembering Nu-sung's indifference, more miserable than he had ever been in his life before.

All day Green Jade had been playing merrily near the pagoda, and soon she climbed over the rock and begged Grandfather to sing for her, but since he said nothing and only disregarded her, and seemed to be dejected, she decided to go down to the creek; and Grandfather, noticing her dark face and her happy-go-lucky air, smiled disdainfully. Someone was calling to him from the other side. He pulled the boat over, saying nothing until he reached midstream, and then for some reason he burst out into loud singing. Afterwards he left the boat and came to where Green Jade was sitting. He kept on rubbing his forehead with his hands.

"What is the matter, Grandfather?" she asked. "Have you sunstroke? Lie down in the shade—I'll take care of the boat!"

"You take care of the boat? Nothing could be better. I leave the boat entirely in your charge!"

Yes, she was sure he was suffering from sunstroke! He was so strange! He went back to the house, and finding some pieces of broken china he deliberately pressed them into his own arms and legs until a little black blood flowed; then he lay down on the bed.

Green Jade continued to look after the boat. She was still

quite cheerful. "Grandfather won't sing for me, so I shall sing for myself." And, saying this, she began to sing songs for herself.

The old ferryman heard them as he lay in bed with his eyes closed. His mind was in turmoil, but he thought he was suffering from no serious disease, and he made plans for getting up in the morning, wandering down to the city and calling upon the people in River Road. But the next day he was really ill; his body lay heavily on the bed, and when Green Jade saw him she was oppressed by the sense of something strange and insecure in her life. She boiled some herbs and made him drink them. She plucked garlic in the garden and soaked them in rice wine to ferment them; and all the time she was running backwards and forwards between the boat and her Grandfather, always asking about his health and how he felt. Grandfather remained perfectly silent, tortured by his secret. For three days he lay in bed, and on the third day he seemed to have recovered so completely that he began to walk round the house; and though his joints seemed to be stiff, he began to make plans to go into the city. Green Jade begged him not to go, for there seemed to be no reason for a long journey when he was still recovering from his fever.

Yet he insisted on going. The only thing that held him back was the thought that he ought to tell her about the purpose of his journey. Gazing at her beautiful oval face shaped like a melon-seed and at her liquid eyes, he murmured:

"No, really, I must go—most urgent—mustn't fail——"

Green Jade laughed a little sadly.

"Is it so urgent? I suppose you are going to——?"

He knew her ways, he knew the rising note of displeasure in her voice, and at last he laid the black sack on the table and said with a faltering laugh:

"All right. If you say so, I'm not going. You're afraid I'll fall down and die. Well, I'm not going. I thought if I went in the morning it would be cooler, and then I could come back as soon as my business was done . . I won't go to-day. I'll go to-morrow."

"Your legs are still very weak," Green Jade whispered.

He was still very feeble, and he would walk about with his arms dangling in front of him a little like a marionette. Once he stumbled over a small mallet used for beating sandals into shape, and as he steadied himself, Green Jade said with her frail little laugh:

"Yes, you won't submit—that's good!"

He picked up the mallet and threw it in the corner with all his strength.

"I'm not getting old," he said fiercely. "Some day, you see, I'll kill a leopard yet!"

In the afternoon it began to rain. Although it was raining he was determined to go into the city, and for a long while he argued the matter with Green Jade; and at last, when she saw that her pleas were unavailing, she begged him to take the yellow dog, since she would have to remain. On the way the old ferryman met a friend of his, with whom he discussed the prices of salt and rice, and later they went to the yamen to see the new blood-horses, and finally they made their way towards Shun-shun's house in River Road. Shun-shun was playing cards with three other men. They were the oblong cards which are only found in Hunan. And because Shun-shun was absorbed in contemplation of the game, Grandfather stood behind him and looked over his shoulder. When Shun-shun offered him some wine, he begged to be excused and said that he had only recently recovered from fever. The game went on and on, the old ferryman had no desire to leave, and Shun-shun seemed not to have realised that the old ferryman was waiting to talk to him. Shun-shun was absorbed in the game of cards. At last one of the players, noticing his grief-stricken appearance, asked him whether there was anything he wanted to say; and in reply the old man, rubbing his hands together according to his usual custom, said that he would like to have a word with the river-judge. It was only then that Shun-shun realised why the man had been standing behind him for such a long time. He turned round and burst out laughing:

"Why didn't you tell me earlier? You just stood there silently, and I thought you were looking at my cards to learn how to play!"

"Just a few words—no more than a few words—— I didn't want to disturb your enjoyment——"

Shun-shun slammed the cards on the table and went into a small adjoining room, still laughing. The old ferryman followed him.

"Well, what's happened?" Shun-shun asked, and it was as though he knew exactly what the old man was going to say, and therefore felt sorry for him.

"They say—they say you're going to marry your son to Captain Wang's daughter. I've come to ask whether it is true?"

Noticing the terrible tension on the old man's face, Shun-shun answered "Yes?" and in saying this he meant: "What about it? Suppose it were true?" He did not mean that this was in fact his real intention.

"Is it true?" the old ferryman asked in a quavering voice.

"Yes, yes, of course it's true," Shun-shun answered, but once again he meant no more than that it was something he would like to see, though he had few enough hopes in its fulfilment.

"Where's Nu-sung nowadays?" the old man asked, pretending to be perfectly at ease.

"The boy went to Taoyuan some days ago."

The boy had gone downstream because he had quarrelled with his father, for the river-judge had refused to consider that the boy should marry the girl who was indirectly responsible for his brother's death. According to the custom of the place, marriages were decided by the children themselves, and the parents had nothing to do with the matter. If

Nu-sung loved Green Jade, and Green Jade loved Nu-sung, there was no more to be said; he could not interfere, and it was only because Grandfather showed so much concern and was always worrying about his grand-daughter's future that father and son had grown to dislike him, and even to distrust him, and they both believed he was responsible for T'ien Pao's death.

Grandfather was about to say something, but Shun-shun begged him to restrain himself and said gruffly:

"Look, Uncle, it's best to forget such things. Our mouths are only fit to drink wine—it is time we stopped singing our children's praises. I know you, and I know all your intentions are for the best; but I do beg you to understand my own position. We should live for ourselves now, and not try to plan our children's lives."

Once again Grandfather felt that he had been struck down by a mortal blow. There was still something he wanted to say, but already Shun-shun was returning to the card-table and the cards. He dealt the cards heavily, as though he, too, was weighed down with a great grief; and, seeing this, the old ferryman decided that nothing was to be gained by staying longer; he threw the sack over his shoulders and went on his way.

It was still early. Disheartened and weighed down with grief and remorse, he made his way to Stableman Yang. The stableman was drinking wine, and though Grandfather insisted that he had only recently recovered from fever, he was compelled to drink three or four cups of distilled spirits. When he returned to Blue Stream Valley he was hot and covered with dust, so he bathed in the stream. He felt exhausted now. Asking Green Jade to look after the boat, he returned to the house and fell asleep.

Twilight came on. Red dragonflies flew low over the stream, and clouds were gathering in the sky, while a hot wind blew through the bamboo groves so that they rustled like lions roaring. A storm was coming. Meanwhile, Green

Jade remained in the boat, gazing distractedly at the dragonflies, utterly confused. She was uneasy at the thought of Grandfather's great pallor, and suddenly she decided to run up to the house and see how he was.

She thought he had gone to bed long ago, but she found him sitting on the threshold and weaving sandals.

"Oh, Grandfather, how many sandals do you want? There are already fourteen pairs hanging over your bed? Why don't you rest now that you are ill?"

For a while he was silent, then he raised his head and gazed at the sky.

"Green Jade, there will be a storm to-night. Haul the boat in under the cliffs, because there is going to be heavy rain."

"I'm afraid," she whispered, and it seemed to her that she was not afraid of the coming storm but of something else.

He seemed to understand her, for he answered: "Why should you be afraid? Everything must come as it comes. There is no need to fear."

XX

At night the storm came as he had promised. Lightning grazed the roof of the cottage, thunder clapped overhead, and then more lightning and more thunder. Green Jade was trembling with fear in the darkness. Grandfather had also awakened, and, now, thinking that she might catch cold, he got up, threw a coverlet over her and whispered:

"Darling, there is no need to be afraid."

"No, I am not afraid," she answered, and she meant to add: "Because you are with me—that's why I am not afraid."

The thunder roared. There were peals of thunder, and then the sound of something falling above the noise of the rain. She imagined that the cliffs were falling into the river and the boat was crushed under them.

They lay in bed, silently listening to the wind and the rain. Soon Green Jade fell asleep. When she awoke it was already daybreak; the rain had ceased, but torrents of water were still pouring down the hillsides into the stream. She got up. Grandfather seemed to be lying in a deep sleep. She opened the door and went out. A rivulet was flowing past the door, and this muddy stream of yellow water was rushing headlong down the slope and over the cliffs. There were rivers flowing everywhere. The vegetable garden had disappeared, carried down in the torrent, the young shoots buried under coarse sand and mud. She walked down to the cliffs and saw the stream in flood, the level of the water only a little way below the tea-jar which stood on the bank. The road leading down the bank was a small river, the yellow muddy water murmuring as it rushed down the steep slope. The rope across the river had been carried away, and what was still more surprising was that the ferryboat, which she had hauled under the cliffs and securely fastened, had also disappeared.

The cliff which lay in front of the house was still standing, but the white pagoda had entirely disappeared. She was extremely astonished, and hurried in the direction where it had been. It had collapsed under the weight of the storm, and there was only a great heap of stones and muddy rubble to remind her of the proud tower that once existed there. She began to cry out to her Grandfather in a loud voice. She heard no reply, and ran home. When she reached his bed, she shook him for a long time, but he remained quite still, speechless and dead. He had died at the moment when the storm was about to cease. She burst out into wild tears which seemed to have no end, so bitterly did she cry and so continual was her wailing.

She began to heat some water in the oven in order to bathe her Grandfather's body. She was still weeping when an errand boy from Ch'a-t'ung on his way to East Szechuan hailed her from the creek. He thought they were still asleep in the cottage, for no one answered him; and since he was anxious to cross as quickly as possible he threw a pebble over the stream which hit the roof of the cottage. Green Jade went out with tears streaming down her face and stood on the cliff.

"Hey! It's getting late! Come and pull the boat across!"

"The boat has run away!"

"What's the matter with your Grandfather? Isn't he supposed to look after the boat?"

"Yes, he looks after the boat, he has looked after it for fifty years. He's dead now!"

As soon as she said this she began to burst out again in interminable lamentations. The boy knew that it was now impossible to cross the stream, and he would have to return to the frontier city to report what had happened on the ferry. So he shouted:

"Is he really dead? I'll go back and tell them, and perhaps they'll send up another boat."

He ran back to the city and informed everyone he met that the old ferryman had died. It was not long before everyone heard about it. Shun-shun sent a man to find a boat and bring it to the valley; on the boat there was an unpainted wooden coffin. Meanwhile Stableman Yang and another old soldier hurried up to the cottage, and there they began to hack down some of the bamboos, which they bound together with rattan; and when this was finished they brought it down the hillside so that passengers could be taken across, and while the old soldier was left to take care of the raft, Yang himself went to pay his respects to the dead man in the cottage. His eyes were filled with tears as he stroked the hands of the dead man lying hard and stiff on the bed. More men came to help, the coffin arrived, and an old taoist priest crossed the stream on the raft, bringing the musical instruments and a cock by which the rites could be performed. Everywhere people were hurrying on strange errands, but Green Jade sat on a bench near the oven weeping interminably.

At noon Shun-shun arrived, followed by a labourer bearing

a sack of rice, a jar of wine and a leg of pork. As soon as he saw Green Jade he said:

"Your Grandfather is dead, but everything will be all right. The old must die, and there is no reason to worry. Depend on me for everything you want."

He stayed a few minutes and then returned. In the afternoon the body was placed in the coffin. Some of the people in the cottage wanted to return home, and when evening came only the Taoist priest, Stableman Yang and two young labourers sent up by Shun-shun remained in the house. The Taoist priest was snipping green and red paper flowers and making candlesticks with a kind of yellow clay. When night came, these ritual candles together with some joss-sticks were lit and placed on a little table beside the coffin; the priest wore his dark blue ceremonial robes, and now he began to lead the procession round and round the coffin with a paper pennon in his hand; Green Jade followed him and the old stableman came up in the rear. Meanwhile the labourers standing near the oven were pounding the cymbals and beating gongs. The priest walked with his eyes closed, singing and humming softly to himself, consoling the dead man, speaking of the western paradise where flowers bloom all the year round, and while he sang of these things, the stableman threw flowers from the tray on the dead body in the coffin.

At midnight, when all the ceremonies were over, firecrackers were lit. The candles were burning low. Green Jade ran to the oven and prepared refreshments for them; and after they had eaten, the priest lay down in the dead man's bed and fell asleep, while the others continued to watch over the coffin, in accordance with immemorial custom, singing songs and beating on a small drum made from an overturned rice-measure, singing the song "Wang Hsiang Lying on the Ice" and "Huang Hsiang Fanning the Pillow," both songs from the "Famous Twenty-four Filial Sons," an ancient Taoist book.

All day Green Jade had been weeping, but now she was

exhausted, and she leaned her head against the coffin and dozed off to sleep. The labourers and the stableman were still singing, and they woke up Green Jade. Tears filled her eyes as she remembered that her Grandfather lay dead in the coffin.

"Don't weep, don't cry any more," the stableman said. "He is dead now, and you cannot cry him back into life!"

He began to tell her stories which were sometimes interlarded with oaths, and these made the labourers laugh in delight. The yellow dog could be heard barking outside the house, and after a while Green Jade opened the door and stood on the threshold. She heard the thrumming of the winged insects. The moon was bright in the heavens, and the clear stars shone in the quiet air.

"Is all this really happening?" she asked herself. "Is it really true that he is dead?"

The old stableman had followed her out, afraid that she would jump over a cliff or hang herself on a beam. She paid no attention to him and seemed to be oblivious of his presence. He coughed quietly and said:

"Green Jade, the dew is falling. Don't you feel cold?"

"No, I'm not cold."

"The weather is fine now," he murmured, and at that moment a great hollow "Ah-h-h!" came from her lips as she watched an immense shooting star followed by another descending in the southern sky. It seemed to split the sky in two. From the distance they heard the moaning of a grave-owl.

"Green Jade," he said, standing beside her. "Go back to the house. Don't let your mind wander."

She returned to the coffin, and, sitting on the earth-floor, she began to whimper again. The labourers had fallen asleep on a heap of straw beside the oven. The stableman was still talking:

"Don't cry, don't cry! He would be sad if he heard you. There is no use in crying—it only makes your eyes swell out.

Listen to me. I know all the things that your Grandfather was thinking about. Depend on me. I will arrange everything—the ferryboat and the boy who loves you—everything. And if things do not happen as they should, I'll fight them to the death, even though I am an old man! Green Jade, set your mind at rest and depend on me!"

Somewhere in the distance a cock crowed. The old Taoist lying on the bed whispered:

"Is it daybreak already?"

XXI

In the early morning men came from the city with ropes and poles.

The unpainted wooden coffin was carried by six men into the hills behind the ruined pagoda, followed by Shun-shun, Stableman Yang, Green Jade, the Taoist priest, and the yellow dog. They were all silent and weighed down with melancholy. When they reached the square grave which had already been dug, the old Taoist priest followed the custom which has been handed down from past ages and leaped down and sprinkled the four corners and the middle with a few grains of cinnabar and white rice; then, still in the grave, he burnt some paper money and recited the requiem. A little while later he climbed out and ordered the carriers to let the coffin into the grave, but Green Jade threw herself on the coffin, wailing in a strident voice, without tears, and would not rise. At last Stableman Yang succeeded in dragging her away. Soon the coffin had disappeared under the earth, and Green Jade remained sobbing beside the grave. It was necessary for the old priest to return to the city, where he had other rites to perform; he crossed the ferry and disappeared. Shun-shun entrusted everything to the stableman and himself departed, while the others went down to the creek to wash the mud from their hands, remembering that they had their own business in the city and knowing that the cottage was too poor to provide any more meals, and so they, too, departed. In Blue Stream Valley only three people were left—the old stableman, Green Jade, and Baldhead Chen, who was sent by Shun-shun to take charge of the ferryboat until new arrangements could be made. Baldhead had been throwing stones at the yellow dog, which kept on barking viciously at him.

In the afternoon Green Jade begged the stableman to return to the city so that his horses could be placed in the care of someone in the barracks, and so leave him free to return to keep her company. When he returned, Baldhead decided to leave for the city, and Green Jade continued to tend the ferry with the yellow dog, while the old stableman idled on the cliff beside the stream and sang songs to her in his husky voice.

Three days later Shun-shun came to invite Green Jade to stay in his house in the city. Green Jade refused; she said she wanted to keep guard over her Grandfather's grave. She begged only that he would ask the people at the yamen to allow Stableman Yang to stay with her for a while. Shun-shun promised to do this, and returned to the city.

Stableman Yang was a man of about fifty, and he told stories better even than Grandfather, and, moreover, he was unusually careful and diligent; and while he stayed with her it seemed to Green Jade that she had lost a grandfather but found an uncle. People crossing the ferry might talk of her Grandfather, and she herself would think of him often at dusk, and at such times she felt loaded with grief. Then they would sit together on the cliffs, talking in soft voices of the old man who lay in the wet earth. From him Green Jade learnt much she had never known before about her father, once a soldier in the Green Army, who was beloved by the girls and who sought both love and a good reputation; and of her mother who sang so sweetly. Now times had changed. There was no longer an Emperor on the throne, and sometimes the old man could not help smiling at the swift passage of time, thinking of the day when he brought his horse and sang to Green Jade's mother at Blue Stream Valley when he was only a young groom. Her mother had never loved him; yet now the daughter leaned against him and trusted him more than anyone else. So they would talk at twilight, reviving their memories, lost in their recollections of Nu-sung's singing, the death of T'ien Pao, the man who had come down from Captain Wang with the offer of the mill, and how Nu-sung, in his anger, had disappeared downstream, unable to decide whether he wanted the mill or the ferry, and of how Green Jade herself was partly responsible for her Grandfather's death. All these things they spoke about until light shone on all the dark places, and now that she knew these things, Green Jade wept the whole night.

According to ceremonial usage, the families of the dead must guard over the coffin for seven weeks. In the fourth week Shun-shun sent for the stableman to discuss whether Green Jade could be brought to the house and prepare for her marriage with Nu-sung. Because Nu-sung was still at Chenshow nothing could be decided about the marriage, but once again Green Jade was asked to make her home in River Road, and this was the message which the stableman brought back to Green Jade, and he advised Green Jade to stay where she was, for nothing could be worse than living at the house of a man unrelated to her, without any settled name. They would wait there until news came from Nu-sung or the boy returned.

So it was settled; and the stableman arranged that someone else should look after his horses while he returned to keep Green Jade company.

The white pagoda in Blue Stream Valley was one of the landmarks of Ch'a-t'ung. It had collapsed; another must be built. Accordingly, the officers in the army, the revenue officers, the shopkeepers and all the inhabitants of the city contributed money, and books were sent round to the neighbouring villages inviting subscriptions. No one would gain by the erection of the new pagoda, but the whole community felt that without it something had passed from their lives. There was even a bamboo box on the ferryboat where money could be placed for rebuilding the pagoda. When the box was filled the stableman would go off to the city and bring it back empty. And when people came from the country and found that there was no sign of the old ferryman, and Green Jade had white mourning threads in her pigtail, they knew that he had done his duty in the world and lay buried in a small grave for the worms to eat, and looking gently at Green Jade, they would fumble in their purses for some money to put into the bamboo box. "May Heaven bless you, may the dead go to the western paradise and may the living have peace." Green Jade understood the motives for their generosity, and she would turn away, her heart still aching.

During the winter the ruined pagoda was erected again, but still there was no sign of the young man who had sung on these cliffs on a moonlight night and who, by his songs, had lifted her heart to the stars. He had not returned. Some thought he would never return and others that he might come on the morrow. Where he was, or what he was doing, no one knew.

THE END

ABOUT THE AUTHOR

SHEN Ts'ung-wen (Shen Congwen in the new official *pinyin* romanization) was born on December 28, 1902 in the small town of Feng-huang (Phoenix City) in the mountainous western part of Hunan Province, near the provincial borders of Szechuan and Kweichow, in West Central China. Feng-huang was populated largely by native Miao people and by Chinese garrison troops, most of whom were sentenced criminals. Shen, the fourth of nine children, came from a military family which had fallen on hard times. His grandfather had been a local official. His grandmother was a Miao. His father, an official in the local military administration, was often away for long periods and thus unable to look after the education of his children.

Shen hated school. After graduating from elementary school, he held a number of short-term jobs, employed most of the time by local army units, first as an irregular soldier, then as a first sergeant. Since he knew how to write, he kept records for the army. During the intervals between his army jobs, he assisted local administrators with the collection of taxes and read proofs at a local newspaper. For five years he traveled up and down the Yüan River and its tributaries, by boat and on foot. He loved to observe the life of the local people, and witnessed much killing. His health suffered, and he found he had no future in his native region. Inspired by the Literary Revolution which had grown out of the Movement of May 4, 1919, he went to the center of that Movement, Peking, in 1922.

There he was fascinated by the daily life, the shops, and arts, and the intellectual ferment of the great metropolis. He met university students, scholars, and writers, and sat in on some classes at National Peking University. He experimented with creative writing, trying his hand at different forms, including poems and plays. He finally settled on fiction and essays. He got a small clerical job at the office of the magazine *Hsien-tai p'ing-lun* (*Modern Criticism*).

In 1928, Shen went to Shanghai, the center of the publishing world. There he taught creative writing and contemporary Chinese literature at China National University, and also at Chinan University on the outskirts of Shanghai, and continued to write. In 1930 and 1931 he taught at National Wuhan University and Tsingtao University. In 1933 he went back to Peking and married there his former student Chang Chao-ho on September 9, 1933. He got a job with the Ministry of Education, compiling high school textbooks. After the outbreak of the Sino-Japanese War on July 7, 1937, Shen evaded the Japanese occupation of North China by traveling to Tientsin, from there to Wuhan, then to Yuanling (in western Hunan Province), and finally to Kunming in Yunnan Province, southwestern China, where he arrived in 1938, to stay for eight years. His wife had to stay in Peking and endure the Japanese occupation because when war broke out she had just given birth to her second son. She left Peking with her two sons in October 1938, making the long and difficult trip to Kunming. In Kunming, Shen Ts'ung-wen held two jobs: he continued his work of textbook compilation for the Ministry of Education, and he became a professor at the National Southwestern Associated University. He taught creative writing and the history of Chinese fiction there from 1938 to 1946. Many Chinese who are now professors or writers or active in other fields were his students in Kunming. After the end of the war, Shen Ts'ung-wen accepted an invitation to teach at National Peking University.

After the establishment of the People's Republic on October 1, 1949, Shen found he could no longer teach, nor write fiction, to suit the requirements of the new society. He got a job as a researcher in the Museum of History in Peking in 1950. He had long been interested in the history of Chinese arts and crafts and material culture, and now built a new career in this field, publishing books and reports, and collecting a great deal of material which is as yet unpublished. In May 1978 he was transferred from the Museum of History to the Institute of History of the Chinese Academy of Social Sciences in Peking, with the title of Researcher, and put in charge of his own research unit for the study of the history of Chinese costumes and ornaments.

In 1980, Shen came to the United States as a Visiting Scholar at the invitation of Yale and other American universities, accompanied by his wife Chang Chao-ho. This was their first visit to the West. During his stay in the United States, Shen gave lectures on his contacts with the Chinese literary world in the 1920s and 1930s, and on the history of Chinese costumes, ornaments, and fans.

HANS H. FRANKEL
(with the assistance of Shen Ts'ung-wen)